AF478094

Internationalising China's Financial Markets

Internationalising China's Financial Markets

Svenja Schlichting

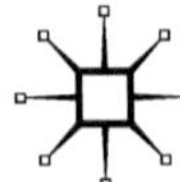

First published 2008 by
PALGRAVE MACMILLAN
Houndmills, Basingstoke, Hampshire RG21 6XS and
175 Fifth Avenue, New York, N.Y. 10010
Companies and representatives throughout the world

PALGRAVE MACMILLAN is the global academic imprint of the Palgrave Macmillan division of St. Martin's Press, LLC and of Palgrave Macmillan Ltd. Macmillan® is a registered trademark in the United States, United Kingdom and other countries. Palgrave is a registered trademark in the European Union and other countries.

ISBN-13: 978–0–230–55198–5   hardback
ISBN-10: 0–230–55198–X   hardback

This book is printed on paper suitable for recycling and made from fully managed and sustained forest sources. Logging, pulping and manufacturing processes are expected to conform to the environmental regulations of the country of origin.

A catalogue record for this book is available from the British Library.

Library of Congress Cataloging-in-Publication Data

Schlichting, Svenja, 1976–
    Internationalising China's financial markets / Svenja Schlichting.
        p. cm.
    Includes bibliographical references and index.
    ISBN 0–230–55198–X (alk. paper)
    1. Finance—China.   2. Investments, Foreign—China.   I. Title.
    HG187.C6S35 2008
    332′.0420951—dc22

                                                        2008016324

10   9   8   7   6   5   4   3   2   1
17 16 15 14 13 12 11 10 09 08

Printed and bound in Great Britain by
CPI Antony Rowe, Chippenham and Eastbourne

Contents

List of Figures

Abbreviations

ABC	Agricultural Bank of China
AFC	Asian financial crisis
AMC	Asset management company
AmCham	American Chamber of Commerce
A-share	Chinese share, denominated in RMB
AustCham	Australian Chamber of Commerce
BaFin	Bundesanstalt für Finanzdienstleistungsaufsicht (Federal Financial Supervisory Authority, Germany)
BIS	Bank for International Settlements
BOC	Bank of China
BOCHK	Bank of China (Hong Kong)
BoComm	Bank of Communication
B-share	Chinese share, denominated in foreign currency
CBRC	China Banking Regulatory Commission
CCB	China Construction Bank
CCP	Chinese Communist Party
CDF	China Development Forum
CDHK	Chinese German University Cooperation (Chinesisch-Deutsches Hochschulkolleg)
CEIBS	China European International Business School
CEO	Chief executive officer
CESL	China Euro Securities Limited
CICC	China International Capital Corporation
CIRC	China Insurance Regulatory Commission
CITIC	China International Trade and Investment Company
CSRC	China Securities Regulatory Commission
DRC	Development Research Centre of the State Council
EBRD	European Bank for Reconstruction and Development
EME	Emerging market economies
EU	European Union
EUCCC	European Union Chamber of Commerce in China
F-bond	Financial bond
FDI	Foreign direct investment
FIRST	Financial Sector Reform and Strengthening Initiative
FSA	Financial Services Authority
FSF	Financial Stability Forum

GDP	Gross domestic product
GITIC	Guangdong International Trade and Investment Company
GTZ	German Development Cooperation Agency
HSBC	Hong Kong and Shanghai Banking Corporation
H-share	Chinese share, issued on the Hong Kong Stock Exchange
IAIS	International Association of Insurance Supervisors
IC	Integrated circuits
ICBC	Industrial and Commercial Bank of China
IFC	International Finance Corporation
IMF	International Monetary Fund
IOSCO	International Organisation of Securities Commissions
IPO	Initial public offering
ITIC	International trade and investment company
JSCB	Joint-stock commercial bank
JV	Joint venture
M&A	Merger and acquisition
MNC	Multinational corporation
MOF	Ministry of Finance
MOFCOM	Ministry of Commerce
MOFTEC	Ministry of Foreign Trade and Economic Cooperation
MOST	Ministry of Science and Technology
MOU	Memorandum of understanding
NAFTA	North American Free Trade Agreement
NPA	Non-performing asset
NPL	Non-performing loan
N-share	Chinese share, issued on the New York Stock Exchange
OECD	Organisation of Economic Development and Cooperation
PBC	People's Bank of China
PE	Private equity
QDII	Qualified Domestic Institutional Investor
QFII	Qualified Foreign Institutional Investor
RMB	Renminbi (Chinese Currency)
ROA	Return on assets
ROE	Return on equity
ROI	Return on investment
SAC	Securities Association of China
SAFE	State Administration of Foreign Exchange
SBA	Shanghai Banking Association
SEC	Securities and Exchange Commission
SETC	State Economic and Trade Commission
SEZ	Special economic zone

SIBFI	Shanghai International Banking and Finance Institute
SME	Small and medium-sized enterprise
SOB	State-owned bank
SOCB	State-owned commercial bank
SOE	State-owned enterprise
T-bond	Treasury bond
TIC	Trade and investment company
TVE	Township and village enterprise
UNDP	United Nations Development Programme
WFOE	Wholly foreign-owned enterprise
WTO	World Trade Organisation

Acknowledgements

This book started out as a PhD project in 2001 and there are many people who contributed significantly to the success of this project. First of all, I would like to thank my supervisor and the spiritual mentor of the project, Professor Dr Sebastian Heilmann, Trier University, who encouraged me to follow my ideas and was a constant source of support as well as a role model during the project. I also thank my second supervisor Professor Dr Peter Molt, Trier University, who agreed to join my PhD committee despite many other commitments.

In the course of my work, Jörn-Carsten Gottwald, at the time also at Trier University, proved an indispensable lighthouse while navigating numerous challenges. I believe that without his constant support, advice and friendship, this work would not have been completed. I would also like to thank the group of graduates, students and assistants around the chair of Professor Heilmann as well as the members of the Research Group on the Political Economy of China who provided an inspiring environment for my work in Trier.

I owe a lot to the people who encouraged me to follow my inclination for interdisciplinary work and to study Chinese in my early years at university. Among them, I would particularly like to thank Dr Zhu, my Mandarin teacher at Hamburg University during my undergraduate years, as well as Professor Weiss, Free University of Berlin. Professor Geis, also at FU Berlin, got me hooked on to financial markets, their institutional specifics and their regulation. Professor Sandschneider's seminar on the integration of China into the world economy prepared me to study China's internationalisation.

More directly linked to the research process for this book, I would like to thank all interviewees in China, the UK, Germany and the US for their time and patience. The interviews made my study of financial market internationalisation fruitful, vivid and fascinating. Also, I am indebted to my Chinese friends, as well as their parents and families with whom I stayed sometimes during field trips to China. In particular, I would like to thank those friends who helped to arrange interviews and those interviewees who became friends over the course of repeated dinners during my stay in Beijing in 2005–6. Thanks also to my German and American friends in China who provided moral support in times when I needed it. Thank you for making field work successful and fun!

On the institutional side, I would like to express my gratitude for the hospitality of the Institute of World Economics and Politics at the Chinese Academy of Social Science in Beijing where I spent a year as a Visiting Research Scholar in 2005–6. To Mrs Gao Haihong, I owe numerous contacts and different perspectives on single issues related to my work.

For financial support, I thank the German Academic Foundation (Studienstiftung des deutschen Volkes) which funded my undergraduate and graduate studies as well as numerous travels to China. The Carlo-Schmid Scholarship Programme allowed me to stay at the World Bank Financial Sector Department for a couple of months at the outset of my studies. Also, I would like to thank the Department of Political Science at Trier University for financing my trip to a conference in Hong Kong which proved very valuable for completing the manuscript.

A warm 'thank you' goes to the people who have reviewed earlier versions of this manuscript. Any remaining mistakes and shortcomings are my responsibility alone.

Finally, I thank my family – the people who shared most closely my joy and as well as the ups and downs of this work. To them, my book is dedicated.

Introduction

More than 25 years after China started its economic reform process, few people in the business and academic communities dispute its overwhelming success: long years of high and comparatively stable economic growth have fuelled beliefs that the Chinese economy avoided the pitfalls of other transition economies and managed – remaining problems notwithstanding – to embark on a long and comparatively steady growth path. Due to favourable initial conditions or clever policy choices (or both), Chinese gradualism under the comparatively firm grip of political leaders has proven superior to Big Bang transitions so far.

The relative success of the economic reforms is reflected in skyrocketing new apartment and office buildings, seemingly growing into the sky everywhere in Beijing and Shanghai. Yet, one might ask, what do we actually see there? Are these the landmarks of a strong and solid newly evolving market economy or empty signs of a destabilising investment bubble? Do we see (foreign) investors' money sunk into non-sellable office space? As someone put it during the interviews conducted for this research project, it is easy to hammer out a rough framework for a market economy on paper (or build some skyscrapers), but much more difficult to build the formal and informal institutions to carry and support it. What are, then, the newly emerging institutional foundations of the Chinese market economy? How are the institutions to guide and govern the emerging markets built, how are rules set for markets and how do markets in turn affect the Chinese political system? What about the contradictions inherent in the emerging economic system that is run and governed by political actors who still operate under the logic of top-down administrative commands and under the control of the Chinese Communist Party (CCP)? Considering the pervasive state ownership in the economy, which actors are able to foster market-oriented institutional change?

A distinct characteristic of the Chinese economic reform process has been the opening of markets for foreign participation and the integration of China into the world economy: within the last 25 years, China not only became a successful example for gradual transition, it has also become so deeply integrated into the world economic system that it is now already regarded as one of its powerhouses. Selling its growth story well to the international community, China has emerged as one of the most important (consumer) markets and has attracted large sums of foreign direct investment (FDI). Therefore, among the new actors, who have been able to enter China's economy during the reform process, transnational corporations were prominent. Entry into the World Trade Organisation (WTO) in 2001 has further strengthened foreign market actors' access to China. Yet, although it is understood quite well that the opening policy of China has contributed largely to its economic reform success (and that, in fact, China has depended heavily on the outside world in modernising its economy), there is little theoretical account of the role of transnational actors, the impact of new incentives created through the integration into international markets, and the impact of increasing internationalisation on Chinese economic policy making.

The role of internationalisation in creating the new institutional foundation of the Chinese market economy is the key theme of this book. Internationalisation here is understood as a process in which new (external) actors enter markets and in which the incentives and market environment of domestic actors are altered simultaneously. Internationalisation affects both market conduct and the rule-setting for markets, and through both contributes to market development. Altered incentives and constraints, new actors and actors' constellations, and new modes of interaction between regulators and industry players in the domestic market are key elements of this process. Therefore this book identifies key actors both on the side of commercial market actors and regulators, analyses the impact of external players' market entry, and discusses changes in the institutional environment of domestic actors. In doing so, the book focuses on financial markets that are one of the hottest spots for transnational market actors in China *and* the single most problematic area in China's economic reforms.

The analysis is centred around the following questions; how has internationalisation shaped the institutional development of financial markets in China so far through the market entry of transnational actors and the changing market environment of domestic ones, and how is it likely to do so in the future? In order to explain financial market development, the book looks both at the political creation and control of financial markets in an internationalising context. Understanding financial markets and their development as a case study of the creation of the institutions of a market economy and the redefinition of the role of state actors in it, the book also looks at the emerging new regulatory regime in China's financial markets.

The Chinese case displays distinct institutional characteristics that make the analysis of its financial market internationalisation both particularly interesting and promising *vis-à-vis* other transition countries: China's financial markets are not only highly distorted hybrids in the transition from a command to a market economy, but have remained dominated by state actors and – due to the absence of political transition – incorporated in the control structures of the CCP. Still, numerous foreign financial firms have entered this complex institutional setting and Chinese regulators over time started to eagerly encourage the market entry of foreign firms. By the end of 2006, having a foreign strategic investor had become a mandatory condition to receive a licence for creating a new Chinese bank or to conduct an initial public offering (IPO).

The overall picture of the Chinese financial markets in 2006 suggested *prima facie* that foreign financial firms had already gained a strong foothold in the Chinese economy and that the Chinese financial markets were, in fact, to a great extent already integrated into world markets. More than 300 representative offices and branches of foreign financial firms were present in China in December 2006, when the WTO phase-in ended. Two stock exchanges were open for foreign investment through the Qualified Foreign Institutional Investors' Scheme (QFII), and international IPOs of Chinese enterprises were frequently underwritten by international investment banks. Numerous Chinese SOEs have been listed overseas, including some domestic financial firms. Three of the four large state-owned commercial banks (SOCBs), plus the Bank of Communications, had secured foreign strategic investments of prestigious foreign financial institutions and were listed in Hong Kong. Yet, the net of control over foreign financial firms' activities, structuring their presence and impact on market development, has so far only been dismantled reluctantly and slowly. Over the past years, much ground has been gained with regard to market access. However, some parts of the control and 'over-regulation' remain in effect. In sum, China's financial markets remain much more closed than the large international component of its real economy would suggest. Ample anecdotal evidence on the arbitrary and discretionary nature of government and regulatory decisions can be cited in this regard, from unfair competition to political interference with business, suggesting that foreign financial firms' business in China depends more on 'leadership access', high-level lobbying and a general ability to respond to unexpected events than on anything else, let alone true competitive advantages. There are numerous ambivalent regulations, such as limitations on refinancing for foreign financial firms that make it hard to judge the true nature of the emerging, presumably more liberal, regulatory regime in the financial markets. Are these prudential or protectionist policies?

WTO entry has changed and will continue to change the overall picture to a large extent. Most importantly, the Chinese WTO commitments for the first time provided a rules-based timeline for further opening that creates a more reliable business environment for domestic and international actors alike. Additional to WTO commitments, there have been changes in the financial market internationalisation strategy of the Chinese government: regulators and bank reformers have started to 'actively play the international card' by encouraging foreign firms' market entry as well as strategic investments in domestic financial firms. In other words, Chinese regulators have started to use foreign financial firms to reform and repair China's fragile financial markets and firms. This has increased the scope of action for foreign firms in China and has led to new modes of interaction between them and the Chinese regulators as well as domestic firms. At the same time, domestic firms have gained commercial strength and international orientation and have started to differentiate themselves from each other. In their board meetings, representatives of their foreign strategic investors meet with state employees and the party secretary to discuss the business of the domestic firm and its value to overseas equity holders.

On the whole, there is a remarkable dynamic as well as a complex institutional structure in China's financial markets. Therefore, it is a promising case to analyse the process of the redefinition of state agencies' roles in an emerging market economy, the commercialisation of domestic financial firms and the interaction between commercial market actors and regulators. In addition, financial market internationalisation is of crucial relevance not only for financial market development, but also for the process and success of economic reforms in China as a whole and thus the economic, political and social stability which in turn is highly relevant for world politics and markets. The relevance of the questions raised in this book for the international economy as well as international politics can thus hardly be overestimated. Over the following pages, this book examines China's financial market internationalisation using four perspectives:

1. *Financial market internationalisation as a catalyst or the Achilles' heel of financial market development.* Within the process of financial market development, market opening and internationalisation is a key component, reflecting both the international competitiveness of domestic financial firms and the alignment of the domestic financial markets with international standards. On the other hand, while offering opportunities for development, market opening also contains risks, especially if internal reforms have not been completed (Chan-Lee, Liu and Yoshitomi, 2002). Therefore, internationalisation can be a catalyst for or the Achilles' heel of financial market development. Looking at financial market internationalisation from the perspective of its contribution to financial market development leads to the question of how internationalisation has fostered and created new incentives for market-oriented reforms and in how far it has influenced domestic actors.
2. *Financial market internationalisation and the interdependence of political and economic institutions.* Political rules, structures and actors shape markets. In China, this is particularly evident because ownership of financial firms is largely public and financial firms are incorporated in the structure of party control. They are an important instrument of political control over the economy and are key in the CCP's policies to ensure economic, social and political stability. This leads to political interference in financial firms and a political logic of resource allocation. It increases the likelihood of a strong, party-politically motivated role of financial market regulation. Based on numerous signs of continued financial repression and ample evidence for political lending, it seems reasonable to consider China's financial firms not only as parts of the economic but also of the political system. Since financial market internationalisation challenges this politicised order and the established channels of control, its analysis contributes to understanding the development and change of the political system in China. Looking at financial market internationalisation this way, the case of China contributes to understanding the role of political systems in economic transition, the connections between finance and political power over resources, as well as the chances for institutional and political change in this regard. In which ways does internationalisation alter the scope of action of political actors, the modes of interaction between industry players and regulators, and how does

it impact the new definition of the role of state actors in financial markets?

3. *Financial market internationalisation and the role and relevance of transnational economic actors in China.* The market entry of foreign actors has been highly regulated and politicised in China. Driven by the desire to mobilise economic resources, control has been loosened and decentralised to some degree and measures have been taken to attract more foreign capital in the form of foreign direct investment (FDI). As the market presence of foreign enterprises has altered existing market structures, what has been their impact on further internationalising the markets they operate in? What lessons can be learnt from financial markets about the impact of internationalisation on market development and regulation, with regard to the market entry of foreign actors, their market conduct and their lobbying? What can be learnt from this for the emerging modes of governance in China's market economy, the emergence of a new Chinese regulatory state and the relation between marketisation and internationalisation?

4. *Financial market internationalisation and the integration of China into global markets.* During the course of opening, foreign actors have entered the financial markets and domestic financial firms and regulatory agencies have started to operate in an increasingly international setting. Standards and rules are (partly) imported and increasingly aligned with international best practices, as China integrates more deeply with international financial markets and tries to attract foreign capital and know-how. China's financial firms also increasingly conduct business in international markets, for example through the international issuance of US$-denominated bonds. Where Chinese decision-makers access international markets, such as in internationally issuing treasury bonds, they also have to come to grips with the established rules of the game in international finance. How does this integration into global financial markets shape national financial market policies? How are standards transferred, what problems arise in the process and how does the mode of interaction between international and domestic actors impact financial market development in China?

Part I
Explaining Financial Market Internationalisation in China

1
Financial Market Internationalisation and Institutional Change in China

What is the role of internationalisation in the process of financial market development and reform in China, a country that has secluded its economy from the outside world for most of the last century and has only reluctantly started to reform and open its financial markets during the economic reform process? How is China building the new institutional foundations for its reforming and opening of financial markets despite its persistent and overwhelming state control over financial assets and domestic financial firms? How do new actors in the financial markets impact their development, how do new market trends change the behaviour of domestic actors? In order to answer these questions, this book applies institutional theories on (financial) market development and regulation to the case of China's financial market opening. The foundations of these are briefly reviewed in this chapter before locating China within the set of other emerging market and transition economies whose experiences in financial market opening might provide useful insights for the case of China.

Explaining institutional change in emerging economies' financial markets

Analytically, financial markets can be approached in different ways. Most economic theories have regarded *markets* in general as given and have focused on market outcome in terms of prices and quantities, allocative efficiency and cases of market failure. Neo-institutional theory, however, has conceptualised markets as a set of rules and contracts, called institutions.[1] Based on North (1990), who analysed the relevance of political and economic institutions for economic competition and the performance of economic systems, institutions are understood to be the rules of the (economic) game, more specifically a set of rules structuring the incentives and behaviour of actors without predetermining their actual conduct. These rules encompass both formal and informal ones (North, 1990, p. 97). This institutional approach will be used as the analytical foundation for this book. A brief overview of the points most relevant for the analysis in the following chapters is presented here.

Scholars in the tradition of Douglas North have analysed how (economic) institutions emerge and change, as well as how they impact economic outcomes and performance over time, adding fruitful insights to questions that traditional economic theory could not answer. One reason for the stronger explanatory power of analysing *markets as institutions* is that the institutional approach renders the structure of markets accessible for analysis, as it illuminates the rules by which market actors interact as well as their incentive structures. Understanding markets as a set of rules rather than a mere (imaginary) location of exchange highlights the variation between different markets and the convertibility of rules as well as the relevance of actors who can influence this process. Markets are not simply the way they are, they are created and formed in a historical context through different configurations of (public and private) actors, varying degrees of government intervention, as well as interest groups' bargaining power and leverage in a political process (North, 1990; Scharpf, 1997).

This approach has drawn attention to the actors, their constellations and their interaction in the process of market creation and development. Here, actors and institutions as structures that govern behaviour are interlocked: institutions structure behaviour, but at the same time behaviour (re-)structures institutions. Institutions hence are dependent and independent variables at the same time. The institutional framework acts as the structure, in which actors operate and create new structures, an interdependence explicitly reflected in the concept of actor-centric institutionalism that combines the analysis of institutions and actors (Mayntz and Scharpf, 1995).

Actors are thus a central component of this framework and can be either individual or collective. Actors are characterised by capabilities, preferences and perceptions *vis-à-vis* specific options or policy outcomes and while some of the preferences and perceptions are of a permanent (stable) nature, others may be changeable over time through learning and persuasion (Scharpf, 1997, pp. 38ff). Alterations both in the actors' incentives and their constellation as well as changes in the preferences, perceptions and configurations of actors in this context are important sources of *institutional change*. Market development, the dependent variable in this book, can thus best be understood as institutional change in reaction to changes in the incentives actors face, in the actor configuration and constellation as well as in changed modes of their interaction. One of the most significant theoretical contributions of this literature has been to emphasise the role of state agencies in the analysis of markets and to disaggregate 'the state', replacing the cryptic monolithic model predominantly used in economic theory with a closer look at specific state agencies, governments, regulators and the bureaucracy (Evans, Ruschemeyer and Skocpol, 1985). In other words, instead of assuming the state to be a unitary actor, acting like a benevolent dictator in the best interests of its subordinates, several parts of the state involved in economic policy decision-making and rule-setting are specified and assumed to follow their own organisational interests. For the aims of this book, the most important actors in this regard are regulators.[2]

Other important market actors include commercial players, often understood to be private actors as opposed to actors in the public sphere, as well as individuals such as consumers of products and services. For the aims of this book, there are two important characteristics to distinguish between regulators and commercial players, also called industry players in this book: firstly, commercial players in general do not have formal rule-setting capacity; secondly, while commercial players may also engage in behaviour that aims at influencing the regulators and the process of rule-making, their primary action is market conduct in the sense that they engage in market transactions such as the exchange and trade of products and services. In their market conduct, they react to the incentives and constraints created by the trends and dynamics of the market environment. Together, regulators who set and enforce formal rules and industry players who primarily react to the market environment form the two important categories of *market actors*. Their respective behaviour in rule-setting and market conduct, as well as the constellation and interaction among them, determines market development.

In addition, differentiating between national and transnational actors and institutions is essential for the analysis in this book. Developments in international markets and transnational market actors increasingly alter and influence the interests of domestic actors.[3] In the process of internationalisation, new actors enter the stage, and the position and weight of domestic actors change (Haggard and Maxfield, 1996). Shifts in the configuration of actors and their interests as well as in the level of economic interdependence frequently lead to changes in policy-making and outcome. Transnational actors as well as an increasingly international environment of domestic actors have an important impact on domestic institutions – that is, the domestic rules of the game.

A major consequence of conceptualising markets as institutions in an international context is that political and economic institutions and their change can only be analysed together; in looking at both the relevance of rule-making and market conduct for market development, the interdependence of political and economic institutions and their change moves into the centre of analysis, thus leading to a combination of the neo-institutionalist approach with theories of new political economy and public choice (Olson, 2000). After all, regulators as the rule-setters for markets are part of the political realm, as is the case for policy-making politicians and parliamentarians. Political and economic institutions influence each other. They both shape the incentives and constraints of different market actors as well as their power, resources and organisational capabilities. This implies that the political system and process of any country has important consequences for the economic institutions and that, for example, the economic strength of commercial actors has a significant impact on their political bargaining power while at the same time the political power of politicians is impacted by their economic might. Analysing markets, as well as the actor constellations and the strategies and interests of key commercial players, thus allows an assessment of power relations and the impact of commercial actors on market development. In this, markets are understood to be shaped by policies, in line with the canon of literature on the political creation, shaping and control of markets (Czada and Lütz, 2000), and are seen to have an important impact on politics in return.

In short, markets can be understood as institutions. Institutions structure incentives and incentive structures vary greatly within different economic settings, leading to different economic outcomes. Understanding markets as institutions draws attention both to the (formal and informal) rules that govern economic interactions, as well as to changes in the rules and the different actors involved in this process. Political and economic institutions need to be analysed together. Changing interests, incentives and constraints of actors (including regulators and industry players) are key to understanding market development, while the sources of these changes can be national or transnational in nature.

Financial markets and their regulation

Turning to financial markets, neo-institutional theory highlights that these are complex institutions structuring and governing the exchange of financial services.[4] Two characteristics make these markets particularly interesting for analysis; firstly, based on the nature of financial transactions and the systematic importance of financial markets in the economy, they are characterised by a higher degree of government intervention (regulation) than other markets (Carmichael and Pomerleano, 2002). Secondly, financial markets are regarded as particularly internationalised markets; due to technological advancements, changes in the mode of transactions and altered consumer behaviour, borders between national financial markets have considerably lost significance (Lütz, 2003, pp. 19ff).

Based on the institutional approach, this book conceptualises financial market regulation in the tradition of positive theories on regulation.[5] These include a disaggregating look at the nature of regulatory organisations, processes of regulation and market-actor constellations.[6] Positive theories of regulation trace the origin of regulatory decisions not only to the search for efficiency, but also to the requests and interests of (powerful) commercial actors as well as to self-interested regulators (Stigler, 1971). Alterations of regulation in this context become politically determined and depend on the relative power of interest groups as well as their ability to organise for collective action (Peltzman, 1976).

Applying a positive theory of regulation, the regulatory framework, based on regulatory organisations (the regulators) and the regulations they use to govern the market, moves into the centre of analysis. Carmichael and Pomerleano (2002, pp. 21ff) defined the regulatory framework to consist of regulatory objectives, the regulatory structure, regulatory backing and regulatory implementation. Vogel (1998, pp. 20ff) understood the *regulatory regime* to describe the combination of the ideational background of regulation with its organisational aspects. His definition of a regulatory regime thus highlights the interrelation of ideas (regime orientation) with the structure of regulatory bodies (regime organisation). The dimensions of the regulatory regime include the means, aims, priorities and instruments of regulation, as well as the overall spirit in which regulation is conducted, also called the *regulatory culture* (Meidinger, 1987). Focusing on the role of common ideas, judgments and knowledge among policy makers, Haas (1992) identified the significance of epistemic communities for this process. Coleman (1990) and Underhill (1997) have developed these ideas further and have analysed policy communities and their role in the change of financial markets in particular.[7] This is a point that will be taken up in Part III of this book when looking at China's regulatory regime change.

There is much debate on just how much and what kind of regulation should be applied to a specific financial market. Opinions have been oscillating between the extremes of regulatory micro-management of financial firms and transactions and a general laissez-faire approach. In principle, this debate highlights the basic tension between two processes in every financial market: the regulatory process of rule-setting and political control, and the process of spontaneous and uncontrolled market development among financial firms and their customers. Both are essential in the process of market development. It is not possible to create a market merely by rules, because financial firms have to fill the framework with their actions and market conduct; nor can a financial market develop stably without rules.

Different institutional dynamics in emerging market economies

In emerging market economies (EMEs)[8], however, regulation takes place mainly as a reform of financial markets in the context of reducing overly strong government interference. Here, internationalisation is closely linked to the internal liberalisation of financial markets and both regulators and external actors are key actors in initiating and fostering it.[9]

While the institutional setting of EMEs varies greatly, there are two common legacies of the typical structures of financial repression as well as incomplete and problematic liberalisation policies; firstly, there is a history of strong state interference in the economy, resulting in remnants of state ownership in financial firms and a resulting closeness between state and commercial actors in mainly bank-dominated financial markets. Banks are often organisationally weak and credit markets segmented. This legacy is most pronounced in emerging market economies that are transition countries. Secondly, due to the recent, incomplete and partly problematic nature of liberalisation policies, financial markets are immature (Beim and Calomiris, 2001). As securities markets are often newly developing, they typically play a less important role in financial intermediation than in industrialised countries, while at the same time displaying high volatility and speculative behaviour within an unclear legal framework. Regulatory implementation and enforcement are among the major problems of these markets, and banks as well as securities markets are often simultaneously under- and over-regulated. Another important feature of financial markets in EMEs are rapidly expanding international links after earlier isolation from international capital markets, reflected in capital account controls and pervasive entry restrictions on foreign financial firms, has been ended during liberalisation. Problems that result from the partial reduction of excessive state control, the ensuing struggle to re-regulate markets and the problems inherent in a 'young' market with new and inexperienced market participants are thus characteristic of financial markets in EMEs. In this context, it is hard to differentiate between developmental problems and problems of the institutional setting (Opper, 2003). Most important for the further analysis in this book, however, is the fact that state actors (regulators) and commercial actors (financial firms) are typically very closely linked in this setting, as are the regulation and reform of the financial markets. Regulators are not only regulating but often actively reforming financial markets.

Conceptualising internationalisation

Following Claessens and Glaessner (1998), internationalisation can be understood as, on the one hand, the elimination of discriminating treatment between foreign and domestic financial services providers, the removal of barriers to the cross-border provision of financial services, and the subsequent market entry of foreign financial firms in domestic markets. On the other hand, it also encompasses the broader processes of changing the market environment and incentives of domestic financial market actors through the development of both new international contacts and interaction, and changes in business opportunities due to an increasingly international framework of action. This book follows this broader definition. Therefore, the market entry of external actors *and* less tangible processes such as the changing market environment of domestic actors and the inflow of new ideas, concepts, and new standards of operation are accounted for here. Transnational actors and international market forces are analysed, understanding the abstract concept of 'market forces' as those factors that create and change the incentives and constraints of domestic firms.

In theories on financial markets, internationalisation is a controversial topic with regard to its impact on domestic financial markets. However, the academic discussion is unevenly split, with a majority of authors pointing to its (potential) benefits; financial market opening is predominantly expected to lead to the increased efficiency and stability of the host countries' financial markets (Pomerleano and Vojta, 2001). Also, the quantity and quality of financial services provided are expected to increase due to the introduction of new products and services by foreign firms, the import of better technology and the provision of sophisticated management skills (Lardy, 2001, p. 2). In addition, in this line of argument, foreign banks are seen to promote capital flows to emerging markets.[10]

With regard to the actors driving financial market internationalisation, it can be noted that on the side of industry players, important actors favouring financial market internationalisation include the new market entrants (foreign financial firms) as well as some domestic financial firms. In their work on the driving forces for financial market development, Rajan and Zingales (2003b) show that the process can also be heavily constrained by the structure of the old, incumbent financial firms, their concentration (and resulting bargaining power) and their interests and preferences; powerful domestic interest groups might also oppose changes in the financial market structure and openness. The constellation of actors and interests is likely to depend on the suggested mode of internationalisation. As Haggard and Maxfield (1996, p. 39) observe with regard to capital account opening and entry deregulation, domestic financial intermediaries primarily benefit from liberalised capital inflows and outflows, which open new opportunities but lose out from a liberalisation of the entry regime. The typically concentrated and state-close nature of the financial industry in EMEs tends to foster domestic firms' resistance to external liberalisation.

To sum up, this book conceptualises financial market development as institutional change. The creation, shaping and control of markets are understood to be eminently political tasks and markets in return are regarded as increasingly important in shaping the scope and context of political action. However, while regulation is crucial, it is not sufficient on its own to create vibrant financial markets; markets also depend on commercial players, their market conduct and the patterns of behaviour between them. *Internationalisation* is an important component of the change and reform of financial markets and it impacts financial market development both via changing the market environment and conduct of industry players and via influencing the regulatory regime. Processes of internationalisation, such as the market entry of foreign financial firms as external actors in these markets or changes in the market environment of domestic actors, are thus driving forces for institutional change. Internationalisation can be used to analyse the relation and interaction between regulatory and commercial actors (and through this, the potentials and limits of the political design of markets), as well as the relation between national and transnational actors and their influence on domestic institutions. EMEs often display a distinct institutional foundation due to their history and reform process. The analysis in the following section will explore how far China fits into this pattern and what lessons can be learnt from other EMEs.

China's financial market internationalisation in international perspective

What can be learnt from other countries for the analysis of China's financial market internationalisation? Two things should be kept in mind when approaching this question; firstly, lessons may in general not be easily transferable from one country to another. This is particularly true in the case of China as it displays some unique institutional characteristics in its institutional setting.[11] Secondly, when looking for lessons to be learnt from others, it should be kept in mind that there is neither agreed 'best practice' with regard to financial market openness nor an internationally agreed optimal level of financial market internationalisation. What may be good for one country may not function well in another.[12]

In many ways, however, China's experiences with financial market internationalisation has not differed vastly from those of other countries; in most countries around the world, the market entry of foreign financial firms was restricted by, above all other restraining factors, regulation. This was driven by the need to balance the perceived benefits and risks of internationalisation. From the perspective of foreign financial firms, the decision to enter an emerging market economy has been dominated by considerations of business opportunities relative to regulatory constraints in the context of their global business strategies. Studies show that in general, two motivations have driven banks to enter emerging financial markets; the first was to serve multinationals or home-based companies, the second to become part of the fabric of domestic banking, thus depending much more on the host countries' growth perspectives and industry structure (Pomerleano and Vojta, 2001).

On the side of the regulators, the benefits and risks of financial market internationalisation need to be carefully managed. The main policy challenge is the implementation of internal financial market reform and the creation of an enabling environment for market development while upgrading prudential regulation and monitoring capacity. Making foreign entry a part of the solution of financial market problems (and of the restructuring of domestic financial firms) has worked well in some central and eastern European countries, such as Hungary and Poland. However, it makes the tasks of the regulators more complex, especially with regard to cross-border supervision and regulation, large complex banking organisations and financial conglomerates, the regulation of derivatives, banking system concentration, and contagion risks (Mathieson and Roldos, 2001).

Historically, there were three circumstances that led to significant shifts in the regulation of foreign firms' market entry around the world and consequently to a steep increase in their market participation; the privatisation of state-owned domestic financial firms in the course of economic transition, their radical restructuring after financial crisis, and rapid internationalisation of the entire economy. This is an interesting observation for the case of China, because as the Chinese economy is internationalising rapidly, regulators face a pending financial crisis and are reformulating policies on privatising financial firms. The interrelatedness of financial market policies with broader economic policies – particularly in the case of the reform of state-owned enterprises (SOEs) – and the importance of single events such as a financial crisis for policy shifts is highlighted through this historical perspective. However, while the impetus for financial market internationalisation in other countries typically came from the side of the regulators, the process of internationalisation has been driven both by regulators as well as domestic and foreign industry actors.

In what ways then is the Chinese case different from other countries' experiences? China has a much higher savings rate than other countries. Its large size and rapid economic growth translate into strong interest and trust from foreign investors, reflected in the high level of inflowing FDI even in spite of a certain lack of institutional foundations that have been deemed prerequisites for foreign market entry in other countries, such as the rule of law. China's economy displays both growth and stability, and China sells this success well to international investors. On the other hand, the private sector is much less developed than in other countries. China is atypical among other transition countries because privatisation with regard to financial firms has not occurred on a large scale so far. In addition, there has been no capital account liberalisation. Leaving theoretical problems in relation to the comparability of China with other EMEs aside, it can be stated that with regard to policy *challenges* and *options* in financial market internationalisation, there has been a strong similarity that has been outweighed by dissimilarities with regard to policy *choices* and *outcomes*. It remains to be shown in the following chapters that this striking contrast was largely based on different political institutions and actors' constellations, in particular the continuing firm grip of the Chinese 'state' on financial markets. As a consequence of this, China's current level of financial market internationalisation stands in clear contrast to that in most transition countries in central and eastern Europe where parallel economic and political transition has led to a rapid evolution of less state-dominated and – in most cases – more open and internationally integrated financial markets.[13] The remaining chapters of this book aim to contribute to explaining this phenomenon with respect to China.

Based on the framework presented so far, how does international comparison help answer the question as to who the important actors are in the process of China's financial market internationalisation – domestic or international actors? Inspired by the experiences of other countries, theories on economic globalisation have developed a common view that domestic governments and regulatory bodies have mainly reacted to external pressure when deregulating financial markets (Cowles and Risse, 2001). However, others have argued that this view overlooks the strong interests of domestic actors *in favour of* deregulation and financial market liberalisation. In fact, as Kroszner (1998) points out, domestic governments played an active role in financial market internationalisation and the financial interests and needs of governments have determined to a large extent the way global capital flows evolved. Empirically, financial market liberalisation has proven to be particularly attractive to governments in times of macroeconomic downswing (Vogel, 1998). Mosley (2003) states that, while governments found their ability to act altered by the more internationalised financial markets, considerable policy freedoms remain. Government bodies, on the basis of changed preferences, therefore can be identified as key in initiating financial market liberalisation; the original preferences of governments for controlling financial markets and using them for industrial policy changed in favour of new financing modes and sources (Haggard and Maxfield, 1996, p. 61). Is this the case for China as well?

Research question, design and problems

As China opens up its financial markets and integrates itself internationally, a number of questions arise that will be addressed in this book. How has financial market internationalisation taken place in China and how has it contributed to financial market development? Who has driven the process and in what ways and to what extent has internationalisation had an impact on it? Can the case of financial market development show that processes of internationalisation have significantly contributed to the establishment of new institutions in China?

The book approaches these themes by addressing the following three questions:

1. What are important institutional particularities of China's financial markets and what has been their relevance for structuring the process of internationalisation?
2. In what ways has internationalisation led to the market entry of new actors, as well as altered actor constellations among domestic actors, new modes of interaction between actors and increased transparency in China's financial markets?
3. How far has internationalisation impacted the domestic financial market participants, in particular with regard to the process of rule-setting for and regulation and the market environment of domestic financial firms?

In a first step, the book therefore approaches foreign financial firms as external actors in China's financial markets and asks what role and relevance they have in the Chinese markets. How do they operate in different market segments, what determines their market entry, business strategies and actual market conduct? In what way do they impact market development? Here, the analysis focuses on firm-level decisions and strategies and analyses both market conduct and lobbying strategies of foreign financial firms in China. Have foreign financial firms – as a group – become powerful and important actors in initiating and fostering institutional change in China's financial markets? Are they going to be the cornerstones of a level playing field for domestic and foreign market participants in an increasingly open and internationally integrated financial market?

In a second step, the book addresses domestic financial market players. Two groups of actors are looked at in this respect; firstly, with regard to regulators, the book asks how internationalisation impacts the development of the regulatory regime of China's financial markets. Secondly, it asks how internationalisation impacts the market environment of domestic industry players and how they respond to the changed incentives and constraints in this environment. What can be learnt about the role and importance of informal institutions, policy communities and new professional elites in financial market reforms? What about changes in actor constellations, bargaining power and modes of interaction through the increased interaction of foreign and domestic actors?

By answering these questions, there are three broad areas of interest that this book contributes to. Firstly, it gathers new knowledge and provides analysis of the process and dynamic of financial market development in China, adding insight to the question of how transnational actors and international influences have shaped and structured an essential part of the newly established market economy in China. Secondly, the book develops new ideas with regard to financial market development theory and particularly the political economy of financial market liberalisation. Finally, illuminating the role of international actors and markets in China's financial system reform, it sheds light on the often underestimated (and under-researched) question of international forces in economic and political transition.

Some issues that are explicitly not within the scope of this book need to be pointed out here. This work's perspective is limited to transnational actors as well as international forces and dynamics in the development and reform of the Chinese financial markets. It is therefore *not* a book on the domestic side of the reform process and as such does not focus on inner-party dynamics or elite politics involved in financial sector reform. While both are clearly important and are naturally interlinked, purely domestic actor constellations and driving forces are not analysed in detail here. Changes of informal rules among domestic players, for example, have to be left for further research. Additionally, this book is not concerned with the prospects and likelihood of profound change in the Chinese political system in the sense of democratisation.[14] Yet, this book remains sceptical regarding the democratising effects of international market integration *per se*.

Financial market internationalisation has historically been closely linked to domestic financial liberalisation and the liberalisation of the capital account, which includes the removal of capital controls and restrictions on the convertibility of the currency. While the internationalisation of financial services is to some degree a substitute for capital account liberalisation, as Claessens, Demirgüç-Kunt and Huizinga (2001) argue, this book leaves currency-related problems and questions regarding the liberalisation of the capital account for further research. And as the main focus of the book is the institutional foundation of the emerging financial markets in China, international financial transactions that are conducted from outside China are only looked at and commented on where they are important for the structure of domestic institutions.

This book does not look at the distributional effects of financial market internationalisation and therefore only gives some partial, inconclusive and preliminary hints at possible detrimental effects of internationalisation in this regard. Further research needs to be conducted on this issue, especially as the economic reform process in China is increasingly subject to well-founded critiques with regard to its polarising impact on income distribution.

While trying to be as up-to-date as possible, the time horizon covered by this book ends in mid to late 2006, a time of rapid and profound change in foreign financial firms' access to China's financial markets and the time of the formal completion of WTO entry phase-in. It is clear, however, that the effects of those last steps, most notably the access of foreign banks to local private customer RMB-business, can only be judged in the future. Therefore, no final conclusions on these developments can be drawn here.

The book is thus a detailed snapshot but not a final evaluation of financial market internationalisation in China.

Research design

As explained above, this book approaches its research questions on the basis of neo-institutional and New Political Economy theories on markets and their development. This perspective functions as a lens to structure the data and material, highlighting the institutional character of markets and the interrelation of political and economic institutions. In using this approach, the book explicitly focuses on the market conduct of commercial actors and on processes of rule-setting for markets through regulatory actors in the context of financial market development in China. It thus combines theories and categories originally used in political science as well as in economics to approach the complex topic of how Chinese financial markets have developed on a foundation of post-Leninist political institutions.

The analysis is based on the assumption that the Chinese economy is in the middle of transition towards a market economy, a process in which regulatory actors and industry players differentiate themselves and regulators define new modes of governance in an international context. At the heart of the economic transition is a change in incentive structures and in formal as well as informal institutions. In this regard, China is understood as a case study for the analysis of market development in economic transition. This is done – notwithstanding the fact that China stands apart from other transition economies, most notably due to its the political system and the preserved CCP rule – because it allows an emphasis to be placed on similarities and differences and helps to specify the particularities of the Chinese institutional setting and their impact on market development.

The analysis is inspired by theories on regulation and the political control of markets (Czada and Lütz, 2000). It follows the approach of Rajan and Zingales (2003a) and focuses on the political economy and the process of financial market development rather than the outcome. With regard to analysing the development of China's financial markets from a neo-institutional and New Political Economy perspective, the book stands in the tradition of Green (2004b), Heilmann (2001) and Shih (2004b). In analysing the role of foreign financial firms in China, it further develops the approaches of Lees and Liaw (1996), Lardy (2001) and He (2004). Most accounts of financial market internationalisation have focused on the role of single groups of actors or single market segments, for example in the course of WTO entry (see Bonin and Huang 2002; He and Fan 2004; Pei and Qiu 2002). However, the approach in this book is broader as it incorporates different market segments, allowing a comparison between different regulatory settings and groups of actors. It also stands out from other studies in its focus on the impact of internationalisation on market development, thus extending the perspectives of Katz (1997) and Harner (2001), who concentrated on the business opportunities for foreign financial firms in China.

Research methods

The research in this book follows a qualitative approach. It is primarily founded on text-based research, using both primary and secondary sources, including laws, regulations, research notes from inhouse think tanks of regulatory bodies, and media reports in English, German and Chinese. As current events comprise a large part of the analysis, newspaper articles have been important sources of information. Newspapers used in this regard include most prominently *Caijing, China Daily, Business Weekly, People's Daily, Southern Daily* and occasionally *21st Century, South China Morning Post* and *The Economist*. Helpful insights into the process of international advisory services in China, the international debate on China's financial markets development and international regulatory and advisory cooperation were gathered during a research internship at the Financial Sector Development Department of the World Bank in Washington, DC in 2002. Most important, though, were the interviews conducted in Beijing and Shanghai during separate field trips to China in October–November 2003 and June–July 2004 as well as a long-term research fellowship in Beijing from April 2005 to June 2006 at the Institute for World Economics and Politics. On these trips experts' and market participants' comments and an in-depth knowledge of the issues at hand were gathered. More than 120 interviews were conducted. Interview partners were domestic and foreign financial firms' representatives, regulators and other experts in the financial community, including consultants, officials from international financial institutions, academics and representatives of research and training as well as educational institutions. These interviews were arranged through a growing network of contacts and were conducted in German, English and Mandarin. Regardless of what information was discussed during an interview, everything was said under the guarantee of anonymity. Therefore no names of interviewees are revealed throughout this book. Visits to conferences and records of speeches by high-ranking officials in China rounded out the picture. Outside China, this material was embedded into its greater context through interviews with experts and financial firms' representatives in Germany, London and New York, some via telephone. Quantitative sources have been used for this research project wherever their meaningful employment was possible. Statistics and numbers used were mainly provided by Chinese official sources.

Limits of the theoretical approach and research problems

Some limits of the theoretical approach and problems that have emerged during the course of writing this book have to be mentioned. Firstly, the institutional approach to financial market internationalisation chosen for this book has no way of accounting thoroughly for the non-financially motivated incentives that govern politicians, regulators and industry players' actions. Secondly, the qualitative perspective does not allow an accurate measure and quantification of the impact of the observations. Judgments of the relative importance of certain developments are thus hard to make. Thirdly, it remains unclear which standards can reasonably be applied to the case of China; in other words, how can Chinese success or failure in financial market development and reform be assessed? Can we employ the standards of industrialised financial markets to judge the problems of China? Fourthly, one of the largest problems in social science research is to establish well-founded comparisons between national settings and across time. On what terms exactly can we compare China with other countries, keeping in mind the unique, historically developed and complex nature of its institutional settings?

Is China's financial market internationalising more quickly and thoroughly than the financial market of, say, India or Brazil? Still, this book shows that even with such relatively tentative and incomplete comparisons, an analysis of the institutional specifics of China contributes to understanding other emerging and transition countries. A well-founded identification of structural parallels and differences sharpens the analysis and enhances the overall understanding of relevant processes, while overly generalising statements should be avoided.

On a practical level, the most pressing problem that occurred during the research for this book was the opaqueness of data. Some data was just not there or not publicly available and often sources contradicted each other. Applying general caution in handling Chinese statistics, it has been attempted throughout the book to find a way through and around the problems burdening quantitative research. Last but not least, financial market development is quickly evolving and its complexity calls for caution when making statements on the nature of its process. It is not always possible to isolate the influence of foreign financial firms from other influences.

Preview of the argument

Internationalisation has had a considerable impact on the development of China's financial markets both with regard to foreign financial firms and domestic market actors. However, the importance of foreign financial firms in China is still limited in terms of relative business scope and scale. Thus, they have only limited business interests (compared to their worldwide business and profits) and bargaining power (compared to domestic players) in China; both obstruct their chances to successfully influence the development of the Chinese regulatory regime in an active way. Instead, financial market internationalisation, as it occurs today, mirrors the newly emerging attempt of the Chinese government to use foreign financial firms (especially their credit and risk assessment technologies, management expertise and corporate governance systems) for their goals to restructure Chinese financial firms and markets. While this does not mean that some foreign financial firms will not be making considerable profits (and expanding their business in China) in the future, financial market reform and opening thus remains largely dominated by regulators and therefore determined by domestic priorities (rather than by external market players' interests and international influences). Yet, while foreign financial firms in China have *not* emerged as a group of politically relevant, sufficiently powerful independent market actors so far, their presence and broader aspects of internationalisation are changing the underlying nature of Chinese financial markets and China's regulatory regime to a far greater extent than might have been expected.

Besides new products, new management styles and increased transparency brought to China's financial markets by foreign financial firms, internationalisation has also had a large impact on domestic market actors. Most importantly, it has led to an internationalisation of Chinese regulators and considerable changes in the regulatory regime of China's financial markets. In this regard, the increased influx of international ideas and cooperation with international regulatory bodies has been important. On the side of domestic industry players, an important differentiation among domestic actors due to the changed market environment has occurred. These processes are leading to the emergence of new internationally inspired policy and business communities that nurture the very foundation of financial markets, but are often neglected by financial market theories – professional personnel. Already, the reference system for the members of these communities is ideal-type, textbook liberal financial markets; these individuals are intellectually in some ways more closely linked to Wall Street than to any place in China. While they still operate (with admittedly limited political leverage) within the transitionary structures of the Chinese financial system, they form the professional foundation of a new financial market order and support significant change in informal institutions.

Up to 2006, the pace of financial market reform in China, especially in the banking sector, resembled the crisis mode of operation more than any 'normal' reform speed, leading to an underestimation of the extent and relevance of changes in the regulatory regime and the actor constellation. For example, considerable conflicts with regard to modernising corporate governance and control structures are to be expected in foreign-invested domestic financial firms once day-to-day business operations dominate. Therefore, it is only *after* phases of concentrated leadership-generated reform peak that the changes in formal and informal institutions become visible. Still, the new (institutional and professional) foundations of the financial markets that emerge under continued and increasing internationalisation can already be seen in the area of securities business and especially in fund management companies, where reforms have moved from a leadership-generated mode to a more market-driven one in recent years. Here, while some domestic market players have opted for passive and resistant strategies towards reform and further opening, an increasing number of more active actors who oppose administrative interference can be identified. Redefining their interests leads many of them to opt for dynamic, even aggressive, internationalisation.

Agents of change, initialising institutional change in the context of financial market internationalisation and reform, are therefore internationally oriented regulators, foreign firms and some domestic firms, as well as reform-minded employees of those domestic financial firms that are facing increased incentives to call for a separation of government and business interests. On the domestic level, these agents of change emerge from within the *public* sphere, contrary to the conventional wisdom of institutional economics that private actors initiate institutional change. However, this is plausible within the Chinese setting, where private financial market actors have been heavily suppressed.

Besides the changes in actor configuration, constellation and interaction, the positive systemic impact of financial market internationalisation in China lies in the increased assertion of commercial principles in business relations and efficiency-oriented principles of allocation *vis-à-vis* political considerations. Modes of socialist market regulation and direct government interference through established channels of control and co-option become less and less feasible as increasingly independent actors emerge. Together, private or public domestic financial firms – hungry for independence – and foreign financial firms necessitate new modes of governance, regulation and supervision. These are, in the end, challenging one of the pillars of the current Chinese political system, namely state control over economic resources. Herein lies the political significance of financial market internationalisation.

Policies of financial market liberalisation and internationalisation have been criticised as leading to a severe negative impact on economic stability and to detrimental distributionary effects. This book argues that while policy mistakes can never be ruled out, the case of China gives considerable insight into the *opportunities* presented by financial market internationalisation; it alters existing equilibria of interests in favour of a depoliticised resource allocation, fosters domestic financial market reform and allows for the emergence of independent (domestic and transnational) industry players. An adequate taxation and fiscal system would, on this basis, allow the achievement of distributional goals as well, given sufficient political will.

Chapter plan

This book is divided into three parts. Part I, including this and the next chapter, presents the theoretical framework of this book as well as an introduction to China's institutional framework for financial markets and an outline of financial market internationalisation from the beginning of the economic reform and opening process through to 2006.

Part II turns to the analysis of foreign financial firms as external actors in China's financial markets. Chapters 3 and 4 present the market segments of commercial banking and the securities business respectively and focus on the market environment as well as the market participation, problems and prospects of transnational financial firms. They are followed in Chapter 5 by a deeper look into the lobbying strategies employed by foreign financial firms. Together, the chapters in Part II present an assessment of the systemic contributions and impact of foreign financial firms on China's financial market development.

In Part III, domestic market actors are analysed. Chapter 6 focuses on the internationalisation of the regulatory regime and assesses changes in regulation and regulatory organisations. Chapter 7 turns to domestic industry players, changes in their market environment due to internationalisation and their reactions to this. These chapters also look at the emergence of new social groups, communities and professional elites within the context of China's financial markets. Together, they present an analysis of the domestic side of financial market internationalisation. In conclusion, Chapter 8 provides an overview of the main findings of this book, as well as developing further conclusions with regard to the theoretical framework and laying out perspectives for China's financial markets and their internationalisation.

2
Actors and Interests in China's Financial Market Internationalisation

In this chapter, the key actors and interests that influence and determine financial market development in China are reviewed along with the basic features of China's emerging financial market regulatory regime. It will be shown that the institutional framework of China's financial markets displays several remarkable characteristics that need to be kept in mind when analysing its internationalisation. Among these, the institutional legacy of the command economy, the structures of China's political system and the path dependencies created by decisions made in the early reform years stand out as particularly important because they structure both the actor constellation and the incentives these actors face. In this setting, commercial and international actors that have become more powerful during the economic reform process face a peculiar market environment and regulatory dynamics that need to be understood before moving to the analysis of single market segments in the next chapter.

The institutional legacy of the command economy and early reforms

Among the major characteristics of China's financial markets' institutional foundation, the specific institutional legacy of the command economy stands out as particularly important because it is determined by both its state-owned structure and by its centralised nature. At the beginning of the economic reforms in 1978, financial markets in China closely resembled those of any socialist market economy. The banking sector was dominant and was structured as a monobank system, primarily fulfilling accounting tasks for a planned economy. With regard to the types of financial firms, there was virtually no diversity. The People's

Bank of China (PBC) was the most important organisation in the financial markets, acting as a fiscal agent (Bowles and White, 1993, p. 58). In this system, banks financed the working capital needs of state-owned enterprises because investments were primarily allocated through the fiscal system. While there was some variation in the institutional setting between 1949 and 1979, financial markets in general were ideologically and practically subordinated to real-sector economic development. In day-to-day transactions, there were two largely separated money circles – one among the enterprises and one among households. This indicated that, as is typical in planned economies, financial markets did not perform genuine tasks of financial intermediation (Schüller, 2002, p. 6). As in any repressed financial system, political ties and networks were most important in securing access to finance.

In this system, government ownership of enterprises and banks as well as administratively set interest rates led to soft budget constraints, giving the concept of credit little practical meaning. All variables on a macro-economic level were *de facto* controlled through the (central) planning apparatus: interest rates, inflation and growth rates, as well as credit amount and distribution. During the Cultural Revolution, as the institutional framework was shaken, banks increasingly became treasuries for local governments (Byrd, 1983) and were used in their favour, a phenomenon that became even more important after the beginning of the reform policies.

Starting from this institutional basis, early decisions in SOE reform in fact determined the direction of financial market reform: contrary to most transition economies, state-owned enterprises (and banks) were not privatised quickly in China. Instead, the gradual reform path allowed state-owned enterprises to remain at the core of the Chinese economic structure. At the same time, however, market-oriented reforms in the economy reinforced the economic problems and competitive inferiority of (large) SOEs. As budgetary transfers to SOEs were radically replaced by credits, the need for SOEs to borrow heavily from state-owned banks increased, a process that developed in parallel to the overall expansion of total credit relative to the gross domestic product (GDP) (Schüller, 2002, p. 10). Consequently, on the part of the state-owned banks, non-performing loans (NPLs) accumulated, laying the foundation of the NPL problem and perpetuating the banks' dependency on state protection and intervention. Organisationally and financially, state-owned enterprises and banks remained weak and under the control of state agencies. So, the single most crucial early reform decision was *not* to break sharply with the past structures, thus leading to a muddling through on the basis of the institutional legacy of the command economy. This decision was primarily intended to secure stability, ensure employment, and guarantee continued control over production, both at the expense of the true commercialisation of economic actors.

The decisions in SOE reform necessitated control over financial firms and markets in order to ensure SOEs' access to liquidity and capital. Therefore, as a two-tier banking system was established during the early reform years and commercial banking grew in importance (Dipchand, Zhang and Ma, 1994), interest rates remained administratively controlled. Interbank and money markets developed, but the degree of state interference remained high. Early reform years also saw some internal banking decentralisation, but insufficient regulation led to inflationary trends (Byrd, 1983; Huang, 1996). In parallel to the banking sector, capital markets emerged, also heavily influenced by SOE policies: after the establishment of the stock exchanges, only SOEs were allowed to apply for listing, and the proclaimed aim of stock market development was to help SOEs with their financing problems.[15] Therefore, in 95 per cent of the cases, listed companies remained ultimately controlled by the state as often only less than half of their shares became tradable after listing. The stock market did not develop into a market for corporate control (Green, 2003a) and a newly emerging capital market was thus integrated into the old structure rather than made a measure to create new means of resource allocation independent of state interference.

As Chinese authorities made the strategic choice to restructure borrowers before solving the problems in the banking sector, the financial markets remained dependent on real-economy developments. The chosen reform path came at the price of SOBs continuing to allocate capital inefficiently, while at the same time creating volatile and inefficient capital markets.[16] Therefore, while the Chinese financial system indeed has become deepened to some degree in the sense of McKinnon and Shaw (Xu, 1998, p. 155), it also remained repressed where it was key to ensuring the social and political viability of the reform policies (Li, 1994). Most importantly, the policies came at the expense of creating sounder micro-foundations for the financial markets, where incentives remained disturbed, information lacking and informal institutions underdeveloped.

Additionally, the emergence of private financial firms was greatly restricted, rendering the financial markets largely dominated by publicly owned and controlled firms as well as dominated by regulation and politics. However, some differentiation among existing firms, for example through spin-offs, occurred, leading to an increase in institutional diversity on the side of industry players. The reduction of planning, the gradual introduction of competition among financial firms and the changes in regulatory style and organisation also signified tremendous changes *vis-à-vis* the pre-reform order.

The order of China's political institutions that governed this economy resembled and still resemble a post-Leninist one-party state, with the typical double structure of party and bureaucracy, a centralised administrative structure, and a key role for the party in policy and decision-making. Most significantly, from the perspective of economic policy-making and reform, all means of production were originally owned by state agencies. As state ownership was divided between central and local levels, each level of government owned its own enterprises and financial firms. Even though this is often overlooked in analyses of China's political system that focus on the institutional order and processes of decision-making, the political control over production and the allocation of resources through a plan in the command economy made state-owned enterprises and financial firms crucial components of the political system and assigned them political tasks. State agencies and industry players were hardly distinguishable. From the perspective of this book, this is the first important observation with regard to the actor constellation in China's economy.

The second important observation is derived from the fact that the Chinese political system operates on the basis of the central role of the Communist Party in policy and decision-making. Party mechanisms of coercion and control are important steering mechanisms in the Chinese political system, and as far as the state-owned enterprises are concerned, also in the economy. They have secured the undiminished claim of CCP leadership to rule as a single, unitary party and have been identified as the basis of the high state capacity and the ability of the Chinese state to act decisively.[17] As the CCP laid the foundations for the initial reform experiments, and displayed a widely recognised ability to learn and adapt during the reform, it can thus be seen to have enabled the development of markets and the expansion of entrepreneurial activities.[18] At the same time, the party has controlled the development of markets. The second important observation for economic policy-making and reform is thus the central role of the Communist Party and the ambivalent nature of its involvement in the economy between the enabling of markets and their control.

Thirdly, the political system allowed only for incremental, gradual and slow reforms without the guidance of an overall comprehensive plan for the new economic structure. On the level of policy-making, as put forth famously by Lieberthal and Lampton (1992, p. 12), one of the most important characteristics of the Chinese political system is its fragmented authoritarianism that leads to a need for compromise and consensus in policy-making, rather than static top-down hierarchies.[19] This structure results in strong and continuous bargaining among the ministries, government branches and localities, in particular in the process of resource allocation and economic planning (Naughton, 1992). *De facto* requirements of overall consent on important policy issues (such as the introduction of reform policies) in such a system only allow for incremental policy changes and reforms. As Shirk (1993) pointed out, policy-making and implementation in China is a process with limited pluralist characteristics, involving hundreds of officials, rather than a process only involving a few leaders at the top. The result of this structure for economic reform has been a gradual and incrementalist reform path. A main characteristic of this course was that it allowed policies to emerge slowly, while minimising opposition and compensating disadvantaged interest groups extensively. Also, while there was a strong leadership commitment to reform (personified in the leader of economic reforms, Deng Xiaoping), a general plan for reforms was missing, and the vision for a new economic structure in China emerged only slowly.

From an ex-post perspective, problematic aspects of all three of these observations are apparent: the state-ownership of enterprises as well as the continued political control over them has led to severe conflicts of interest in the economic reforms. In addition, the interdependence of *newly established* businesses and local state agencies has become firmly institutionalised (Lau, 1998; Rawski, 1999). Important reform steps have been delayed and problems have been aggravated by the need for consensus and by the gradual and slow reform policies. The actor constellation in this process has remained dominated by state-actors under CCP control.

The emerging regulatory framework

The need to change formal and informal rules in the transition to a market economy has resulted in the change of the organisational structure of state agencies and a re-configuration of state actors in the financial markets and elsewhere. Compared to the pre-reform era, a number of considerable changes have taken place with regard to the overall governance of the economic system: firstly, new administrative institutions have been created that govern the economic reform process and the emerging market economy. Old state organs, notably the powerful centrepieces of the planned economy, have been reformed and partly dismantled in three waves of administrative reform (Liu, 2001). Administrative reforms have included a separation of administration and industry, the abolition of industry ministries, and the creation of business associations. New regulatory bodies have been established in order to regulate specific economic sectors. Secondly, the spheres of the state and the party have been increasingly separated. Thirdly, a process of modernisation and professionalisation of Chinese cadres has changed the underlying personnel foundations. It was accompanied by generational change and induced a perceived reduction in the role of ideology in (economic) policy-making. Key mechanisms of personnel control have changed accordingly, away from coercion, ideology and direct control towards party control, rapid rotation and short tenure periods, as well as selective integration of local leadership with central leadership mainly intended to enforce compliance. Additionally, the development of the legal system has had a great effect on the relations between state agencies and the economy.

The growth of new formal institutions and organisations in order to govern the transition to a market economy has been accompanied by changes in the informal structure of the Chinese economy and state: the reform years witnessed an upsurge of the shadow economy, processes of informal privatisation and corruption. The emerging system of cadre capitalism has further undermined the separation of state actors and industry actors (Duckett, 1996). Continued political interference has fostered informal networks and rent-seeking coalitions. These trends are essential for understanding the persistent importance of the state sector in China's economy. They have two important consequences: firstly, in the context of the close connection of political–public interests and the interests of publicly owned enterprises and financial firms, independent (market) actors have a hard time in emerging. Secondly, the policies generated in this way have contributed significantly to the distortion of the micro-foundations of the new market economy. This is particularly visible in the case of corporate governance (Tenev and Zhang, 2002).

Who are the main actors on the side of central and local governments in regulating financial market reform on this basis? How has the regulatory regime for the Chinese financial markets evolved? In answering these questions, it is important to note that all main financial market and macroeconomic policies in China are decided upon at a central level by the State Council under the guidance of CCP commissions and leading groups.[20] On the administrative level, the Ministry of Finance (MOF) is concerned with formulating macroeconomic policies. It also manages government finances and prepares the annual budget, sets taxes and coordinates tax collection through the State Administration of Taxation. With regard to the financial markets, the MOF is important in issuing treasury notes and bonds as well as determining overall economic policies. It plays an important role in the recapitalisation of state-owned banks. China's central bank, the People's Bank of China (PBC) is the key actor with regard to monetary policy and control. Until 1992, the PBC also was the sole regulator for the financial markets, supervising the banking as well as the securities sector. As the institutional diversity of China's financial markets increased, parts of the regulatory tasks have been transferred to other, newly created regulatory bodies, 'shifting functions and capabilities of the Chinese state toward greater compatibility with a market economy' (Naughton, 2003b, p. 2). Since 2003, the PBC has concentrated solely on the implementation of monetary policy and financial market stability, while the newly established China Banking Regulatory Commission (CBRC) concentrates on the regulation of banks. It is noteworthy, however, that the PBC is no independent central bank but remains under the explicit control of the State Council (Holz, 1992).

Additionally, there are three specialised regulatory commissions operating directly under the State Council with ministerial rank (*zhiye lingdao*). The China Securities Regulatory Commission (CSRC) emerged from the securities market department inside the PBC in 1992, inheriting oversight and regulatory power over the securities firms and their business. While the CSRC today is judged to be a powerful and progressive regulatory institution, It has been troubled by conflicting mandates of regulation and industrial policy (Green, 2003c, p. 168; Heilmann, 2001). The second regulatory body in the financial markets, the Chinese Insurance Regulatory Commission (CIRC) was founded in November 1998 and thus also is a comparatively young regulatory body. The CIRC has regulated and supervised the domestic insurance sector, including domestic and foreign companies and their business, since responsibilities were transferred to it from the PBC. The CIRC has attracted far less attention than the CSRC, and has generally been regarded to be much more conservative and less internationally oriented. The third regulatory body, the CBRC, was created in 2003, incorporating functions of the China Financial Working Commission, an important CCP panel, and the regulatory responsibilities for the banking sector transferred to it from the PBC. Its main task is to supervise the banking sector, but the actual division of work and power between the PBC and the CBRC in bank restructuring has so far remained blurry.

Additionally, all regulatory bodies have subsidiaries on the sub-national level. The regulatory bodies each have regional-level branches; for example, the CSRC has offices for securities supervision in ten cities and authorised agents in 26. They are controlled by their head offices. Following the traditional structure of Leninist administration (*kuai/tiao*), this results in overlapping responsibilities and powers, as highlighted by the reform of the regional structure of the PBC in 1998, intended to break the direct link between provincial governments and provincial branches of the PBC (Shih, 2001; Saich, 2001). Following the reform, the PBC now has nine regional offices, in Chengdu, Guangzhou, Jinan, Nanjing, Shanghai, Shenyang, Tianjin, Wuhan and Xi'an. In addition, there are the self-regulatory bodies such as the Securities Association and the Banking Association, which complete the emerging three-tier structure of regulation in the markets. However, self-regulatory bodies in China have remained weak and have primarily created channels for information and discussion, while at times also being used by regulatory bodies to impose discipline and foster market development.

As a general characteristic of the regulatory structure, financial market regulators have continuously been confronted with new challenges over the reform years, as the financial markets became more and more diversified (Xu, 1998, p. 156). The regulatory framework itself thus remained under reform. The ability of the central-level government to control the market has not been seriously questioned yet (at least not in times of crisis) and while scandals have been an important driving force in financial market development, they have so far not endangered the credibility of the government's claim to guarantee residents' deposits in state-owned commercial banks.[21] Overall, during the reform years, the configuration of regulatory actors in China's financial markets therefore has changed considerably and regulatory bodies have specialised along the lines of their formal functions. They form the regulatory counter-part of the state-owned financial firms on the industry side of financial markets.

Market actors and motives for internationalisation

In this context of partially introduced markets and a state-dominated actor constellation, who have been the key actors on the commercial side of financial markets? What can be said about their interests with regard to financial market internationalisation? Powerful players and interests in the financial markets include SOEs and influential state-owned financial firms, both very well represented *vis-à-vis* the political decision makers.

Local governments and their enterprises (and financial firms) are also key players in financial market development, because an important feature of the economic reform process was to partly decentralise the allocation of funds to the sub-national level (Huang, 1996; Shirk, 1993).[22] Throughout most of the reform period, there were virtually no independent financial firms capable of acting on a commercial level outside the state-dominated fields of interest. Central and local state organisations dominated through their ownership and control structures within the commercial realm of China's financial markets.

The main motivation behind financial market policies and regulation in this setting included the protection of SOEs, the implementation of industrial policy as well as the retention of control over resource allocation. In addition, market development was impacted by the central-local dynamic, which was particularly important in periods of monetary expansion, such as in 1993 and during the closure of the GITIC in 1997, as well as for the reform of the Central Bank along regional instead of provincial lines in 1998.[23] On top of this, during certain time periods, the financial interests of the central government, budgetary problems and the implementation of wider social policies became important because the diversification of financial firms, the new role of banks, as well as the slow start to the capital markets' development, for example, were all driven heavily by the financial needs of the central government after the decline of budgetary income from SOEs. In this system, artificially low interest rates on deposits rendered saving deposits a quasi-fiscal income, and continuing financial repression enabled the central government to control and use the (cheap and abundant) deposits (Schüller, 2002, p. 28). As Kumar (1997) points out, capital markets initially primarily helped finance the government's deficit. In total, financial markets during the reform years played a semi-fiscal role for central and local governments, helping them to implement policies and to systematically transfer funds among provinces (Hu and Zhou, 2001). Among the actors, ideological disputes and clashes of interest as well as power relations have dominated the process.[24] Both a power-driven dynamic and an ideological dynamic have been the main driving forces on the process of financial market reform for most of the reform process.[25] While this constellation explains the persistent structural problems of the financial market in China with regard to financial market internationalisation, it highlights that new market entrants, in the form of domestic private or foreign financial firms, challenge it. Restrictions imposed on them can therefore be explained through this framework and the reluctant and gradual reform policies can be interpreted as attempts by the regulatory bodies to maximise their interest within this equilibrium.[26] Lardy (1998, p. 221) pointed out that the financial system is the last remaining powerful instrument for the Chinese state organisations to influence resource allocation. Therefore they are naturally reluctant to give up control over it.

However, changes in the power balances between actors have also occurred to some extent. An increase in the power of (certain) provincial governments was observed during the reform years (Shirk, 1993). Market-oriented reforms have also led to the increased power and political weight of market actors within the realm of publicly owned firms and large and well-connected market players have increasingly become important forces in the hybrid financial markets. Both groups, however, do not have a clear motive for challenging the existing order. The considerable stability of the equilibrium then can also be understood as the reason why financial market internationalisation is so difficult and progressing only slowly in China: the market entry of external actors challenges the existing equilibrium of interests that domestic actors seek to preserve. They are thus very likely to oppose such policies.

The differentiation among state actors on the industry side and the increasing relevance of markets in the Chinese economy during the reform course also had important repercussions for the interaction of state agencies and state-owned firms. The role of economic interest groups increased during the organisational differentiation among ministries, enterprises and associations. An interesting point is that lobbying in this context occurs not primarily between state and private actors, but also among state and state-close industry actors.[27] They reflect a change in the constellation of market actors primarily within the group of state-actors and, in particular, a differentiation between regulators and state-owned industry players (Kennedy, 2005). In redefining their role in the emerging market economy, state actors increasingly position themselves as commercial industry players, referees or policy-makers. These functions were less clearly separated in the command economy.

In this process, large state-owned enterprises are among the most powerful entities lobbying for their own interests. They traditionally maintain very close connections to the bureaucracy, as they were incorporated in the monolithic and monomorphic nature of the command economy (Naughton, 1995). While the administrative reforms discussed above have loosened the connection, and significant changes in the priorities of industrial policies have reduced the political leverage of these enterprises (Heilmann, 2002; Green, 2004b), in general, large SOEs still have a strong bargaining position.[28] State-owned financial firms are a similarly strong lobby group. They are heavily interested in the protection of their economic interests, more aggressively so since the reforms in the enterprise sector have accelerated and financial firms have been put under increasing pressure to become competitive.

Summing up, it can be said that the institutional legacy of the command economy has created an actor constellation in the financial markets parallel to that of the years prior to 1978. Early decisions in SOE and financial market reform have reinforced these structures. While differentiation among domestic actors – both regulators and state-owned industry players – occurred despite continued financial repression and political control over the financial markets, internationalisation poses a credible threat to the existing political economy equilibrium: new (private) market participants outside the established balance of interests endanger both the flow of funds and the political control over resources. This is what makes internationalisation so difficult and simultaneously so interesting to analyse: it allows an assessment of the impact of independent external actors on the development of the financial markets as well as their impact on the political economy equilibrium in China's financial markets. At the same time it allows analysis of the change of the regulatory regime and the operation of state-owned domestic financial firms in an increasingly international environment. In as far as it confronts the hybrid domestic markets with the logic and strategies of foreign financial firms, analysing internationalisation allows one to address the tension between domestic and foreign actors as well as the tension between industry players and regulators in a setting where domestic actors are almost exclusively state-owned or state-controlled.

Transnational actors and international influences

Starting from the introduction of special economic zones (SEZs), the opening of the economy has been an important component of the Chinese reform strategy (*gaige kaifang*). Transnational corporations were encouraged to enter the newly emerging Chinese markets and the influx of FDI contributed greatly to the economic success story of the Chinese reforms. However, in academic accounts of the reform process, the impact of internationalisation on domestic markets, both with regard to changes of the incentives of domestic actors and the role of foreign actors entering China, remains under-accounted for.[29] Consequently, there is only a limited understanding of how the opening affected the overall reform course.

However, the impact on domestic markets clearly depended on how the opening policies were constructed. In this respect, it has been argued that, both with regard to the SEZs and the numerous restrictions foreign enterprises face in China, despite an increasingly open appearance, Chinese policy-makers in fact aimed at using China's comparative advantage (cheap labour) while at the same time insulating its domestic markets from international competition. Zweig (2002, pp. 264ff) identifies a mercantilist flavour to the manner in which China's internationalisation is taking place. In his view, the regulation of opened markets remained high, and internationalisation thus led to an increase in transnational flows, but not to the reduction of state control and the emergence of a liberal-market regulatory regime. Markets therefore also remained dominated by state actors. Huang (2002b) analysed the driving forces behind the patterns of FDI in China and argued that the level and patterns of FDI show the (politically motivated) continuation of state control and primarily reflect the reluctance to allow for a stronger role of private domestic-industry actors.

As for actors in favour of opening and internationalisation, both domestic and transnational ones can be identified; again, policy-makers and regulators are most important in this regard. Additionally, as pointed out by Zweig (2002, p. 39), a number of linkage agents, predominantly new organisations managing the (economic) internationalisation, emerged during the course of the reforms. Internationalisation has also been fostered by domestic corporations engaging in international transactions. On the international level, transnational enterprises, entering Chinese markets either in the form of joint ventures or wholly foreign owned enterprises, had a great interest in further opening China's economy. This was further intensified because Chinese policies fostered equity finance rather than debt finance as part of the economic opening strategy, thus committing incoming investors to a greater degree than other emerging markets to their financial means (Overholt, 2004, p. 2). Foreign governments and institutions that would profit indirectly from a better position for foreign enterprises in China also had a great interest in the Chinese opening process and started to influence economic policies, in particular in regard to licensing and contracting procedures on the central and local level. Internationalisation has thus been fostered by specific actors and has in turn led to changes in the actor constellation in domestic markets.

With regard to bargaining power, however, most studies have noted that it remained limited for international actors in China due to the discretionary trade and investment regime in China and the abundance of FDI. Chinese state agencies, while comparatively accommodating towards foreign investors in general, have therefore often kept an upper hand in business transactions (Rosen, 1999). However, the WTO entry of China is not only seen as a major move towards a more contract- and rules-based market opening, but also as an acknowledgement of the role and rights of foreign market players in China. WTO entry thus indicates the stronger position of foreign investors and transnational industry actors.

From protectionist policy to proactive liberalisation?

Despite the hardly favourable constellation for the participation of foreign financial firms outlined above, a considerable opening of the financial markets occurred between 1978 and 2006. Sketching out phases of financial market internationalisation in post-1978 China, this section provides a preliminary bird's-eye view of the process, progress and problems of financial market internationalisation. It shows that starting from a completely isolated financial market, opening policies evolved gradually and reluctantly. Since 2001, more substantial internationalisation has occurred, in part due to China's WTO entry, and in part unrelated to it. Financial market internationalisation in China is thus a story of the stepwise and reluctant granting of market access to foreign financial firms and integration into international markets through overseas borrowing and lending. Three major points are made in this section: firstly, financial market internationalisation has been initiated and controlled, in fact almost micro-managed, by regulatory bodies, particularly with regard to the market access of foreign financial firms. Secondly, there has been a close connection to the overall reform course in the design and timing of important policy decisions. Thirdly, there is an overall trend towards a more open regime.

Phase 1: Severe restrictions (1978–91)

After China experienced a forceful opening of its financial market after 1851, foreign financial firms were regarded as a sign of imperialism and were largely repressed from 1949 onwards.[30] International capital flows had been restricted to a minimum in the years before 1978, and had mainly taken the form of government loans.[31] Therefore, at the outset of the reform era in 1978, foreign financial firms' market presence in China consisted of remnants of four foreign banks, all in Shanghai and mainly functioning as representative offices.[32] On this basis, the first step to allow the re-emergence of foreign financial firms was to allow representative offices of foreign banks in selected Chinese cities and special economic zones (SEZs). Thus, in 1979, the Bank of Tokyo was the first foreign bank to open a representative office in Beijing in the reform era.[33] However, representative offices were not allowed to conduct directly profit-generating business, and instead had to focus on initiating and facilitating offshore business deals. Representative offices thus acted primarily as facilitators for foreign firms' business in China; this remained largely the case even after the licensing of branches. In 1982, the Nanjang Commercial Bank was the first to open a branch in Shenzhen. From then on, branches could be established and were allowed to conduct non-RMB business (lending and deposits) to foreign customers in the four special economic zones. The SEZs Foreign Banking Regulations formally opened the five SEZs to foreign bank branches in 1985 (including upgraded Hainan). Still, the focus was on the support and consulting of foreign firms and thus foreign banks' market entry was largely restricted to assisting foreign direct investment.[34]

In 1985, the first Sino-foreign JV bank was formed in Xiamen; it was named Xiamen International Bank and had ICBC and ADB (among others) as shareholders. As observed by Solvet (2002), this cooperation, as with other JV banks later, aimed at know-how transfer rather than capital transfer. Before long, though, it became clear that JV banks were hampered by their legal status and were mutually disadvantageous to both foreign and domestic banks, as they were regarded as foreign financial firms, had to be capitalised accordingly, and were subject to restrictions on their branch network and business scope. Their only advantage was that they seemed to be quicker and easier to establish than foreign bank branches. Since 1985, only seven have been established and they seem to have little to offer for their parent banks either financially or strategically (Solvet, 2002, p. 104).

The lack of clarity about the banking system's development (Byrd, 1983), as well as for the financial system as a whole, during the early reform years included a lack of a clear vision for the role of foreign financial firms in it. Yet, it can be said that the reluctant opening was part of a bigger picture of the Chinese authorities' attempt to channel foreign capital in the form of FDI into China and their wooing of foreigners to participate in China's economic reconstruction. Despite the slowdown of the economic reform process after the Tian'anmen Incident in 1989, the 'Shanghai Procedures for the Administration of Foreign Financial Firms and Chinese–Foreign Joint Financial Firms' allowed foreign banks for the first time to enter a non-SEZ coastal city in 1990.

The securities business was developing rapidly during the early 1990s in China and the first official stock market was opened in Shanghai in

1991. The so-called B-share market allowed foreigners to enter the securities business, as B-shares are only available to foreign investors and are denominated in foreign currency. Their introduction started the segmentation of the securities market in China along the lines of the currency in which securities were issued. Foreign securities houses were allowed to enter the domestic market but could trade in B-shares only through a Chinese intermediary. It is noteworthy that before this the offshore China-related business of foreign financial firms, primarily banks, had expanded rapidly during the 1980s (Katz, 1997) just as the international bond issuance of Chinese entities increased after 1990 and helped to establish an international benchmark yield curve for China risk (ACFB, 1990, pp. 135ff).[35]

Overall, the first phase of financial market internationalisation with regard to the opening of domestic markets to international participation is best characterised as heavily restrained and entirely driven by internal forces, although regulatory decisions were based on newly arising market opportunities in the course of the opening policies. However, financial market internationalisation at the same time responded to and mirrored the growing importance of international business linkages to the Chinese reform process as well as the general willingness of Chinese policy-makers to utilise foreign capital and expertise.

Phase 2: The careful opening of a protected market (1992–97/8)

Corresponding to the revived vigour in the economic reform process, financial markets policies gained momentum from 1992 onwards. Domestically, this period was characterised by gradually emerging competition among Chinese banks (Katz, 1997). Externally, the years after 1992 primarily witnessed a geographical expansion of foreign bank presence, although it was still on a limited level in particular due to limited business scope. Foreign banks were establishing branches more actively and in 1992, Standard Chartered, for example, by then already had six branches and four representative offices in China (Lees and Liaw, 1996, p. 32). After 1992, foreign banks were allowed to establish branches outside the SEZs not only in Shanghai but in seven open coastal cities, a regulation extended to inland cities after 1994.[36] Also in 1992, for the first time, foreign-invested insurance companies were allowed to operate in China. In 1993, overseas listing of Chinese shares was legalised and quickly became larger than B-share issues. In general, the development of the B-share market turned out to be far less successful than originally hoped and the participation of foreign securities firms remained lukewarm.[37]

After 1995, foreign banks were allowed to establish branches in five SEZs and 19 large cities (Huang, 2002a, p. 48). With regard to business scope, foreign banks often circumvented the RMB-business restrictions and acted as agents in helping clients to arrange credit access (Lees and Liaw, 1996, p. 35). It is remarkable that, although suggestions had been discussed (Dipchand, Zhang and Ma, 1994: 188f), the expansion of foreign financial firms was not channelled through obligatory JVs as in other industries in China. However, foreign firms were kept from meaningfully engaging in RMB-business with local customers.

After 1993, with Zhu Rongji as the new Central Bank governor, important domestic reforms in the financial market were initiated; these included the reform of the fiscal system, the further development of the stock markets and the unification of the foreign exchange system. Direct government borrowing from the Central Bank was ended, which led to an increase in domestic and international bond issuance. Policy lending was transferred from domestic commercial banks to Policy Banks, starting the long and painful process of separation of commercial and political credit in China. Still, there was no revision of important structural decisions in stock market development, such as the separation of the A- and B-share market or the decision to list only SOEs. In this context, in 1994 and 1995, a new legal footing for foreign financial firms was created, for the first time defining and actively regulating foreign financial firms in total on a nationwide and comprehensive level.[38]

In 1996, RMB-business for the first time became accessible to foreign financial firms, when four foreign banks were allowed to conduct RMB-business in Pudong on a experimental basis. Remarkably, it was only in 1998 that foreign banks were allowed to do the same in Shenzhen. This experiment in RMB-business is of great systemic significance because it introduced competition with domestic banks in their core business – RMB-denominated transactions. However, the experimental stage of foreign banks' RMB-business was marked by an uneven playing field between foreign and domestic firms and numerous restrictions on the foreign banks' business, and especially the speed of business expansion, remained. Shanghai emerged as a financial centre in China during that time while Hong Kong became a southern pole from where most of the offshore business was also conducted.

Chinese overseas bond issues increased considerably during the first half of the 1990s, from less than US$200 million (average per year) in 1989–91 to more than US$2 billion per year in 1992–4. These bond issuances were part of the national credit plan and were conducted with the help of international investment banks in a highly professional manner by the Chinese government (issuing T-bonds) or financial firms (issuing F-bonds which the central government guaranteed). Interestingly, the parallel rise in syndicated loan financing (offshore and onshore) as well as the rise in the amount international banks lent to investment companies in that time contradicted the global trend of decreasing commercial loans to EMEs both before and, especially, after the 1997 Asian financial crisis. Kumar (1997, p. 201) relates this to the excellent track record that China had during that time, a picture that sharply changed with the first large Chinese financial firm defaulting on debts – the collapse of the Guangdong International Trade and Investment Company (GITIC).[39]

On the whole, during the years 1992 to 1997, financial market reform in China was gaining speed, but major microeconomic and institutional issues were not tackled. Financial market internationalisation slowly evolved in a more regulated manner and expanded geographically as well as with regard to business scope. Still, from the Chinese perspective, during this time, maximising foreign capital inflow (FCI) remained more important than developing an overall strategy for financial market development. Accordingly, while regional dynamics in financial market internationalisation emerged around Shanghai and Hong Kong, there was hardly a systemic importance assigned to foreign financial firms.

Phase 3: Towards proactive external financial market liberalisation? (1998–2006)

The single most important event initiating changes in financial market development in China at the end of the 1990s was the Asian financial crisis (AFC), which evolved after mid-1997. It resulted in a reassessment of financial market risks by Chinese decision-makers, and a massive re-centralisation of control to ensure stability from 1998 onwards. This process had a twofold impact on foreign financial firms: as the AFC highlighted the dangers of international bank lending with currency and maturity mismatches and the volatility of portfolio investment under an open capital account, opening the banking market and the capital account seemed less desirable to Chinese decision-makers. The Asian countries' integration into international capital markets was seen to be one major cause of the crisis. Yet, on the other hand, the AFC highlighted the dangers of domestic banking system fragility, an inferior competitive position on an international scale and the problems of domestic Chinese banks (Overholt, 2004). Consequently, the Chinese banking sector lost much of its political backing and major efforts were undertaken both to ensure central control over credit and for the first time to meaningfully reform domestic commercial banks. While this primarily caused an increased domestic impetus towards financial market reform (at that time without an identifiable strategic role of including foreign financial firms in it), the gradual process of opening the financial market proceeded. By 1999, 23 cities had been opened for foreign banks to establish a commercial presence and the number of foreign banks engaging in RMB-business was growing quickly.

The end of the 1990s also saw a change in the structure of foreign banks' presence in China. Most banks changed their perception of country risk in the aftermath of the GITIC collapse and some consequently cut back their lending exposure. Foreign-bank lending to China (mostly offshore/from outside China) peaked in 1997 and then fell sharply, reflecting an overall trend in emerging market finance after the AFC and the country-specific consequences of the GITIC collapse. As banks' business declined, other types of foreign financial firms engaged more strongly in the Chinese market – banks with a stronger focus on retail banking, attracted by expected WTO commitments and a comprehensive framework for foreign banks' market access emerging on the horizon. Rapid growth in the insurance business, part of it also with foreign participation, fostered the development of the securities markets. Zhu Rongji, whose appointment as prime minister in 1998 was seen to confirm the importance of financial market reforms, was warmly welcomed by the international financial community as a reformer.

In 2000, on the eve of China's WTO entry, there were 154 foreign branch banks, as well as 23 foreign funded/joint-venture banks and finance companies in China. Their share of the bank market was low, though, at only 1.3 per cent of all outstanding loans. Economically, foreign banks were thus still extremely marginal players, ever more so in RMB lending.[40] The agreement on WTO entry in 2001 confirmed the Chinese leadership's will to bind itself to an international treaty on a stepwise banking, insurance and capital market opening and a set schedule for the demolition of barriers to (some) foreign financial firms' presence. National treatment in the banking sector was to be achieved within five years of accession (at the end of 2006), based on the WTO-inherent principle of reciprocity. Ownership in the securities business, on the other hand, would remain restrained.[41] From late 2001 onwards, regulatory changes were made according to the WTO commitments, including the immediate licensing of JVs in the securities business leading to an increase in international participation in the formerly sealed-off A-share market and the stepwise opening of the banking business. Yet, in the run-up to the leadership transition after the 16th Party Congress, there was an observable general halt on economic reforms in 2001–2, with financial market reforms significantly slowing down (Naughton, 2003a). Outstandingly, however, the Qualified Foreign Institutional Investor (QFII) scheme was introduced at the end of 2002, opening the capital market to selected foreign institutional investors, a move that was not part of the WTO commitments. Starting in 2002, strategic foreign investments in Chinese financial firms were allowed and the CBRC increasingly encouraged foreign banks to invest in (smaller joint stock) Chinese banks, starting with city commercial banks. The first transaction in this regard was the investment of International Finance Corporation (IFC) in the Xi'an City Commercial Bank in September 2002, marking the beginning of this important new development.

After completion of the leadership succession in 2002–3, domestic financial market reform regained both momentum and urgency, as highlighted in a statement of new premier Wen Jiabao (ChinaOnline, 2004). Leadership attention stuck with banks and financial market stability (Naughton, 2003b, p. 44). Additionally, preparing domestic banks for the market entry of foreign banks became a headline in policy rhetoric. In domestic reforms, critical steps in banking sector reform were taken in 2003, starting off a comprehensive reform of the four large state-owned commercial banks (SOCBs). A new strategic decision to engage foreign banks in the restructuring of the sector became observable in policy statements as well as in an increase of foreign investments in Chinese financial firms on a national scale. Experimental showcases of the new direction of financial market reform included the international listings of insurance companies in 2003 after foreign strategic investors had been introduced and the deal between the Bank of Communications and HSBC in 2004. These were followed by the international listings of three of the four SOCBs in 2005 and 2006 after each of them had introduced foreign strategic investors. Many smaller banks also aimed to follow these examples; by the end of June 2006 27 foreign financial firms had made investments in 20 Chinese banks.

The QFII and the corresponding Qualified Domestic Institutional Investor Scheme (QDII) developed rapidly from late 2003 onwards, when the first selected Chinese social security funds gained their QDII licence. Clearly, all these developments show that there was a more intensive internationalisation evolving in 2003–4, standing in contrast to the previous years of reluctant, gradual and slow financial market opening. The commercial banks market serves best to highlight the extent of market opening achieved at the end of 2006: when the phase-in period for WTO commitments ended, there were 74 foreign banks present in China with

200 branch offices and 74 sub-branches, as well as 186 foreign banks with 242 representative offices. The number of products permitted to foreign banks exceeded 100 and 115 foreign banks had gained a RMB licence. The foreign-funded banks controlled US$103.3 billion in assets, accounting for 1.8 per cent of all banking assets in China (CBRC, 2007).

Summing up, financial market internationalisation before 1997 was highly contradictory in policy and hardly a catalyst for financial market reform, just as the domestic financial market during that time was hardly a motor for economic reforms. External influences were largely shut off or restrained in order to ensure financial market stability, although there were policies designed to facilitate the utilisation of inflows of capital, technology and know-how. In general, the China-related business of foreign financial firms was split into onshore and offshore business, with the latter making up the larger part, mainly conducted from Hong Kong. After 1997, changes in the financial market policies as well as in the structure of foreign financial firms' business in China gradually led to an increased (but quantitatively still almost insignificant) role for foreign financial firms, with a major turning point being the experimental opening of the RMB credit market. WTO entry and the related commitments in 2001 for the first time marked a clear policy commitment to further financial market internationalisation. Practically, however, it was only when the leadership succession was out of the way at the end of 2003 that domestic reform increased and the financial market was hence opened for significantly increased participation by foreign financial firms. The years between 2003 and 2006 have seen rapid and, for most observers, astonishingly rapid reform. However, problems remain on the domestic level as well as with regard to internationalisation and financial market opening.

Part II
International Actors in China's Financial Markets

3
Foreign Banks and the Market for Commercial Banking Services

Foreign banks have become increasingly interested in China's commercial banking sector. Being one of the largest banking markets in the world, China – with its high savings rate and continued high economic growth – has turned into a key market for them. But have foreign banks also become important actors for the Chinese market? Have they been able to grow into successful commercial players in China? Undoubtedly, foreign banks have faced an unusual and challenging market environment: the banking market is a hybrid halfway between a state-controlled command economy and a modern financial market, has pronounced institutional problems, and is characterised by both a peculiar constellation of domestic actors and a large role for regulation in market development. This chapter shows that the market entry of foreign banks in China has been a story of restraint and limitations with regard to business scale and scope and it provides some arguments for the claim that foreign banks are likely to be comparatively small yet well-noted players for the foreseeable future.

The chapter is divided into three sections. The first examines the actor constellation, problems and steps towards reform undertaken by the banking regulator CBRC, since all define the market foreign banks have to act in when entering China. The second section looks at foreign banks' strategies for entering these markets. It shows that the incentives for foreign banks to enter the market have been structured by business opportunities, competition and regulatory restrictions alike. The third section discusses the impact foreign banks have had on the Chinese commercial banking market and presents evidence for the claim that foreign banks have contributed to the development of the market. Despite their limited quantitative market position, they have become significant actors for market development through the introduction of new products and their contribution to an increase in competition. They have altered the constellation of domestic actors considerably, and have contributed to a stronger impetus for market development and reform from the side of industry players. With regard to the last steps of the phase-in of WTO commitments in December 2006, the chapter argues that these did not change the market-access strategies of most foreign banks; cream-skimming, targeting only the highly competitive market segments such as high net wealth clients or credit card business remain in the focus for most banks – even those foreign banks with the largest presence in China.

Actors, problems and reforms in China's commercial banking

The Chinese banking sector is a major pillar of the economic reform process in China. In 2006, it still accounted for the largest part of the Chinese financial markets and made up about 80 per cent of all financial assets. However, as widely agreed in the academic literature and by Chinese policy-makers, it has remained burdened with severe problems.[42] The close linkage between regulators and industry players, the political control of domestic firms and their state-owned and controlled nature have created a domestic banking sector characterised by a peculiar constellation of concentrated, state-controlled and financially weak domestic banks.

Domestic banks under state control

In a structure that developed and diversified after the separation of the central bank (PBC) and state-owned commercial banks (SOCBs) in 1984, state-owned banks remained key commercial players during the reform period. In 2006, the four large state-owned commercial banks, the Bank of China, the Industrial and Commercial Bank of China, the China Construction Bank and the Agricultural Bank of China, accounted for more than half of all banking assets in China. By then, the significantly smaller national joint-stock commercial banks (JSCBs), such as the Bank of Communications and the China Minsheng Bank, as well as regional joint-stock commercial banks and city commercial banks, had grown in size but had not yet overtaken their four large brothers (see Figure 3.1).[43]

The respective operational scopes, as well as their ownership and control structures, makes it possible to highlight the differences between these types of banks; the four SOCBs operate nationally with extensive branch networks and are owned centrally by government agencies,

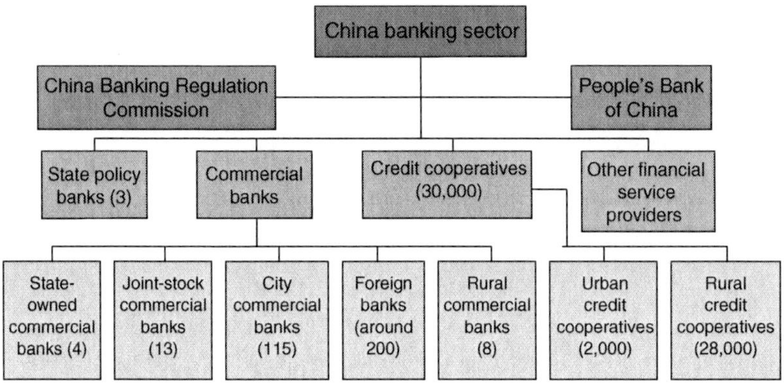

Figure 3.1   Banking sector overview as of 2006
Source: CBRC, KPMG (2005), media reports

such as the Ministry of Finance, whereas joint-stock commercial banks differ in their operational scope according to their national or regional licences.[44] In terms of their ownership structure, the classification 'joint-stock' signifies that their equity is held jointly by state agencies as well as state-owned and non-state-owned enterprises. However, they remain under the control of their respective government level to a varying degree, often as a result of their organisational history. In the case of the city commercial banks, city governments own and largely control the banks. Bank of Shanghai, for example, is controlled by the city government of Shanghai as the main shareholder. Even with dispersed ownership, such as in the case of those banks that are listed on the domestic stock exchange, state agencies remain the ultimately controlling shareholders. There are no officially recognised private banks of a significant scale in China.[45]

Through the structures of state ownership and the control mechanisms of the CCP, domestic banks in China thus have remained under state (and party) control.[46] This has consequently led to – at times severe – interference by local governments in banks' business, especially with regard to inflation and non-performing loan (NPL) creation.[47] In response to these problems, the central government recentralised credit control in a massive reform and reorganisation both after 1994 and after the Asian financial crisis. It is noteworthy that this reform led to a *reallocation of control* rather than to a liberalisation within the banking sector; central government control in Chinese banks remains high especially with regard to the four SOCBs (Shih, Zhang and Liu, 2004). The influence

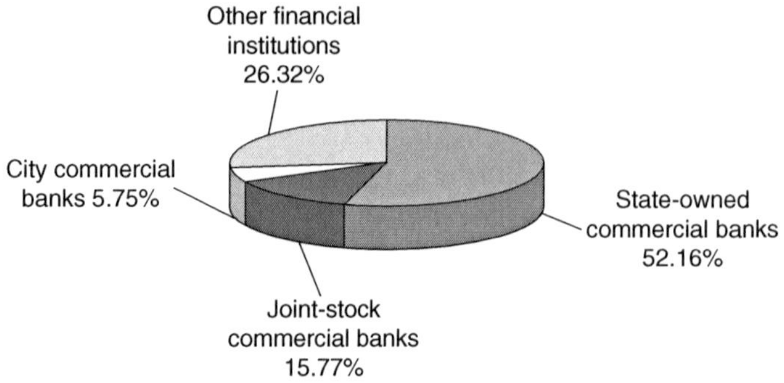

Figure 3.2   Asset allocation in China's banking sector as of 2006
Source: CBRC (2006)

of government agencies on joint-stock commercial banks, on the other hand, depends on the concentration of shareholders and the relation of those shareholders to government agencies on different levels (Wong and Wong, 2001, pp. 33–4). While actual government control over single banks thus varies, the overall state domination of the domestic commercial players and the lack of private banks is the most striking characteristic of the Chinese banking sector.[48]

Concentration and competition

In addition, concentration in the Chinese banking sector has remained high, as highlighted by the combined market share of the four SOCBs. Competition has increased, but remains distorted; regulatory differences in guarantees and refinancing options, for example, often favour of the four large SOCBs, a fact that has further strengthened their dominant position.[49] As a result of market segmentation, competition remained most intense *within* the separate tiers of the banking sector, especially among the joint-stock commercial banks and city commercial banks (Solvet 2002, p. 89; Shirai and Rajasekaran, 2001). The four SOCBs still held three-quarters of credits and four-fifths of savings deposits in 2004 and are, with 120,000 branches and 1.4 million employees, among the largest banks in the world with regard to assets (Lange, 2004) (see Figure 3.2).[50] Business-wise, no domestic bank is in a true position to challenge the large four SOCBs.

Organisational, operational and political weaknesses of domestic banks

Based on state ownership and political control over banks, central and local governments have frequently used banks to foster policy goals, mainly in industrial policy. Despite the establishment of policy banks in 1994, officially intended to end soft policy loans by commercial banks, the SOCBs, primarily, continued to channel their ample deposits towards strategically important SOEs.[51] The central government's use of them as powerful policy instruments to guard against inflation, recession and unemployment had two consequences: firstly, it left resource allocation inefficient on a macroeconomic level, following an administrative logic rather than a profit-oriented one. Secondly, it weakened the domestic banks financially and organisationally, as credits were frequently not repaid, NPL ratios rose and the incentives for internal reform were reduced; this made the domestic banks dependent on political protection. The size of the banks, their corporate governance structure, the lack of modern credit technology and, as some have argued, their ownership structure have contributed to this weak organisational and financial position because the banks found it hard to introduce new credit technologies and effectively reduce the stock and flow of new NPLs. Due to the resulting low efficiency and loan losses, the SOCBs in particular remained financially and operationally weak entities – ongoing reforms and their success notwithstanding.[52] They have remained the insolvent but overly liquid troublesome behemoths of the Chinese financial market and have become the crystallisation point of conflicting policies. Due to their organisational weakness, they are regarded as the largest legacy of the socialist system and the greatest danger to China's economic stability. Solving the problem of the four SOCBs and their NPLs has consequently become the highest priority for the CBRC (Tang, 2004).

The PBC on the other hand continued the repression of the financial markets throughout the economic reform process in order to ensure the liquidity of the four SOCBs (Li, 2001; Li, 1994). The double nature of the banks as commercial actors and policy tools resulted in three additional structural problems of the Chinese banking market that now made reforms more difficult:

1. *Administratively controlled interest rates.* Deposit and lending interest rates have remained administratively controlled. Therefore only limited price competition in the collection of deposits or granting of credit is possible and the structuring of banking products is restricted. It is questionable whether the government will loosen the grip on interest rates as long as the process of SOCB reform is not completed (Bank of East Asia, 2004).
2. *Distortion of risk structures and segmentation of the banking sector.* State guarantees render the fundamentals of enterprises largely irrelevant

for competition, disturbing the risk structure in the market. Giving credit to a low-risk client in China in many cases still means (for Chinese and foreign banks alike) giving it to large SOEs that are unlikely to lose government support rather than giving it to small, opaque but possibly more innovative private-sector companies.[53]

3. *Limited development level of the money market.* The banking sector is essentially still a deposit-driven system and domestic banks depend heavily on their ability to collect deposits, since Chinese money markets remain underdeveloped.[54]

Banking reform and policy-led market development

As described in the previous chapter, banking reform had not been a policy priority for most of the reform years after 1978. It has only been from 1997 onwards in the post-Asian financial crisis setting that the focus of banking-sector reform policies shifted towards the financial strength of banks. The first serious attack on NPLs in 1998 was characterised by capital injections, recapitalisation through bonds issuance and the transfer of NPLs to asset management companies (AMCs).[55] In parallel to a general change in industrial policies away from state-owned enterprises and related interest groups, banking reform policies in general turned towards better credit management, the implementation of new best practices and increasing operational efficiency. Yet, banking reform in China gained true momentum only in 2003–4, and restructuring the banking sector became a top policy priority in 2004. The new impetus was directed at the four large state-owned commercial banks and paved the road for their partial privatisation both to domestic and foreign strategic investors. The proclaimed aim of the CBRC has been to create internationally competitive joint-stock commercial banks, through taking responsibility for past policy-related losses and ending affiliated lending.[56] Strategically, the new impetus of banking reform was to change the incentives that govern domestic banks (Harner, 2004).

The reform of the SOCBs has been conducted in three steps; the first was a bailout, including a recapitalisation through the injection of foreign exchange reserves, in January 2004.[57] The second is the corporatisation and internal restructuring of the banks. The new legal structure will be accompanied by organisational improvements in decision-making, accountability and personnel, potentially assisted by foreign strategic investors. The third was the stock market listing and partial privatisation of the two banks.[58] However, the unique structure of the Chinese banking market had not been altered by the reforms up to 2006; domestic banks remained state-owned and the extent of government control, interference and regulation-driven reform was still remarkable after more than 25 years of economic reforms.

Foreign banks entering a challenging market environment

Foreign financial firms have been largely attracted to the Chinese banking market, but at the same time faced severe regulatory restrictions. The state-dominated structure of the domestic actors and peculiar market structure have created a unique market environment for them. How have foreign banks been willing and able to enter this market? How has their market participation evolved in the triangle of regulation, market opportunities and strategic decisions on the side of foreign banks? This section shows that foreign banks, as external actors in China's banking market, are a heterogeneous group of actors with different market-entry strategies. Only few banks are actively engaging in the Chinese market. They have had to adapt continuously to the evolving market environment, in particular with regard to regulation, and have faced specific operational problems. Restrictive regulation stands out as the single most important limiting factor on their business expansion. Business opportunities and strategic decisions made at their headquarters, however, also account for the actual level of market participation.

Overview

In December 2006, there were 74 foreign banks operating in China, with 200 branches and 79 sub-branches as well as 242 representative offices (CBRC, 2007).[59] In order to understand the heterogeneous nature of these banks and the main differences in their strategies, it is helpful to group them into three broad categories.[60] In the first category there are those foreign banks that regard China as a part of their core business and are eager to engage deeper in consumer banking and RMB-business, a strategy often rooted in their historical ties to the area or set by global strategic aims (or both). In the second category are those banks that have a limited presence and business interest in China, and engage mainly in corporate banking, or are banks that have reduced their presence and exposure after enduring some losses (for example after 1997, there was a collapse of numerous trade and investment companies, to which foreign banks were exposed). These banks tend to be less than globally oriented in their strategy, but remain flexible to adjust to newly emerging business opportunities in China. In the third category are those banks that essentially have followed their customers to China and provide only limited services to them there, without being oriented in a genuine way towards the Chinese market or Chinese customers. While the borders of this categorisation remain blurred and flexible, as new windows of opportunity and reduced regulatory constraints can change business strategies, the categorisation helps to highlight the differences in foreign banks' willingness and ability to take long-term investments as well as differences in their overall commitment to China. Prominent examples of the first group of foreign banks are HSBC, Citibank and Standard Chartered, all historically attached to China. The German Commerzbank and Bank of America are examples of the second category. LBBW is an example of the third type; originally having followed customers from an export-intensive region in southern Germany to China, LBBW offers advice, limited services and help in establishing operations in China, often for medium-sized companies. The market-entry strategies of foreign banks with regard to products offered by them, as well as their branching policies, vary greatly among the categories. Not surprisingly, there are only a few banks in the first category, more in the second, but most of the foreign banks fall into the third category. It is important to note that the overall strategy of the banks is determined both by China-specific factors and by the overall global strategy and size of the respective banks.[61]

Market-entry strategies: regional concentration and branching policies

In general, foreign banks can choose between three modes of market entry on the operational level; the establishment of branches, of wholly foreign-owned subsidiaries or of JV banks.[62] As has been pointed out already, JV banks have been regarded as inferior to other arrangements by both foreign and Chinese banks and have remained rare. Instead, foreign banks have generally preferred to open branches, as confirmed by the list of foreign financial firms' operations in China published by the People's Bank of China (2004c). There is limited evidence relating to the question of why branches have been so popular as a mode of entry in the Chinese banking market, but it can be suspected that the lack of retail orientation in earlier years has made branches a preferred choice.[63]

With regard to genuinely building (and growing) networks in the Chinese market, either through branch opening or through subsidiaries, it has to be pointed out that there are regulatory and economic restrictions on the number of branches or subsidiaries that a foreign bank can set up. Until August 2004, only one branch per year could be opened by a foreign bank and branch establishment remained expensive due to prudential regulations. Therefore, building extensive 'bricks and mortar' branch networks has not occurred (Bonin and Huang, 2002, p. 1090).

Bank	Origin	Branches	Sub-branches	Rep-offices
HSBC	UK	15	28	n.a.
Standard Chartered Bank	UK	12	14	3
Citibank	US	9	17	1

Figure 3.3   The foreign banks with the largest presence in China (as of mid-2007)
Source: EIU (2003), media reports, companies' websites

HSBC, the bank with the largest network of branches in China (see Figure 3.3), had 10 branches, three sub-branches and two representative offices in November 2004; this had grown to 15 branches and 28 sub-branches by 2007 (www.hsbc.com.cn). But as only a small number of foreign banks view the Chinese market as key to their business, most banks have only one or two branches in China.

In expanding their branch networks strategically in high-profile locations in large cities, some of the active foreign banks have been trying to secure first-mover advantages primarily *vis-à-vis* other foreign banks. For this, banks need to have considerable financial strength because regulatory requirements make these business expansion strategies cost-intensive. However, branching out has not been the sole strategy to enlarge their reach to potential customers, as building networks with local partners and investing in Chinese banks has become increasingly important (as discussed below).[64] He (2004) notes that the growth of the number of branches of foreign banks in China after WTO entry in 2001 has not been due to those banks opening *more* branches, but was attributed primarily to Asian banks opening their first or second branch in China. All foreign banks, however, had long been geographically limited in their market entry to those cities that have been opened by regulations. It is noteworthy that these regulations not only restrict geographical specialisation among foreign banks but limit their location to areas near the major international clients as well as the emerging rich middle class and large financially stable SOEs in coastal areas. Banks with many branches are not necessarily the most active, and operating only a representative office does not necessarily indicate a small participation in China business or small profits. On the contrary, representative offices have generally proven to be very valuable for the foreign banks' offshore business, as confirmed by interviews with foreign banks. Additionally, they provide a foothold in the market for later expansion. For a long time they were a prerequisite for applying for a branch. Overall, the branch networks of *all* foreign banks in general have remained very limited, especially when compared to the market presence of domestic banks.

Market entry strategies: products and services

For those banks that actively and directly engage in the Chinese banking sector (which implies having at least one branch), the provision of foreign-currency loans to foreign-invested companies has been a major area of business. Even in 2004, the largest number of foreign banks primarily conducted foreign currency business with an additional focus on syndicated loans and wholesale banking as well as project and trade financing.[65] Additionally, foreign banks offer cash management services and international money transfers.[66] Historically, however, corporate and niche strategies have dominated among foreign banks.[67] Moving towards more comprehensive strategies from their initial starting point in foreign-currency banking, some foreign banks (from the first category and some from the second), have started to extend their presence in retail banking, again with a dominance of foreign-currency services due to regulatory restrictions. Foreign-currency credit to Chinese corporate customers has been allowed since 2002.[68] In retail banking to corporations, the credit business, as well as taking deposits from corporate customers, was additionally extended to RMB-business within geographic restrictions in 2003. By mid-2004, however, only around half of the 190 branches were licensed to conduct RMB-business.

Foreign banks are restricted in their business scope by the 'Regulations of the People's Republic of China on the Administration of Foreign-Funded Financial Firms', allowing for 12 categories of services, including online banking, underwriting of T-bonds, real estate mortgage loans as well as cash and wealth management.[69] While consumer banking in China is still more restricted from the perspective of foreign banks (as of mid-2004), and RMB services to private customers (households) were not allowed before the end of 2006, only a limited number of foreign banks has developed a consumer-oriented strategy (see Figure 3.4). These banks most likely will try to tap the market for the most wealthy private customers, a customer segment where a large share of Chinese savings is concentrated, and offer private wealth-management services. Other new developments in consumer banking have also been attractive to and fostered by foreign banks, such as the market for credit cards (Lange, 2004). Technology-intensive new areas of banking include e-banking and other internet services but the evidence remains inconclusive as to how far many foreign banks will go towards offering these services on a significant scale. In principle, however, from the perspective of foreign banks, e-banking offers a cost-sensible way to substitute for extensive (and expensive) branch networks. If regulations permit, the strong IT position of foreign banks will not only allow foreign banks to operate more efficiently internally, but can also be turned into a qualitative advantage for significant cream-skimming among customers (Lange, 2004).

In general, the new trends and options in retail banking after the granting of RMB licenses have led to more aggressive and comprehensive market approaches only among those foreign banks that intend to be involved and present in the market over the long term (category one and some of category two). It is primarily those banks that have increased their visibility strategically in Shanghai and Beijing over recent years. In total, the quantitative impact of foreign firms in commercial banking has been limited, in regard to RMB lending even more so than with foreign currency.

This broad picture of foreign commercial banks' business in China is completed by a number of smaller foreign banks that have developed specialised services in trade or infrastructure-related finance, positioning themselves as important players in niches. HSH Nordbank, for example, part of the German Landesbanken and a leading bank in maritime finance in the Scandinavian area, has been conducting offshore business focused on harbour infrastructure and related M&A business in China, operating through a representative office in Shanghai.

Foreign banks have also positioned themselves in the newly emerging mortgage business, which is generally considered to have a low risk profile. The German building society and housing finance provider Schwäbisch Hall provides housing finance through a JV with CCB in Tianjin, modelled after the German Bausparkassen. As WTO has opened the door to the provision of consumer finance for automobiles, a number of automobile companies such as GM and VW have moved into credit provision. The impact of these smaller banks and newer developments in consumer finance, however, while significant from the perspective of individual firms and potentially profitable, remains limited for the financial markets.[70]

Overall, the product strategies of foreign banks in China have varied greatly, ranging from corporate and niche strategies to offering value-added services alongside the domestic players in more comprehensive strategies. Foreign banks have thus been competing with domestic banks with different intensity in single market segments. However, they have not only aimed at competing with domestic banks, but also at cooperating with them as partners.

	Pre-WTO entry (before 2001)	During phase-in (2002-Dec. 2006)	Post phase-in (2007 onwards)
Restrictions on business	Branches of foreign banks can 1. Conduct foreign currency business with foreign and foreign invested corporations, including JVs 2. Conduct RMB business with foreign and foreign invested corporations on an experimental basis in Shanghai and Shenzhen Branch opening is limited to opening one branch a year and branches can only be opened in selected cities.	Gradual and step-wise reduction of restrictions on ownership and business scale • Immediately on accession: foreign currency business to all customers (deposits and lending) • Deposits and lending in RMB to Chinese corporations after two years (end of 2003) • Deposits and lending in RMB to Chinese private customers after five years (end of 2006) • Removal of geographic restrictions step-wise until 2006, each year four cities opening • Five years after WTO accession no geographic restrictions remain	National treatment of foreign banks

Figure 3.4   Foreign banks in China, pre- and post-WTO entry
Source: WTO (2001a), WTO (2001b), media reports

Strategies of cooperation: building networks for expansion through localisation

Despite restrictions, foreign banks have long been allowed to enter the Chinese market in a standalone manner. Yet many have engaged in partnership arrangements with Chinese banks on various scales after their entry. Deutsche Bank, for example, linked with local partners with regard to cash transfer systems long before entering into closer cooperation arrangements.[71] It was only after 2001 that PBC and CBRC allowed strategic investment by foreign banks (equity participation) in Chinese banks.[72] Cooperation though strategic foreign investments in Chinese banks has consecutively become a new channel of cooperation and an important part of the entry strategies that foreign banks pursue. Not even mentioned in the WTO agreements, they have been increasingly fostered by the CBRC in order to utilise them for the benefit of the domestic financial market, especially with regard to the recapitalisation and modernisation of Chinese banks (CBRC, 2004b). Two types of investments have to be differentiated in this regard; strategic investment in mid-cap banks and strategic investment in larger banks prior to their IPO. With regard to buying a strategic stake in mid-cap banks, the IFC was the first foreign investor to buy a stake in the Nanjing City Commercial Bank in 2001, and others have followed since.[73] Technically, buying the stake is a legal-person share transfer requiring government consent (Cheong, 2003). Initially, the banks on the Chinese side in these transactions were small city commercial banks with a strong need to expand their capital base. These banks are often called bonsai banks due to the regulatory limitations they face with regard to their geographical mandate and consequently their ability to grow. Since 1 January 2004, foreign financial firms may acquire equity up to 25 per cent of domestic Chinese banks, a limit raised from a previous 15 per cent. The most important motive for acquiring a stake in a domestic bank has been the branch network, as well as access to restricted business activities and the forming of strategic alliances (Cheong, 2003). In the case of HSBC and Citibank, who each bought a small stake in local banks in Shanghai, the ultimate motive was access to the Shanghainese credit card market. Other strategic investments have included an active participation of the foreign investor after concluding the deal, especially with regard to the streamlining of risk-management structures, business development, and the strategic positioning of the bank. Regarding the question of a transfer of control through these strategic investments, it has to be pointed out that only in the case of Shenzhen Development Bank, an important regionally operating joint-stock commercial bank, has the foreign investor been successful in gaining control through buying a 18 per cent stake. This stake allowed for effective control of the firm and the majority of the board due to the (unusually) dispersed ownership structure of Shenzhen Development Bank. While a significant move, it has to be kept in mind that similar deals were judged to be unlikely in the future (*The Economist*, 2004; *China Daily* 2004b).

With regard to buying into large state-owned banks before their IPO, the investment of HSBC in the Bank of Communications in 2004 opened the scene. Bank of Communications is China's fifth-largest lender and thus neither a mid-cap bank, nor – with 2700 branches and outlets in 137 cities – regionally restricted in its operations (Zhang and Cao, 2004). Buying a 19.9 per cent share, HSBC was expected to take an active role in the further streamlining of the BoComm in order to guide it to its IPO (Dolven, Winn and Murphy, 2004). BoComm, on the other hand, gave HSBC access to its nationwide network and licence. The significance of this deal, however, was its exemplary nature; strategic foreign investors were also sought and successfully found for three of the four large SOCBs in the following years (Xu, 2004; Tang, 2004; China Economic Net, 2004; *People's Daily*, 2004c). China Construction Bank, Bank of China and ICBC took on foreign strategic investors and went public internationally in Hong Kong during 2005 and 2006.

However, taking control in any Chinese bank in the sense of majority shareholding is not allowed for foreign banks due to regulatory restrictions. As of 2006 CBRC restricted the investment to just under 20 per cent for a single foreign bank and just under 25 per cent for a consortium of foreign investors. The significance of strategic foreign investments from the perspective of the domestic banks is discussed in Chapter 7.

Business opportunities and regulatory restrictions

The framework for the market entry of foreign banks has been highly restrictive for most of the reform years since 1978, allowing business only within limitations on geographic location, on the types of products that can be offered, on the currency they can be offered in, on the range of potential clients, and on the speed of branch network growth. Gradually, restrictions were released in a move away from the containment and exclusion of foreign banks towards a more liberal market-access regime. The starting point of this evolution was foreign banks' business with foreign-invested enterprises and in foreign currency only. Branch opening was based on regulatory approval, and restricted to opening one branch a year in selected cities. This regulatory framework reinforced foreign banks' position in foreign currency business only. They thus remained at the border of the domestic financial markets. Even in this business area, however, their potential customers have long been limited to internationally invested or foreign corporations. Originally, therefore, foreign banks were allowed to operate on a very limited scale only. From this starting point, their market participation increased in parallel to the extent that restrictive regulations were dismantled, geographically, with regard to RMB lending and also for niche transactions. WTO entry was a major breakthrough in this regard. Still, even the granting of national treatment to foreign banks will not necessarily put them on an equal footing with domestic banks in day-to-day business transactions, as regulatory constraints on the refinancing of RMB loans and even of foreign currency loans continue to restrict actual business expansion. Regulatory restrictions have thus been the single most important factor limiting the expansion of foreign banks' business in China.[74]

Due to regulations, foreign banks have long had to locate in the largest and most open (coastal) Chinese cities, conduct business with internationally connected clients, and refrain from entering the consumer banking market. Since these were market segments in which foreign banks had the largest comparative advantage (as discussed below), the regulations did not necessarily conflict with the business logic of foreign banks. Instead, the regulations have *channelled* the market participation of foreign banks to these market segments and have reinforced the strong competitive position of foreign banks in them. Regulation did conflict with the business logic of foreign banks, however, where they limited their ability to grasp business opportunities, such as in the provision of sophisticated financial services – for example, the hedging of currency risks. In the interviews conducted among foreign bankers for this book, regulatory restrictions were regarded as the single most important factor in determining the range of products offered by foreign banks in China. Overall, the attractiveness of the Chinese market from the perspective of foreign banks was determined to a large degree by regulations that created small accessible segments of the overall market, rendering the myths of the gigantic Chinese banking market largely unfounded.

As highlighted in the discussion of the product and cooperation strategies, it is noteworthy that some new business and cooperation opportunities have rapidly been emerging for foreign banks since 2001, marking a clear contrast with the formerly gradual removal of their containment. In the implementation of WTO commitments and the new strategic investments of foreign banks into Chinese banks, a new regulatory strategy of increased admittance of and cooperation with foreign banks can be identified. From the perspective of Chinese regulatory bodies, foreign banks are increasingly seen to hold a strategic position in the reform of the Chinese banking sector, primarily due to their professional standards as well as their ability to inject new capital. They have been used by the Chinese regulatory bodies not only to create a threat to domestic banks, but have also been encouraged to engage more actively in domestic banks' restructuring (CBRC, 2004b; Liu, 2004a). This strategy of welcoming foreign banks, reducing barriers of entry and actively encouraging their participation was in line with the new impetus on banking reform in 2003–4. Nationalist sentiments about the importance of a genuinely Chinese banking sector have faded and given way to efficiency considerations, as expressed by the following CBRC statement: 'The CBRC shares the view that the most important question is not who provides banking services but who can provide them more efficiently' (Ping, 2003, p. 12).

In the view of a PBC official, interviewed in July 2004, finally solving part of the NPL problem through getting rid of them was much more important than the question who bought them. As a CBRC official stated in November 2003: 'The CBRC is now assisting foreign banks to become niche players in consumer lending, wealth management, asset securitization and resolution of bad loans. It also encourages foreign banks to have equity stake or become strategic investors in Chinese banks, big or small' (p. 12).

These foreign strategic investments, described above as a strategy of foreign banks to cooperate with domestic banks and access their networks, in turn allow the Chinese government to use the 'helping hand of the foreign institutions' (Bank of East Asia, 2004) in reforming the Chinese banking sector. As a side-effect, this strategy also prevents foreign banks from competing fiercely for market share themselves (as they increasingly operate through cooperation), and – due to the minority position of foreign banks – allows the maintenance of political control over the domestic banks. It thus creates a balance between solving the NPL problem and speeding up banking reforms and maintaining the key features of the banking sector. From the perspective of foreign banks, this strategy implies their (partial) cooption by the CBRC while their business opportunities have increased (Zhang, 2004; Chuan, 2004; O'Neill, 2004; Chen Yao, 2004). The CBRC's strategy in dealing with the market presence of foreign banks thus ranges from containment and restriction via coordination to cooperation and cooption.

Competitive strengths and weaknesses of foreign banks in the Chinese market

The second most important factor shaping the market participation of foreign banks in China has been their competitive advantages in the market and the competition they have faced from domestic banks. Here, foreign banks' clearest comparative advantage *vis-à-vis* Chinese banks lies in their international networks and global reach. As international players, they are well positioned to help (foreign and domestic) enterprises in China meet their financial needs internationally. Their global brand and network, sophisticated IT systems, as well as their quality of service and capability of product innovation, gives them a 'huge competitive edge in generating business with global firms operating in China' (Qing, 2001, p. 832). Therefore, foreign banks are well positioned to grasp the opportunities arising in some of the most profitable segments of the Chinese banking sector, namely those of internationally connected domestic enterprises, JVs and multinational corporations (MNCs). As the internationally connected enterprises tend to be more profitable, stable and transparent than other enterprises in China, this also reduces the risks to foreign banks. The growing importance of international economic connections for the Chinese economy naturally coincides with their specialisation, and offers profitable business opportunities. Foreign currency business and related cross-border transactions, the traditional strongholds of foreign banks, have gained importance over the course of the reform years.

However, foreign banks are in a much weaker position with regard to intimate knowledge of the Chinese market and (smaller) Chinese customers. Foreign banks are therefore reluctant to lend on a larger scale to domestic enterprises that display limited transparency, especially since administratively controlled interest rates inhibit adequate pricing of their perceived risks.[75] In addition, foreign banks are competing on an unequal footing with domestic banks in the current regulatory environment. It is uncertain how far they are able to utilise the advantages they have as internationally competitive banks in know-how, credit technologies, business experience, better management and clearer incentives structures (corporate governance). Therefore, due to their competitive position, even if foreign banks were permitted to participate on a broader scale in RMB-business with small local companies, they are likely to keep their strategic focus on internationally connected and large enterprises (Lardy, 2001). Some of the interviewees, notably from smaller banks, pointed out that the lack of transparent, credit-worthy and profitable creditors in China is the largest limitation on their credit growth (and thus might be almost as important in structuring their business as regulation). For foreign banks, there are hence primarily two groups of attractive customers: firstly, large SOEs that profit from state guarantees and protection, and therefore carry limited risks even if their profitability is questionable.[76] Secondly, the better-managed and more transparent foreign-invested enterprises and JVs. However, as domestic banks have repositioned their strategies towards these promising customers as well, competition in the provision of local banking services to MNCs and foreign-invested companies is high.

With regard to consumer banking, foreign banks are not well positioned to collect small-scale deposits through a nationwide network of branches and thus tend to concentrate on specific market segments.[77] Increasing personal wealth and the newly emerging middle class in the urban coastal areas coincides with their competitive advantages in the provision of high-end wealth-management products, with which they have more experience than domestic banks. However, as in corporate banking, domestic banks have increasingly realigned their business in this market segment as well, increasing competition (He, 2004). As regulation of the market entry of foreign banks in consumer banking has so far remained restrictive, this is a good example to highlight the interplay of regulation and business opportunities in the context of comparative advantages and competition. In the market segment of private banking, foreign banks have strong incentives to position themselves at the high end of wealth management, where they have a competitive advantage *vis-à-vis* domestic banks. However, competition is high both between foreign banks and with domestic banks, and regulatory restrictions constrain their ability to utilise their competitive advantages. Still, both the structure of the domestic market and the comparative advantages of foreign banks have been important factors in shaping their market participation on the business side.

Operational problems of foreign banks in China

There are some problems in day-to-day operations that are specific to foreign banks and that have a significant impact on foreign banks' market participation. Firstly, operating costs in the Chinese market have remained high; expanding business in China is mainly a cost-based decision. The cost of setting up branches has long been viewed as extraordinarily expensive,[78] and such long-term investments can only be made by the world's largest banks. In a move to explicitly reduce the operating costs of foreign banks in China, capital requirements for foreign bank branches' corporate and retail RMB-business with Chinese clients were reduced to 300 million RMB and 500 million RMB from 400 million RMB and 600 million respectively from 1 September 2004 ('Rules on the Administration of Foreign Financial Institutions'). Yet, the high working capital requirements, and the unfavourable application of capital adequacy calculations, as well as restrictive foreign exchange approvals and restricted interest rates on foreign currency (and RMB) deposits still render the cost structure problematic (Cheong, 2003).

Secondly, foreign banks have found it very difficult to find suitable personnel. The availability of skilled and experienced personnel is thus a major constraint on the business of foreign banks and its expansion. Local personnel are often not adequately trained and while training and educational initiatives have been set up almost from the beginning of the reforms, the demand has not yet been met (interviews). Training staff in-house entails the risk of losing the trained personnel to other foreign or domestic banks, as job-hopping is frequent in China's financial industry. Foreign banks have thus partially resorted to employing personnel from their Hong Kong operations, which in turn has contributed to the high operational costs.

Refinancing problems are a third area of trouble. Foreign banks in China lend much more than they collect, especially in RMB, so they depend on external funding and refinancing sources. He and Fan (2004) point out that the increase of foreign banks' external liabilities exceeds the increase of their assets, signifying that – with regard to business in foreign currency – foreign banks are actively importing funds, which has been problematic in regard to restrictions on capital imports. In the case of RMB business, foreign banks depend on the money market, which remains underdeveloped (Bonin and Huang, 2002, p. 1090). In effect, this leads to larger costs as well. In addition, regulation has limited refinancing on the money market to 40 per cent of all loans. If foreign banks intend to grow significantly in the RMB credit market, under current regulations they will have to collect more domestic RMB deposits. However, doing so is not a comparative advantage to foreign banks due to their limited branch structure, as pointed out above. Refinancing is thus likely to remain a limiting factor to business expansion.

Fourthly, the risks of the banking business in China remain high and can increase in the course of SOE reform – for example, if state guarantees for SOEs are withdrawn. Foreign banks therefore hold an ambivalent position towards SOE reform; they seek better customers elsewhere, but encounter lower risks with state-owned Chinese enterprises. High regulatory risks and risks related to the ongoing banking reform are another problem because the regulatory framework is still incomplete and constantly evolving.

This section has shown that regulatory restrictions, market opportunities based on comparative advantages and competition, and operational problems have shaped the incentives and constraints of foreign banks. These incentives and constraints explain the market-entry strategies and the pattern of actual market participation of foreign banks in China. In their business strategy, foreign banks take the institutional context as given and operate within the regulatory framework. In order to understand their position as commercial actors in the domestic actor constellation, a position that is determined by their business expansion, market share and commercial weight in the market, it is important to understand the double dynamic behind their market entry. Foreign banks position themselves where regulation allows them to be *and* where it is profitable for them to operate. In this regard, it is an important finding of the analysis that while regulation so far has been the most important factor in limiting the market entry of foreign banks, commercial considerations have also limited the business expansion of foreign banks. This implies that even after lifting restrictions, only the high-end, geographically concentrated and internationally connected market segments will be of substantial commercial interest to foreign banks, making a branch-based expansion of their business in China comparatively unlikely. Still, the more cooperative and coopting approach of the CBRC and PBC that has also been identified in this section creates new options for foreign banks and has been an important factor in initiating stronger market participation as well as changes in the pattern of foreign banks' operation.

Impact on China's commercial banking sector

After assessing what drove foreign banks' market participation, this section turns to the impact foreign banks' business conduct has had on the market they participate in. As highlighted by their limited market shares in lending and deposit-taking, the quantitative impact of foreign banks on lending and deposits in China has been small. But in what ways has foreign banks' business had a direct, qualitative effect on market development?

1. Introducing new products and new standards in service provision

The above discussion of the product dimension of foreign banks' market entry strategies emphasised that they have positioned themselves

	Product description
Wealth management	Consumer banking for wealthy customers, as of 2004 still restricted to foreign currency business and foreign customers
Cash management	Offered to private and corporate customers alike
E-banking and phone banking	Available both for private and corporate customers, facilitating and accelerating basic banking services
Factoring	Sale on credit, accounts receivable management, credit risk guarantee and trade financing
Credit cards	Foreign currency account credit cards as opposed to Chinese debit card system
Specialised foreign-exchange services	Account settlement, guarantees, cross-border money transfers, multi-currency savings accounts

Figure 3.5   New products offered
Sources: Company's websites, product brochures, Lange (2004), Huang (2002a)

along two lines; either they have developed a niche strategy or they have attempted to provide value-added services in parallel to domestic competitors. Looking at their contribution to the overall range of products available within the Chinese banking market, they have thus either offered products that were previously unavailable or products that have been significantly improved.[79] Figure 3.5 depicts some examples of products that foreign banks have introduced to the Chinese market. While some domestic banks later picked up these product lines, it was foreign banks that contributed significantly to their initial development and diffusion. That foreign banks may not be the single providers of these products does not diminish their contribution to market development. On the contrary, it can be argued that the effect on the domestic banking market was particularly strong in cases where domestic banks developed similar products after foreign banks had introduced them. However, not all of the products introduced by foreign banks have been copied and replicated by domestic banks. It is noteworthy with regard to cooperation that some of the products have been offered in strategic alliances (*zhanlüe lianmeng*) with domestic banks, such as in the cash-management products offered by Deutsche Bank and Minsheng Bank (Huang, 2003).

As Figure 3.5 shows, the product lines in which foreign bank participation have been significant are varied. Some of the products and services, such as e-banking, have application to corporate banking and consumer

	General account services	**Premium services**	**Services with foreign exchange linkage**
Citibank	Basic checking account Junior account	CitiGold account	Premium account
HSBC	Standard account	HSBC Premier account	
Standard Chartered	Standard account	Priority banking	Integrated banking

Figure 3.6   Account services of foreign banks
Sources: Companies' websites

banking alike. Foreign banks have also contributed to the differentiation of products and a more customer-oriented approach to banking, such as in the case of account services. The tailoring of products towards specific customer groups in consumer banking has in fact been a new approach in China that foreign banks are widely credited for, as confirmed by interviews with domestic and foreign bankers (see also Hu, 2003). It is noteworthy that the products offered by foreign banks in this regard are based on their internationally available products and are part of their global strategy, rather than being made for the Chinese market in particular. International linkages, including international availability of services and easy transfer of funds, and international features of products, such as in savings deposits that are bound to foreign currency baskets, for example, have become important dimensions of foreign banks' value-added strategies.

In addition to single products, foreign banks have contributed to the introduction of a generally stronger service orientation to banking in China.[80] The broad service spectrum of some of the more active foreign banks in China and their strategic use of their international links (such as in the case of Citibank advertising with its branches in more than 100 countries, 'the world's most global bank') has also set new benchmarks. Foreign banks have thus exerted competitive pressures on domestic banks, not only with regard to product lines, marketing and service but also with regard to efficiency, settlement speed and internationally oriented products. As they are allowed to conduct consumer banking with Chinese private customers after 2006, it remains to be seen how and to what extent they will be able to transfer this qualitative advantage to a broader quantitative level.

2.   Challenging domestic actors as strong and independent firms

In addition, foreign banks have challenged domestic banks due to their organisational characteristics. As globally operating and internationally competitive firms, they are – as a group of actors – well capitalised and regulated and exhibit strong internal management structures.[81] At least, it can reasonably be argued that they are superior in this regard *vis-à-vis* the organisationally, financially and politically weaker domestic banks. They are thus distinctively different commercial actors. Comparing foreign banks with Chinese domestic banks confirms that their Capital Adequacy Ratio is significantly higher. It can reasonably be argued that foreign banks in China have a capital ratio above 8 per cent, whereas the domestic banks have significantly lower rates.[82] It has been widely suspected that the exact capital adequacy ratios for the domestic banks are much lower (interviews).

A similar comparison can be made with regard to asset quality, reflected in the NPL ratio of foreign and domestic banks. Again, the exact numbers on the asset quality of single foreign banks are not available. The CBRC states, however, that foreign banks as a group have an NPL ratio of 1.3 per cent (CBRC, 2004b). As discussed during the interviews with representatives of foreign banks and regulatory bodies in 2004, the low NPL ratio is a great advantage for foreign banks. The rates of the domestic banks, however, are impressive in a negative sense, depending on the respective estimation. Even allowing for some variation with regard to different types of banks, as shown by Shih, Zhang and Liu (2004), the NPL ratios indicate a bad asset quality in (most) domestic banks.

With regard to the management structure, foreign banks exhibit clear advantages. As their (private) ownership is clearly defined, they operate under hard budget constraints, with a strong profit orientation and without political interference from domestic government entities.[83] Another strength of foreign banks is their loan growth; this is significant both with regard to assessing their earnings potential and their organisational stability. With regard to earnings, loan growth reflects the ability of the bank to lend and generate interest income. However, it has been discussed widely that the breakneck speed of loan growth of some domestic banks was in fact a sign of their weakness.[84] Foreign banks on the other hand have reported positive but viable rates of loan growth (interviews). However, refinancing options and liquidity have been the soft spot for foreign banks, due to their limited position in deposit taking. The limited refinancing options on the interbank market come only at higher costs, thus reducing the margins of foreign banks. Turning to the profitability of foreign banks, it has to be pointed out that in this regard statistical data is also missing on both a group and an individual level.[85] Available evidence, such as press reports on internal PBC data with regard to Beijing, suggest that foreign banks are (among) the most profitable banks in China (also see Lange, 2004). Overall, the picture confirms the notion that foreign banks are strong and healthy firms. They are politically independent, in contrast to domestic banks, and operate under profit considerations only. On these grounds it can be concluded that foreign banks are financially and politically stronger than domestic firms. They are thus organisationally strong and independent unique actors in the Chinese banking sector.

This stronger and independent position is important for the market in two ways. Firstly, it is important because foreign banks' behaviour on this basis differs from domestic banks' behaviour and thus changes the resulting allocation of resources and provision of services as well as increasing the efficiency and the stability of the financial markets. Arguably, this aspect largely depends on the scale of market entry and is thus limited, due to the limited quantitative level of foreign banks' operations in China. Secondly, foreign banks have become role models for domestic banks on this basis. Outlining the merits of foreign banks, a study by Shanghai Pudong Development Bank, for example, highlights that they are regarded as prominent examples and offer respected guidelines for introducing new internal management structures, better corporate governance, and more sophisticated risk management and human resource management structures (Shanhai Pudong Fazhan Yinhang, 2002).[86] Foreign banks have impacted the market development indirectly through fostering changes in the operations of domestic actors. In the case of commercial actors the adaptation process has taken place through competition and cooperation (see below). As will be discussed in Chapter 6, the impact on the domestic market has not only included domestic banks and their operations but also modes of regulation in the Chinese financial markets. Since the strong and independent position of foreign banks has meant that they are positioned outside regulatory control and coercion where it is exerted through mechanisms of party control, they have also challenged some aspects of the regulatory regime in China's financial markets.

3.   Fostering change in Chinese banks through cooperation and competition

Foreign banks have also had an impact on the Chinese banking market through their engagement in cooperation agreements and through the stimulating effect their market access has had on domestic competition.

It has already been pointed out that engaging in cooperation agreements and building strategic alliances through investments in Chinese banks has been part of foreign banks' strategies for entering the Chinese market. This has had a significant impact on the domestic banks engaged in this cooperation and on their operations. Competition has been the other main channel for influencing domestic banks' incentives and market environment and for thus effecting the development of the domestic market. Foreign banks' market entry has led to increased competition in certain market segments, such as the provision of specific corporate finance products as well as wealth-management services. As the effects of both cooperation and competition are of a more indirect nature, highlighting the changes in domestic banks more than the direct contributions of foreign banks to market development, they are discussed in more detail in Chapter 7.

This section has thus identified and discussed aspects of the impact that foreign banks' market entry and actual market participation has had on the development of the domestic banking sector despite the limited quantitative scale of foreign banks' business in China. Foreign banks have introduced new and better products, and they have challenged domestic actors through the provision of new benchmarks and role models, and through increased competition. Cooperation between foreign and domestic banks has also been identified as an important means through which foreign banks have impacted domestic markets, but analysis of the exact way in which domestic banks have responded to these impacts shall be postponed to Part III.

Overall, foreign banks have thus contributed to the development of China's banking market. However, the limits to foreign banks' influence also need to be kept in mind. They are independent, but they also occupy a weak position as outsiders with limited connections to Chinese firms and regulators. They operate in markets with distorted competition, and are discriminated against by regulation. The CBRC and the PBC have imposed severe limits on their market participation and thus have curtailed their impact on the domestic market. It is therefore justified to say that the impact foreign banks have had on the domestic Chinese banking sector occurred only within the tight framework set by the CBRC and by challenging market conditions. Foreign banks have accordingly emerged as important actors for market development but have been hindered by their limited quantitative position, and have not been able to make the most out of their qualitative potential. It is only in the limited or niche areas where they managed to enter the market that they have increased competition, introduced new products and imported international standards of service provision and service quality. Their important position as new and organisationally strong market actors has so far only been exploited to a limited degree.

Concluding remarks

The analysis of foreign banks' business in China has shown that only a limited number of foreign banks has engaged deeply in the domestic market for credit and savings deposits in China and that their quantitative impact has been limited with regard to credit offered and deposits taken. Foreign banks have positioned themselves in only limited segments of the Chinese market, a process driven both by the regulatory restrictions that have been identified as the single most important limiting force on the business of foreign banks in China, as well as by the challenging market environment. Except for some small market segments, foreign banks have not been in a position to increase their market share quickly due to their forced geographical concentration, restrictions on eligible customers and the costs of expanding their own branch networks. Empirically, there has been a more active participation of foreign banks in the Chinese banking sector since 2001 with regard to the extension of services offered, the number of branch openings per year, the acquisition of stakes in Chinese banks and the forming of new co-operations (He, 2004). In addition, there has also been a trend for foreign strategic investors to buy larger shares in larger domestic firms. As shown above, this trend has coincided with a more cooperative and cooptive approach by the CBRC and PBC *vis-à-vis* foreign banks. Does this new approach and related changes in regulation mean that the doors of the Chinese banking sector are finally wide open for foreign banks? Will we see more foreign control and market participation in the near future? What are the prospects for foreign banks in China's banking market?

The single most significant factor influencing the perspectives for foreign banks in China, both with regard to regulatory restrictions and market opportunities, is the success or failure of the domestic Chinese banking sector reform, particularly of the four large SOCBs; this will also determine further liberalisation measures, for example, with regard to interest rates. WTO commitments and their full implementation after 2006 will allow for a greater degree of differentiation in foreign banks' strategies. However, the actual market participation will also depend on the development of internationally competitive firms in China, as well as on the ability of Chinese banks to operate internationally, and on the overall economic growth and international integration of the Chinese economy. With regard to the development of the inland provinces and their banking infrastructure, foreign banks' participation remains unlikely on a large scale as long as strong incentives remain to focus on the richer coastal provinces and potential customers there. Unless a redistribution of growth, wealth and savings among China's provinces occurs, foreign banks will have little incentive to engage in the Western inland provinces, as well as rural and remote areas.

Three conditions are of significance in determining foreign banks' abilities to grasp opportunities arising in China's banking market: firstly, the further development of refinancing options for RMB business and the development of the money market will be very important for the liquidity of foreign banks. Secondly, the training and qualification of more professional staff in financial services will be a crucial factor and, thirdly, the evolving structures of electronic data-processing in banking in China will contribute to determining foreign banks' competitive edge. Although not the focus of this book, it has additionally to be pointed out that the chances of foreign banks participating in the banking sector also depend on the evolution of the Chinese currency system and current account convertability.

Overall, based primarily on assumptions about the development and reform of the domestic banking sector, two scenarios for foreign banks in China can be sketched out. Depending on the success of domestic banking sector reform, foreign banks' share in total bank profits may increase if Chinese banks remain essentially unreformed and largely unprofitable. Alternatively, with more effective reforms and opening, foreign banks' market share might go up, while their profit share might stay the same or decrease as domestic banks become more sophisticated (OECD, 2002). However, foreign banks in any case are unlikely to dominate the banking market except in limited market segments. Most importantly, however, it should be pointed out that foreign banks' market access is likely to be shaped by regulation and the role regulatory bodies assign to foreign banks in the process of banking reform. If the shift of regulation from coercion to cooperation with domestic banks continues and proves complementary to the strategies of foreign banks in China, foreign bank entry will continue to increase. The options for foreign banks continue to depend primarily on regulation.

4
Foreign Firms and the Market for Securities

Securities markets are the second largest pillar of the Chinese financial market. Despite the notion that they – as core institutions of a market economy – contradict the socialist nature of China's economic order, they have gained significance and size over the reform course and have become a symbol of market-oriented reforms. However, equity markets are still burdened with the consequences of incomplete SOE reform and the resulting hybrid market order. Bond markets have remained underdeveloped and largely dominated by government and quasi-government financial bonds. In addition, a distinct feature of the Chinese securities markets had been their closed character, until WTO entry in 2001 brought a breakthrough for the market participation of foreign firms. How have these firms entered the Chinese securities markets since then? Have they become important actors in their development?

This chapter analyses the participation of foreign firms in China's securities markets. Following the structure of the previous chapter, it focuses on the role and relevance of foreign firms as external actors in the hybrid markets, and assesses the impact and importance of foreign firms for their development. In a first step, it lays out the basic characteristics of the domestic industry and market environment that foreign firms face when entering the Chinese markets. Then, it assesses the different modes and strategies of the market entry of foreign firms as well as the main incentives and constraints behind their participation. Finally, it analyses how foreign firms have positioned themselves in the markets and what their impact on market development has been so far.

It is shown in this chapter that highly restrictive regulation has led to a limited quantitative scale of the market entry of foreign financial firms, and that the new options in the context of the WTO commitments have channelled foreign participation exclusively into JV structures. However, the introduction of the Qualified Foreign Institutional Investor (QFII) scheme shortly after the historic opening of the market has also opened new ways of market participation. Both aspects together highlight that regulatory policies have shifted to allowing more foreign participation, and that the CSRC, as the main regulator in the Chinese securities markets, now in fact actively uses foreign securities firms in order to foster market development. Remaining restrictions notwithstanding, foreign firms have been able to become significant actors in China's securities markets in this context and have contributed to market development through the introduction of new management techniques and research capabilities. If the CSRC continues its liberal approach, foreign firms' impact on market development is likely to increase. This chapter also identifies strong similarities – compared to the banking sector – in foreign firms' strategies and actual market participation, making differences in the regulatory framework for market entry less significant than they appear on first sight.

China's emerging domestic securities industry

The Chinese equity and bond markets have grown in importance and volume in recent years and have attracted considerable international attention based primarily on their potential for future growth, as the Chinese market is projected to become the largest securities market in Asia (see Wilson and Purushothaman, 2003). Still, they accounted only for a comparatively small portion of overall financial transactions in 2004. As a market environment for foreign firms, they display a number of distinct characteristics with regard to market structure, main commercial actors and ongoing reforms. Highlighting important historical legacies and conflicting policies, this section develops the basis to understand the state of the Chinese securities industry and its development dynamic, and thus the framework for foreign firms' market participation. It shows that the securities markets exhibit a larger organisational diversity with regard to domestic firms, but that these firms are also mainly state-owned or state-controlled.[87] The markets themselves display both developmental and institutional problems, and their development is mainly driven by regulation. The CSRC has employed a more comprehensive strategy for regulation and reform since 2001, but foreign firms still face a hybrid and distorted dynamic institutional environment when entering the Chinese markets.

Actors in Chinese securities markets

Whereas in the banking sector the position of Chinese banks – however fragile their balance sheets might be – is dominant and well established by size and organisational history, in the securities industry the organisational foundation of the domestic players shows greater variation and fewer historical burdens. The securities industry is developing much faster than the banking sector, which is partly due to the fact that there are – notwithstanding all existing problems – fewer monolithic structures among domestic intermediaries. The main industry players include the following groups of actors.

Securities companies

Securities companies (*zhengquan gongsi*) are one of the main groups of intermediaries in the Chinese securities markets. Their major lines of business include underwriting of securities, brokerage of shares and bonds as well as proprietary trading. As several authors note, some securities companies have also moved into asset management (Green, 2003c, p. 80; Kim, Ho and St Giles, 2003). Among securities companies, the CSRC distinguishes between comprehensive firms and brokerages (CSRC, 2004a). According to their (original) ownership, securities houses can be divided into those under the influence and control of the central government and those controlled by local governments or other state-owned enterprises, as most of the securities houses existing in mid-2004 were state-owned or controlled (Walter and Howie, 2003). Historically, securities companies emerged as spin-offs from trade and investments companies (TICs) and other financial firms, or were set up by local governments and local branches of the Ministry of Finance (Green, 2003c, pp. 80ff). In mid-2004, Huaxia, Guotai and Nanfang Securities were the three national brokerages in China.

Operationally, each securities company operates a number of brokerage branches, which are regionally dispersed primarily across the eastern and southern part of China. At the end of 2003, there were 133 securities companies in China with more than 3000 brokerage outlets. They managed assets of RMB51 billion for their clients.[88] With their concentrated revenue sources, all of the securities companies are vulnerable to market downturn (Green, 2003c, pp. 79ff), and since 2001, the industry has seen considerable restructuring and consolidation among players. While the reduction of overcapacity is widely acknowledged as necessary, restructuring is hindered by the protectionism of local governments and other state-close entities who own the securities companies.[89]

	1998	1999	2000	2001	2002	2003	2004	2005
Fund management companies	6	10	10	15	21	34	45	52

Figure 4.1   Number of intermediaries in the securities markets (1998–2005)
Source: CSRC (2004a); PWC (2006)

Securities companies in China have been subject to scandals as some were actively engaging in insider trading and extensive stock-price manipulation in the past. A stricter regulation of the industry and an increase in professional standards is thus regarded as necessary.

Investment fund management companies

Another important group of intermediaries in the Chinese securities markets are investment fund management companies, offering closed as well as open-ended investment funds. Establishing investment funds in their present form has been allowed since 1997; therefore the funds and their management companies are relatively young firms.[90] They require RMB10 million in registered capital. As depicted in Figure 4.1, the total number of fund management firms in 2003 was 34. In 2002, the then 21 fund management firms managed 71 funds, aggregating RMB123 billion or 1.21 per cent of GDP (Bolland, 2004). With only 3–4 per cent of tradable market capitalisation invested through funds in 2003, according to the CSRC, the relevance of investment fund management companies is based primarily on their rapid expansion and the increase of funds under their management rather than their current share of the securities market.

Trade and investment companies

Historically, some 200 trade and investment companies (TICs) have been involved in the securities business. In the last ten years, these troubled financial firms have been reformed continuously, and today do not resemble their former selves. Their under-regulated interconnected business areas created serious systemic threats to the financial market in the past, so their securities and other business arms were separated in 1999, and the spun-off securities business parts of several TICs were merged, creating new securities companies. There are, however, remaining areas of business that include capital trust, investment fund business, the intermediation of M&A activities, asset management, and underwriting of bonds that allow TICs to operate in the sphere of traditional investment banking business (Kim, Ho and St Giles, 2003, pp. 22ff).

Asset management companies

The four large asset management companies (AMCs), founded in 1999 in order to relieve the four large state-owned banks from their stock of NPLs, also operate in the securities markets. As they mostly opted for debt-for-equity swaps in NPL restructuring, they hold large amounts of shares as minority positions, mostly in poor-quality SOEs (Ma and Fung, 2002). Originally intended to be of transitionary nature with the single purpose of solving the NPL stock problem, they are, as Green (2003c, pp. 113ff) points out, well positioned to transform themselves into investment banks. Cinda and Huarong Asset Management have been granted underwriting licences already.

Insurance companies

Insurance companies are important players in securities markets as their investment side resembles that of long-term-oriented investment funds, collecting and channelling their clients' money into securities investments. In China, for a long time insurance companies were practically forced to invest their funds in central government bonds and bank deposits. Investment in selected 'high-quality' corporate bonds has been allowed since 1999 up to the limit of 2 per cent of their assets. Investment in equity (A-shares) through funds has also been allowed since 1999, originally limited to 5 per cent of their total assets, but since November 2002, the quantitative restriction has been lifted to 15 per cent. Just before the limit was lifted in 2002, the investment in A-shares accounted for 30 per cent of total funds value. Insurance companies have also been allowed to set up their own investment funds since 2001 and they have become important institutional investors. The special needs of insurance companies for long-term investments let them stand out from other intermediaries in the securities markets.[91]

Overall, domestic intermediaries in the securities markets are thus much more diversified organisationally than they are in the commercial banking sector. There are no equivalents to the four large SOCBs, neither with regard to size, their dominant position nor their problems. What about ownership, control and competition in the securities markets?

Ownership, control and competition among domestic intermediaries

While detailed information on the ownership of single companies in China's securities markets is often hard to obtain, local and central governments as well as state-owned enterprises stand out as important owners of domestic intermediaries. Galaxy Securities, for example, is owned by the MOF (Green, 2003c, p. 80). As most securities companies were SOEs and founded by central or local governments or SOEs, their later transformation into limited liability or shareholding companies only in some cases altered the predominant position of state agencies or SOEs in ownership and control. Two characteristics of the ownership structure are significant; firstly, there are privately owned companies among the market intermediaries. Private ownership of securities companies has been allowed since the start of the more active restructuring and recapitalisation of the industry in 2001 and accounts for about 10 per cent of the total ownership (Green, 2003c, p. 82). Large private enterprises have invested heavily in securities firms (Pang, 2005). Secondly, even among state-owned and controlled intermediaries, ownership structures vary to a larger extent than they do in the banking sector. This also leads to varying levels of political control. Green (2003, p. 83) noticed the increasing dispersal of ownership and states that '[t]his dispersal trend is important since it makes it more difficult for government officials to interfere in the operations of these companies'. Historically, fund management firms and securities companies also had close ties to banks, as some of them were founded as their arms, a legacy that might – regulation permitting – be revived in the emergence of financial conglomerates.

Depending on ownership concentration, the level of state ownership and the effectiveness of party control over firms, state agencies have been able to exert significant influence on the business of intermediaries in ways similar to their influence in other (non-financial) SOEs. Personnel decisions are controlled by CCP organs, and each financial firm has a party committee, of which the enterprise's chief executive officer (CEO) often is the secretary. Party influence extended to day-to-day business and politically inspired buy-orders were not uncommon for most of the Chinese stock market's history (interviews). Additionally, regulatory oversight and regulation are far-reaching; CSRC powers included the approval of personnel decisions. As fund management companies are mostly set up and controlled by securities or insurance firms, they are also included in this system. As the CSRC approves the appointments of CEOs and fund managers, it retained 'some influence over their trading strategies and the market's indices' (Green 2003c, p. 101). As discussed in more detail below, the resulting interlinkage of industry policy implementation and prudential regulation have been a cause of major problems in the securities market.

With regard to competition, it has to be noted that the securities markets are much less concentrated than markets in the banking sector.

There is no single dominant market player. A study by China International Economic Consultants notes, however, that competition varies with regard to business segments; in the market for securities underwriting they identify decreased competition whereas securities brokerage was a market with much fiercer competition (CIEC, 2000). The consolidation among the intermediaries due to the crisis in the securities markets since 2001 may change this picture and lead to more concentration (Green and He, 2004). While state ownership thus prevailed, ownership has been much more diversified, there is more competition and markets are less concentrated than the commercial banking sector.

Segmented markets driven by regulation

The market intermediaries discussed above operate in two large market segments, the equity and the bond market, and both have distinct characteristics. Most notably, they are strongly segmented and driven by regulation, and are characterised by problems that result from the legacy of the planned economy, mostly with regard to the enterprise sector. Since securities markets emerged as new markets from the 1980s onwards, their emergence has been driven both by unregulated decentralised development and by the policies designed to regulate these markets and bring them under (central) control.

The equity market

The equity market developed gradually from decentralised regional trading centres into national stock exchanges (see Figure 4.2).[92] Its most important characteristics include, first of all, its strongly segmented structure (Walter and Howie, 2003, p. 177). The market is divided into A, B, H and N shares, defined according to place of issuance and the eligibility of issuers and investors. From the perspective of foreign firms, B-shares, as the only domestic shares available to them, and internationally listed shares, including H- and N-shares, are of interest. A-shares are denominated in RMB and could originally only be bought by Chinese investors. They have become available for foreign investors through the QFII scheme since 2003. In terms of segmentation, however, domestically issued shares are also subdivided into publicly traded shares, legal person shares and state shares, rendering the total amount of tradable shares as considerably less than domestic market capitalisation. Most companies' holding of non-tradable state shares is over 50 per cent; therefore a transition of control is only possible through legal person or state share transfers. As a result, the stock market has not become a market for corporate control (Green, 2003a; Green, 2003e; Green and Black, 2003; Green, 2004a).

	1992	1994	1996	1998	2000	2002
Total shares issued (100 million shares)	68.87	684.54	1219.54	2526.79	3791.71	5875.45
Tradable shares (100 million shares)	21.18	226.04	429.85	861.94	1354.26	2036.9
Total capital raised (RMB 100 million yuan)	94.09	326.78	425.08	841.52	2103.08	961.75
Total stock market cap. (RMB 100 million yuan)	1048.13	3690.61	9842.38	19505.64	48090.94	38329.12
Total stock trading volume (100 million shares)	37.95	2013.34	2533.14	2154.11	4758.4	3016.19
Total stock turnover (RMB 100 million yuan)	681.25	8127.63	21332.16	23544.25	60826.65	27990.46
Number of listed companies – A, B shares	53	291	530	851	1088	1224
Number of stock investment accounts (10,000)	216.65	1058.98	2307.23	3911.13	5801.14	6881.76

Figure 4.2 Early years of the equity market (1992–2002)
Source: CSRC (2004a)

Both lines of segmentation have caused problems for the valuation of shares, highlighted, for instance, by the trading of B-shares at a discount. Segmentation additionally narrows the market and further aggravates problems of undersupply (or over-demand), stock market overvaluation and pricing of IPOs (Su, 2003). As pointed out by Gao (2002), this over-demand was a causal factor in the long boom of the Chinese stock markets before 2001. Another problem inherent in state shares is that the state-owned nature of listed enterprises led to continuous conflicts of interest and double mandates in regulation, oscillating between fostering a positive economic climate through rising stock market prices and enforcing regulations; this was confirmed by interviews with domestic and JV securities firms. Regulation was not driven by a comprehensive approach and the equity developmentalism of local governments contributed to the problems because it came at the expense of tight prudent regulations (Green, 2004b).

Based on this structure, the equity market has consequently not been able to fulfil expectations with regard to financing firms' productive investment, improving firms' corporate governance and signalling information about issuers, as pointed out by Shirai (2004). This is due to the fact that the politically controlled and highly administrative listing process secures access to capital for the SOE sector, rather than selecting profitable and efficient enterprises and fostering efficient allocation of capital. The performance of listed firms often has declined after listing, indicating that the secondary market for shares has not set the right incentives for better management (Green, 2004a). The problems have led to an excessive volatility of stock prices in China that is attributed to speculative behaviour on the part of intermediaries and investors as well as to the former laissez-faire approach to regulation (Neoh, 2000). It can therefore be said that the stock market enabled state agencies as the majority shareholders in listed SOEs to leverage their investments better, but did not improve the efficiency of capital allocation. An interesting feature of the Chinese stock market is that its share prices and indices are largely uncorrelated to international stock price developments, signifying that the capital controls and market segmentation successfully isolates the Chinese market from international markets and developments (Gao, 2002). Overall, the Chinese equity market is strongly driven by state interference and regulation.

The bond market

With regard to the Chinese bond market, it has first of all to be noted that it is much smaller than the equity market.[93] The small size, especially of the corporate bond market segment in relation to GDP, highlights the structural problems of the market as well as the fact that bond market expansion is not keeping track with the fast-growing economy (Kim, Ho and St Giles, 2003, p. 28). The small size also reflects the limited availability of fixed-income securities in the Chinese securities markets.

The bond market as such is dominated by government bonds (T-bonds) and bonds issued by state-owned financial firms, so called financial bonds (F-bonds), whereas enterprise bonds account only for a small fraction of total bond issuance and outstanding amount. Again, the issuing enterprises in the corporate bond market are state-owned. The dominance of T-bond issues discriminates against enterprises, whose (potential) issuances are crowded out. Primarily, the structure of the bond market reflects the developmental preferences of policy-makers and the CSRC for the securities markets; these have been characterised by the intention to create refinancing options for the State Council's budget deficit through government bonds and to prioritise the development of the equity market within the securities markets (Schlichting, 2004). Accordingly, the primary effect of the bond market, as with the equity market, has been to collect money for the State Council and the SOEs, either in the form of T-bonds financing the rising budget deficit domestically or in the form of channelling funds to SOEs.

In line with these policy priorities, the market remained driven by regulations and arguably the financial interests of the State Council. The issuing process is tightly controlled, interest on bonds is administratively determined and the distribution of issued bonds is heavily influenced by statutory restrictions, leading to a partly captive market. Through the low interest rates on savings deposits and limited alternative investment opportunities the demand for bonds remained high and the cost of refinancing state debt low. In addition, the bond markets are segmented to a similar degree as the equity markets; domestic issuance and trading are split into the inter-bank market and the general stock exchange market, with detrimental effects for liquidity and market performance (Kim, Ho and St Giles, 2003, pp. 29ff).

Just as Chinese investors have been prohibited from transferring funds overseas, the domestic bond market has been locked off from international investment. QFII was the first instance where foreign firms were allowed to invest in Chinese bonds. In fact, T-bonds have become very popular among foreign investors, due to expectations of a revaluation of the Chinese currency that encouraged these seemingly risk-free investments. In 2003, treasury bonds worth US$21.1 billion were purchased, 11.6 times more than the year before (*China Daily*, 2004c).

As discussed below, the opening of the domestic bond market for foreign investors is part of an overall reform impetus in the bond market that emerged after the Asian financial crisis, as outlined by Zhou Xiaochuan in 2003 (also see Overholt, 2004; Zhou, 2003). Since systematic progress remained slow during 2004, however, the bond market has remained a troubled segment of the Chinese securities markets and continues to create problems for other market segments.

In order to fully portray the complex dynamic of Chinese securities markets, the demand and supply side have to be taken into account, as they have distinct characteristics. On the demand side, the investors in Chinese securities are mostly individual investors (Walter and Howie 2003). There are few formal institutional investors that conduct professional investments with long-term strategies and thus foster market development (Kim, Ho and St Giles, 2003; HKEx, 2004). In 2003, China's formal institutional investors' assets made up only 10.6 per cent of GDP, indicating ample room to increase their share when compared to institutional investors in OECD countries and other EMEs (Kim, Ho and St Giles, 2003). It has been argued that the weak fundamentals of the listed enterprises, the selection criteria of the listing process and the overall unstable development of the securities markets have inhibited the development of institutional investors. Indeed, as briefly mentioned above, the business and financial performance of many listed enterprises has remained weak.

On the supply side of the Chinese securities markets are primarily SOEs of varying quality, often with a small but highly leveraged equity basis. Some have deteriorated in their commercial results after their listing. The undersupply of high-quality shares that could function as benchmarks and guide the market is partly a consequence of better-performing enterprises listing overseas as well as of the problems of domestic enterprise reform (Gao, 2002). Privatisation has been proceeding slowly for listed enterprises after the first serious attempt to sell off state shares failed in 2001 (Naughton, 2002; Wu, 2002). However, there will be no healthy securities' markets without a healthy enterprise sector.

As this brief overview shows, the development of the Chinese securities markets has been troubled by severe problems and driven by regulation through the CSRC. The prevailing ownership and control structures in the context of the simultaneous transition from an unregulated to a regulated market and from a planned to a market economy created distinct problems (Hu, Wei and Niu, 2002). The markets have accordingly been characterised both by rapid growth, as well as developmental and institutional problems.

Comprehensive regulatory policies in a bearish market

The problems of the securities markets have revealed themselves in high share-price volatility, loss of investor confidence, and high price-earnings ratios. However, with the stock market downturn since 2001, a time of correction has begun for the Chinese securities markets. The end of the predominately bullish market that China's investors enjoyed for almost ten years before 2001 – marked by a five-year low point in September 2004 – indicates on the one hand the *rites de passage* that every emerging stock market has to grow through, teaching market participants and investors about the risks in securities business (*China Daily*, 2004e). On the other hand, the period since 2001 has seen considerable effort by the CSRC to streamline the market and increase the transparency and quality of regulations. The bearish market, after all, was a 'golden opportunity to reform' (Hu, 2004c). However, worries continue that the market remains a 'policy market' with market recovery based on policy-related news rather than fundamental improvements in companies' data. And while there might be some chances in a bearish market, it has also to be kept in mind that the turndown is not conducive towards the development of intermediaries, such as investment fund management companies and securities companies.

A new comprehensive approach of the State Council to reform the securities markets was marked by the publishing of the Nine Articles (*jiudian yidian*) in January 2004, calling for the 'establishment of transparent, efficient, well-structured, functioning and secure capital markets with the goals of expanding direct financing and giving full play to the market's fundamental role in the distribution of resources' (Naughton, 2004b, pp. 6ff; for the text of the articles see *People's Daily*, 2004a). They encompass all major fields for necessary market corrections and summarise efforts in stock market policy and regulation. As argued by Naughton (2004b), this has also partly aimed to prepare better market conditions for a future reduction of state-owned shares and thus tackle some of the problematic foundations of the Chinese securities markets.

Overall, while securities markets are still underdeveloped, segmented and under constant reform, they are less troubled and in better shape than many domestic firms in the banking sector. In particular, there is more organisational diversity and less market concentration compared to the banking sector; however, among intermediaries in the securities markets state ownership and control still prevail. On the basis of their pronounced institutional and developmental problems, the securities markets have been both dynamic and distorted and remain driven by regulation through the CSRC.[94] It is yet unclear what kind of a regulatory regime will emerge in the securities markets; a liberal market-oriented one or a more coordinated version with more micro-level regulation and (potential) political interference. So far, the securities markets in China have hardly been catalysts for economic transition and development. As of 2004, the distorted markets thus represented a special and challenging market environment for foreign market participants to enter.

Foreign firms in China's securities markets

Compared to the banking sector, China's emerging securities markets have been protected from international influences much longer and to an even greater extent. Essentially following an infant-industry logic in allowing domestic firms to grow before having to compete with international investment banks, the restrictions have been most severe on the (standalone) business of foreign firms in China. Based on CSRC regulations, only the B-share market was accessible for foreign investors and intermediaries and even here entry was channelled through cooperation with domestic firms. From the perspective of foreign firms, the China business hence predominantly consisted of offshore transactions such as the underwriting of international IPOs of Chinese customers and international bond issuances, typically conducted and administered from Hong Kong (Katz, 1997). It was only after WTO entry in 2001 that new channels into the domestic Chinese securities market were opened for foreign firms.

This section analyses the onshore entry of foreign firms in China's securities markets. It looks at the strategies of foreign firms for entering the dynamic and increasingly liberalised market environment after WTO entry. Most importantly, it asks what incentives and constraints have structured the form, extent and patterns of their participation and how they have positioned themselves as external actors in the market. The section shows that foreign firms' market-entry strategies have varied considerably and that despite the trend of liberalisation, the regulatory framework has remained restrictive. Cooperation between foreign and domestic firms in the form of JVs has been a condition for organisational market entry both with regard to securities and fund management companies. Yet, it was only due to newly emerging regulatory policies that foreign market entry was possible on a significant scale at all; therefore – as was the case in the commercial banking sector – regulation has been a key factor for the market entry of securities firms.

Market entry strategies: setting up (mandatory) JVs

Originally, the brokerage of B-shares had been the only business field for foreign financial firms in the Chinese securities markets. While foreign brokerages were allowed to be set up in a standalone manner, their actual business could only be conducted through local brokerages. The much larger and more attractive domestic A-share market, as well as the different sections of the bond market, were sealed off from foreign participation. It is only since 2001 that foreign firms have been allowed to form Sino-foreign JVs in order to access these markets.[95] Therefore, whereas foreign financial firms could enter the Chinese commercial banking market through a number of channels including wholly foreign-owned operations, the channels for entering the securities markets have remained much more restricted.

Investment banking joint ventures

After the promulgation of the new 'Implementing Rules on the Administration of Foreign Financial Institutions' in June 2002, it became possible to routinely found Sino-foreign JV investment banks in China. Before 2002, China's only international investment bank was the China International Capital Corporation (CICC), a JV between China Construction Bank and Morgan Stanley. CICC's establishment in 1995 had been conducted under exceptional circumstances based on connections to high-ranking political officials and had thus remained a singular event. After 2002, however, new securities JVs were licensed, including a JV between XiangCai Securities and CLSA as well as a JV between Changjiang Securities and BNP Paribas (see Figure 4.3).[96] Both JVs aimed to create a 'one-stop shop' for domestic companies wishing to go public in China or internationally (Ogden and Hu, 2002).

In principle, JV securities firms can conduct business in the areas of underwriting stocks and bonds in RMB and foreign currency, brokerage of foreign-currency denominated stocks and bonds including T-bonds and corporate bonds. They may not, however, engage in the trading of A-shares. The share of the foreign JV partner is restricted to 33 per cent and there is no legally secured method of gaining full control. However, market participants expressed the assumption that the ownership controls would be relaxed after 2007 (interviews). Given this lack of control over the JV, European firms have engaged more actively in creating securities JVs and have been more willing to enter minority positions *vis-à-vis* American firms who have tended to set higher requirements for control and compliance (*The Economist*, 2003a). An example of this cooperation

Investment banks	Cooperation with Chinese partner	Name of JV securities firm
Morgan Stanley	China Construction Bank	China International Capital Corporation (CICC)
CLSA	XiangCai Securities	China Europe Securities (CESL)
BNP Paribas	Changjiang Securities	Changjiang BNP Paribas Peregrine
Goldman Sachs	Gaohua Securities	Beijing Gaohua Securities

Figure 4.3   JV securities companies in China
Source: Media reports

is the US-American investment bank Goldman Sachs and Beijing Gaohua Securities, a brokerage that inherited the operating licence from troubled Hainan Securities (Iyengar, 2004). The construction of this particular JV, approved in mid-2004, allows for an untypical way of founding the JV that actually antedates the transfer of control to the minority shareholder. As it is unclear whether this will become generally accepted practice, the construction is primarily seen to put Goldman Sachs on an equal footing with Morgan Stanley (interviews with market participants). This also points to competition among international players rather than the competition with domestic firms.

JV securities firms also include JVs that are limited in their business scope, such as those Sino-foreign brokerages that have a less than comprehensive securities licence. These JVs are not allowed to trade securities on their own account. Technically, instead of setting up a JV, the cooperation may in both cases also be conducted through the acquisition of a share of an existing securities company or brokerage.

Joint venture fund management companies

After WTO entry, the CSRC also allowed for the set-up of fund management JVs with a foreign participation of up to 33 per cent of all shares. Relevant rules were issued in 2002 that foresaw an increase of this share to 49 per cent three years after WTO accession at the end of 2004 ('Rules on the Establishment of Foreign-shared Fund Management Companies', 1 July 2002). Again, this was seen as a transitionary stage to wholly foreign-owned fund management companies by many industry participants, but there is no clear timeline for the establishment of controlling majorities in fund management JVs. Setting up a JV fund management

Foreign partner	Chinese partner	JV fund management company	Date of approval
Société General Asset Management	Fortune Trust & Investment	Fortune SGAM Fund Management	October 2002
Fortis Investment Management	Haitong Securities	Fortis Haitong Investment Management	October 2002
ING Investment Management	China Merchant Securities (and others)	China Merchants Fund Management	December 2002
Invesco Asia	China Great Wall Securities (and others)	Invesco Great Wall Fund Management	February 2003
Allianz Dresdner Asset Management	Guotai Jun'an Securities	Guotai Jun'an Allianz Fund Management	March 2003
Franklin Templeton	Sealand Securities	Franklin Templeton Sealand Fund Management	August 2003
BNP Paribas Asset Management	Shenyin & Wangguo Securities	SW BNP Paribas Asset Management	August 2003
ABN Amro	XiangCai Securities and Shandong Xinyuan	XiangCai Hefeng Fund Management	September 2003

Figure 4.4   Selected Sino-foreign fund management JVs
Source: Bolland (2004), PWC (2006), various media reports, a complete list is provided in Chapter 7

company can either be done with one of the domestic fund management companies that emerged after 1998 or with a domestic securities house that may have a longer organisational history. Fund management JVs can engage in all business that is allowed for wholly domestically owned fund management companies, essentially raising and managing funds inside China (see Figure 4.4).

The main interest of foreign firms in entering these JVs is access to Chinese savings pools. The distribution network of their local partners, as well as their market know-how, is seen as less important than, for example, the branch system of commercial banks. Local partners on the Chinese side have an interest in accessing more investment channels, and increase management expertise and know-how. They also wish to

	Underwriting	**Trading**	**Issuance of funds**
Wholly foreign owned brokerages	No	Yes, but only in (foreign-currency denominated) B-shares	No
JV securities houses	Yes	Only trading foreign currency equity, but all bonds	No
JV fund management companies	No	No	Yes

Figure 4.5   Who can do what type of business?
Source: Own compilation based on WTO documents and Chinese regulations

enhance their reputation by bringing in international partners, thus raising their competitiveness in local markets (Bolland, 2004, p. 21). At the end of 2003, there were 50 fund management companies in China, of which 13 were Sino-foreign JVs.[97]

With these two major channels for foreign market entry – JV securities companies and JV fund management companies (see Figure 4.5) – foreign firms had to cooperate with domestic firms when entering the Chinese market, a striking difference from the banking sector. However, with the expectation of regulatory changes on the majority position of foreign partners in these JVs, there was also a general assumption that after 2007 foreign fund managers and investment banks would be allowed to establish wholly foreign-owned operations (AmCham 2004c, interviews).

The Qualified Foreign Institutional Investor scheme

The Chinese markets for A-shares and bonds have additionally been opened for foreign investors through the Qualified Foreign Institutional Investor (QFII) scheme. For the first time, the scheme offers international investors the option to buy tradable A-shares, as well as RMB-denominated treasury, convertible and corporate bonds through international intermediaries. International investment banks, fund management companies, insurance companies, securities companies and commercial banks can apply for QFII status and engage in the intermediation of these transactions under strict rules set out in the 'Provisional QFII Rules'. QFIIs also can participate in domestic IPOs and secondary share issues. The QFII scheme hence enables foreign institutional investors to trade in Chinese securities without being present in the Chinese market through a JV.

The specific regulation of the QFII scheme requires a minimum capital requirement of US$50 million per QFII account. The upper limit is US$300 million. A single stake in a company may not exceed 10 per cent, while total foreign investment may not exceed 20 per cent. Lock-in periods necessitate that remitted money from an open-ended fund must be held in the account for one year, and money from closed-end funds for three years. While the money is not necessarily to be held in shares, this lock-in period creates a lack of liquidity in QFII transactions, as well as an exposure to exchange rate risk from the investors' perspective. In addition, remittance has to be applied for a period even after the lock-in, creating bureaucratic risks. The custodian banks, through which QFIIs have to apply for licences and quotas and conduct their transactions, include ICBC, BOC, CCB, ABC and BoComm as well as Citibank, HSBC and Standard Chartered (Bei, 2003). Chinese securities companies act as brokerages.[98] There were 20 licensed QFII firms in mid-October 2004 and the sum of total investment under the QFII scheme reached US$2.925 billion (*China Daily*, 2004g). Some firms have already applied for the extension of their quotas, confirming the rapid growth of the scheme.

Since the A-share market has been widely regarded as overvalued and investors can easily obtain desired China exposure through Hong Kong and other overseas markets at much lower costs, the potential success of the QFII scheme was heavily debated before its introduction.[99] The initial phase, however, was marked by strong demand, although some of it was potentially induced by speculations about a potential RMB appreciation. From the foreign perspective, the QFII scheme offers foreign investors an option for market access and allows greater market entry for foreign intermediaries, even if it remains restricted and tightly regulated.[100] On a broader level, the scheme is also regarded as a commitment to open the market further and to reform it with international support.

Two other channels of foreign participation in China's securities markets have emerged as trends. Firstly, there are indications of the emerging participation of foreign financial firms in bad debt recovery and NPL disposal. In principle, with their large toolbox for dealing with NPLs and assets, ranging from restructuring and sale to securitisation, international investment banks are in a strong position to engage in this business. They have thus entered into cooperation agreements with Chinese AMCs, including Deutsche Bank who agreed with Cinda Asset Management on chartering NPLs with a book value of RMB2.55 billion. The founding of a separate asset management JV between

Morgan Stanley and China Construction Bank in order to deal with RMB4.3 billion of NPLs is a direction in which Goldman Sachs and Industrial & Commercial Bank of China moved as well, aiming at bundling and restructuring RMB10 billion. However, both JVs had not yet been approved at the end of 2004 (Solvet, 2002, p. 48; Lange, 2004). Secondly, strategic foreign investment in domestic Chinese firms in the securities business has become another new component of the market entry of foreign financial firms. Structured in parallel to the strategic foreign investments in the commercial banking industry, foreign firms are allowed to buy into Chinese securities market players under certain conditions. Foreign investors will thus be allowed and encouraged to participate in the restructuring of the domestic firms (*China Daily*, 2004a). It is unclear whether this will become a trend.

In sum, foreign firms have had only limited options for market entry into the Chinese securities markets. The Chinese securities business has remained more closed than the banking industry and foreign firms have only been able to enter the Chinese market through cooperative activities such as JVs, or through the QFII scheme. With regard to product strategies, the newly born JVs were still in an early stage. Consequently, it can only tentatively be observed that securities firms have positioned themselves less distinctively with regard to the products and services they offer in the domestic market so far (compared to foreign commercial banks), an observation that can also be made for young fund management JVs.[101] In the interviews conducted for this research, it was repeatedly pointed out that it was only after several years that distinct differences in the behaviour and products of the JV firms and domestic firms would become observable. Evidence based on their products and the specifics of their services is thus still too limited for an in-depth analysis and has to be left for further research. This chapter now turns to assessing both the incentives and constraints behind the choice of market entry strategies.

Regulation and regulatory change

As in the commercial banking sector, the single most important limiting and channelling factor for the market entry of foreign firms has been regulation. In the case of the securities industry, as pointed out above, this has primarily meant that foreign financial firms had to enter JVs in order to be able to access the domestic market at all and that most of the potential business has thus been sealed off from standalone foreign firms through regulatory restrictions. In addition, regulations have been important in shaping the actual business options of the securities firms and fund management JVs in China *after* market entry. This has been the case both with regard to rules that apply for all (domestic and Sino-foreign JVs) financial firms as well as with regard to those that create differences in the range of products that various financial firms can offer. In fund management, for example, investment options have been restricted for all firms alike by regulation, thus making it difficult for *all* firms to develop distinct products and distinguish themselves from their competitors.[102] An example of the second case is the fact that Sino-foreign JVs are not allowed to conduct trade in A-shares on their own account whereas domestic securities companies are, thus discriminating between the types of firms and creating a difference in their product range. With regard to QFII investments, the ways in which regulation has limited, structured and shaped them through quotas and restrictions on the timing of investment and disinvestment have already been discussed above. Yet, it should be noted that it had in fact been the new regulation that *enabled* foreign investors and intermediaries to conduct QFII investments.

In a historical perspective and keeping in mind the almost complete prohibition of onshore business pre-2001, the introduction of QFII and the liberalisation of market entry in the course of the WTO entry constitute distinct changes in the regulatory policies with regard to market opening. Notwithstanding their gradual nature, the new regulatory policies signal a shift away from the restriction and containment of foreign firms' market participation. It is in the context of these policies that the ability of foreign firms to participate in domestic markets and the availability of more business opportunities for them has increased. Yet, there has not only been a reduction of containment of foreign firms, but also a change in the role the CSRC assigns to them, specifically in their strategy to develop the base of institutional investors and to increase financial skills and professional long-term investment in the securities markets (interviews, also see Harner, 2001). Foreign firms are now seen to have assistance and expertise to offer in the reform of domestic markets and are thus regarded as contributors to market development (interview with a CSRC official). This change emerged in parallel to the deepening domestic reform endeavours in the securities markets after 2001. Depending on how the new regulatory priorities of the CSRC develop further, the role of foreign firms will continue to be redefined in the future, and has the potential not unlike the role of foreign strategic investors in domestic commercial banks.[103]

Overall, new regulations have been decisive in the change in market entry options for foreign firms, highlighting the dominant role of regulation in structuring their onshore China business and shaping the constraints on it. In comparison to the commercial banking sector, the trend towards more liberalisation and cooperation is similar in direction, but less marked; as of 2004 JVs remained the dominant mode of market entry, and no foreign strategic investments had been made by then. This is remarkable because the domestic securities markets have been revealed by the above analysis to be less concentrated than the domestic commercial banking sector and less burdened with the problems of single large firms.

Business opportunities versus comparative strengths and weaknesses

In what ways has the market environment been important in shaping foreign firms' incentives and constraints for participation? While regulations define the *options* of foreign firms for market entry, the market conditions and opportunities themselves define and structure incentives to actively engage in the market. In this regard, market attractiveness, competition and competitive advantage are crucial. Overall, the Chinese securities markets have been very attractive for foreign firms due to the generally high and stable growth of the Chinese economy and the prospect of China's stock market growing into one of the largest markets in Asia. The ongoing reforms of the market have increased expectations, although stability during these times might be reduced (interview). Foreign securities firms, which have long been interested in entering these markets as a channel to establish contacts with enterprises that will potentially list internationally, have increasingly been attracted to the domestic market as well. In particular, in the case of fund management, they want a share of the enormous growth market (interviews).

What are the competitive advantages and disadvantages of foreign firms in this regard? For the securities houses or investments banks, their largest advantages are their international experience and their connections for internationally oriented investment banking services. On the local market, their single most important advantage is their international reputation and brand, followed by their professional knowledge and expertise, as well as better management and governance structures.[104] They are capital rich and financially strong companies, operating according to commercial criteria. However, they know little about domestic markets and need to build local knowledge and contacts. On the other hand, they depend less on the establishment of a branch network (as is the case in commercial banking), because investment banking and asset management are less dependent on a branch network.

However, competition within the domestic securities industry is high, especially with regard to the top-end clients that foreign firms are focusing on. In internationally related business, there is fierce competition for leading roles in larger IPOs, almost exclusively among a fixed set of selected domestic players and leading international investment banks, an illustrative example of which is the IPO of China Life in 2003 where competition was exclusively among international firms (Li and Kang, 2003). As discussed above, the domestic market is a tricky environment for foreign firms, as it is dominated by volatile share prices and high risks as well as informal rules.

In actual market conduct, foreign financial firms have positioned themselves in areas of business most profitable for them and where they have the greatest advantage; the underwriting and management of international IPOs of Chinese customers. The far less advantageous position of foreign firms in domestic markets has led to a much less pronounced strategy and presence there. It can be argued in this regard that this structure of business opportunities and comparative advantage is contributing to the reluctance of foreign firms to enter into JV securities firms and the (tentatively observed) lack of a distinct positioning in the domestic market with regard to products. As foreign firms can conduct the international business from representative offices in an offshore mode, the JV securities firms have little to offer, especially when additionally keeping in mind the regulations restricting them to a minority position and the restrictions on A-share trading. In general, however, business for international securities companies is a two-way street – both doing business in China and doing business with Chinese customers overseas. As Slater (2002a) has argued, the domestic presence of foreign firms may therefore have to increase in the future in order to offer potential clients more domestic services (see also SCMP, 2004).

As opposed to the securities companies, the fund management industry has witnessed a growing interest among foreign firms in setting up JVs, reflecting a boom in the industry in China. Even the declining market has not stopped foreign companies from initiating new funds, although the process has slowed down. With regard to QFII investments, it has been argued, however, that it has not been the Chinese markets that necessarily have been of so much interest in a genuine way (last but not least because of the risk, lack of transparency, and problems with enterprise reform) but that strategies of international risk-spreading and speculation on a currency revaluation have been more decisive.

Overall, within the regulatory framework, market considerations and competitive advantages have been very important in shaping the scale and pattern of foreign firms' market entry in the securities market. Foreign securities firms have been strongest in internationally related business and have thus been reluctant to enter the Chinese market on a large scale, a process that has been reinforced by the distorted and troubled structure of the domestic market. The downturn of the securities market has been key in slowing the set-up of fund management JVs.

Problems of foreign companies

In addition to regulation and market opportunities, foreign financial firms' market participation in China's securities markets has been shaped by specific problems in market entry and doing business in China. Most importantly in this regard, as in the case of foreign commercial banks, operating in the Chinese market has been difficult for foreign firms in the securities industry due to a lack of experienced personnel and due to limitations on funding. In addition, again reflecting the experience of foreign commercial banks, weak accounting and corporate governance standards have been a major problem for foreign financial firms. More distinctively, however, in the securities industry, foreign participation has encountered specific problems due to the (mandatory) JV structure. The setting up of JVs has been particularly difficult in the Chinese case because the virtual absence of track records for Chinese fund management companies, for instance, has made the choice of partner and the pricing of each firm's contribution difficult.[105] Additionally, JVs always run the risk of cooperation difficulties after set-up as well as risking the strengthening of a potential competitor. As a critical issue in every JV is control, the caps placed on the share of the JV permitted for foreign partners (and the resulting limits in the design of JV agreements) have also created problems. As revealed during the interviews conducted for this research, however, some innovative arrangements have been made in this respect. In some of the fund management JVs a greater degree of management control was transferred to the foreign partner than the (minority) equity share would have formally mandated. The top management position of the head of operations, and thus the operational control, was in these cases executed by the smaller (foreign) partner.[106] Other solutions included written veto-rights for the minority shareholders on portfolio and risk management, as was the case in the agreement between ABN Amro and XiangCai Hefeng (*The Economist*, 2003a). Still, despite innovative counter-measures, problems related to control issues have been an important factor contributing to the limited number of JV securities firms being set up so far. Given the regulatory restrictions on the business as well as the limited economic opportunities offered by JV securities companies, foreign firms have preferred to wait for the possibility to set up 100 per cent wholly foreign-owned enterprises before engaging more deeply in the market (interviews). With regard to funding, the restrictions on the share of the foreign partner have limited the growth of the JVs that have emerged.

Overall, the market participation of foreign securities firms has been driven by regulatory restrictions, market opportunities and specific problems of foreign firms in China's markets. Regulation has posed severe limits on the degree to which foreign firms have been able to enter the market in the first place as well as on their business expansion. Yet it has not been the only restricting factor; the motivation to set up JV securities firms has been further reduced by the difficulty in transferring the competitive advantages of foreign firms to domestic markets and by problems inherent in the JV structure. JVs have thus offered limited benefits to foreign partners. Fund management JVs, with their more concise business scope, have been more attractive, because the fund management industry is, despite market problems, rapidly growing with regard to the number and size of funds set up. The advantages of foreign firms in fund management are also more pronounced. With regard to the market participation of QFII, it was pointed out above that investments through the QFII scheme in part reflect currency speculation rather than a genuine interest in the Chinese market.

Impact on China's securities markets

Despite the recent nature of the opening of China's securities markets, in what ways has foreign participation been meaningful for domestic market development? Where has it (already) had an impact? To what degree are foreign firms (already) important actors in the domestic markets? Have they altered the constellation of actors, the range of available products and the mode of interaction and business conduct? In approaching these questions, it has to be kept in mind that the JV structure differs considerably from the QFII mode of market entry. Each will be therefore looked at separately. Additionally, besides the impact on the securities market itself, a broader impact on the enterprise sector has to be taken into consideration, due both to foreign firms' role in the internationalisation of Chinese firms through international IPOs or bond issuances and to changes in the enterprise sector that have been initiated by changes in the domestic securities markets.

1. Increased competition

For the commercial banking sector, the provision of new products has been among the most important ways in which foreign banks have had an impact on domestic market development, as was shown in the previous chapter. As already briefly mentioned above, however, this picture can not be decisively confirmed for the securities industry as of 2004, since the securities companies and fund management JVs were both too immature in their organisational development and too restricted by regulation to offer distinct products. Yet there are indications that JV firms have led to an increase in competition in their respective market segments, especially as they are regarded as more professional and experienced in their work, both in fund management and the securities companies' business (interviews with industry participants). As their reputation stands in stark contrast to the distrust *vis-à-vis* some of the domestic players that have been involved in domestic scandals, fund management JVs have, in the view of interviewees, generally been more successful than their non-JV competitors in collecting capital and issuing funds. On the securities firms' side, competition has increased due to JVs' broader and technically more advanced approach to distribution channels in parallel to the overall change in trading mechanisms. They exploit the increased importance of telephone and internet trading, making the establishment of walk-in branches less important and the smaller existing branches redundant. As pointed out by an interviewee, the JVs tend to position themselves more clearly with regard to marketing strategy and technology. Since JV securities firms have in addition been emphasising their international linkages as one of their main strengths, they have also contributed to a further increase in the focus on international services and comprehensive investment banking services among securities companies in China. In the case of the securities JV CESL, the double strategy of strong domestic presence and international connections has been employed quite successfully. This was reflected by its dominant position in the sponsorship of underwriting deals in 2004, which it achieved within its first full business year of operation and which can also be understood as a sign of the relative competitive strength of new JVs.[107] Further conclusions are dependent on a longer-term evaluation of their business development. In contrast to the findings for the commercial banking sector, the effects of foreign financial firms' entry on the securities business on a direct product and strategy level are so far less clear, especially as the indirect effects of increased competition remain hard to measure.

2. New management techniques and expertise

With regard to the effects of foreign firms' entry on the introduction of new management techniques and expertise, the internal set-up of JVs comes into focus because most of this transfer occurs within the JVs themselves. In the cooperation agreements, the aspect of transferring skills and techniques is of high significance, as pointed out by interviewed fund management and securities firms JVs' representatives. The intention behind giving operational control to the foreign minority partner in some fund management JVs, for example, has been to ensure that the learning process be as deep as possible (as confirmed in interviews with the domestic and foreign partners of these JVs). The strong position of the foreign partner in risk management (ensured through the JV agreements) that was consistently mentioned throughout the interviews was motivated by the perceived gap of skills and techniques in this area. As far as it could be observed through the interviews, risk management was thus placed under foreign control in order to ensure the transfer of skills and the smooth operations of the venture. Essentially, the aim of the JV was perceived to be helping the domestic partner become more professional, to apply international standards and to internationalise while simultaneously providing a channel of market access to the foreign partner. The fact that the securities firm JVs in particular were set up as long-term commitments to build an international investment bank, as was the case with CESL, also increased the incentives on the foreign side to engage in longer-term training for JV staff and the establishment of detailed incentive schemes and management structures in the JV (interview). Competition and the threat of industry consolidation significantly increased the motivation of the domestic partner to actively learn in this process, whereas the hope of involvement in the opening of the QDII scheme was an additional motivating factor for the foreign partner.[108] Based on the interviews, there are indications that a significant transfer of skills and techniques as well as management structures and corporate governance standards in the JV took place, for example through the design of internal operational procedure guidelines, in-house training programmes and the standardisation of decision-making procedures in management. While limited on a quantitative scale so far, this is likely to increase if buying into a Chinese securities company along the lines of foreign strategic investment becomes more common, something the CSRC began to foster in 2004, according to a statement by Fang Xinghai, deputy chief executive officer of the Shanghai stock exchange (*China Daily*, 2004a).

3. Increased information and research capacities

Turning to the contribution of QFII to the development of the Chinese securities markets, it has first of all to be pointed out that QFIIs' significance from the Chinese perspective lies mainly in their role as investors (instead of intermediaries). They are a new group of institutional investors and due to their international nature they have distinct characteristics that distinguish them from the already present domestic investors. Their most clearly observable impact in this regard is that they increase the capital for investment and thus the liquidity of the market. QFIIs invested around US$2 billion in China's securities markets in 2004 alone. Due to the professional nature of their investments, there are important signalling effects related to these investments, giving companies that are chosen by QFII investors an external professional approval of their business prospects. As a prospective trend, it is expected that the signalling effects of QFII investment will help to increase corporate governance standards in domestically listed enterprises by raising the benchmark for the performance of listed firms and rewarding improved corporate governance when they report QFII in shareholder lists in annual reports.

In addition to signalling effects, QFII investments have led to an increase in the amount of high-quality research on Chinese companies due to the need of QFIIs to conduct informed investment decisions. The increase in research activities is identifiable in the increased number of (internal) research reports as well as in the increase of investment banking staff in foreign financial firms in China (interviews).[109] On a more indirect level, the QFII scheme has greatly increased the international interest in the Chinese stock market and has highlighted the progress in opening China's securities markets to outsiders, thus creating a positive attitude towards investments in the Chinese financial market. QFIIs increase the linkages of China's securities markets with international markets because they increase the stake of foreign investors in them. For the future, it is thus hoped that QFII will have further positive impacts in stabilising the Chinese markets and increasing their international reputation.

At the same time, two fears of detrimental effects were voiced after the plans for a QFII scheme emerged. Firstly, it was feared that the QFII scheme would contribute to a further segmentation of the equity market and the emergence of a blue-chip bubble (Green and He, 2004). As there may only be a limited number of stocks among the 1300 listed companies that are likely to pass the quality controls of foreign investors, it was feared that the signalling would, while providing a desirable quality selection, also lead to a two-class market. It has been argued that since the mismatch in supply and demand for the best 50 firms would lead to a price surge for those companies, a blue-chip bubble would be unavoidable. Therefore, QFII was seen to harbour the danger of leaving the weaker enterprises behind without solving their problems. By 2004, this had not materialised. The second fear related to QFII was the danger of potential speculative capital inflows through the QFII accounts. Raising doubts about genuine investment interests of foreign investors, it was argued that the expectations of revaluation of the RMB would induce large amounts of foreign currency inflows, thus creating problems for the foreign exchange management system.[110] While in 2004 problems developed along these lines, the Chinese side was able to manage and control the process. Speculative capital inflows, however, highlighted the close relation of the securities market opening to the opening of the capital account and reforming the exchange rate system.

One last point is that the market entry of QFII had an additional impact on the domestic securities companies that act as custodian banks and brokers for international investors. Fierce competition among them created incentives to develop comprehensive QFII platforms as a response to pressures for more international orientation and professionalisation among them.

In sum, while it has to be kept in mind that the overall impact of foreign firms' market entry can only tentatively be assessed so far, channels in which foreign financial firms have had an impact on market development in China have been identified. Most importantly, they have led to an increase in competition, a transfer of management techniques and expertise, and an increase in information and research capabilities in the Chinese markets. The limits to their impact have resulted from the regulatory restrictions placed on their market entry. While foreign firms have thus been able to contribute to market development and have emerged as important actors, they have done so on a limited quantitative scale and have thus remained in a comparatively weak position *vis-à-vis* the CSRC. This has especially been the case because they operate through JV structures and are thus – while themselves operationally strong and independent actors – bound into cooperation with domestic partners. The extent to which this cooperation has had an impact on domestic firms is discussed in Chapter 7. However, the above section has also identified the potential dangers of market opening with regard to QFII and related speculative inflows of capital. The future depth and breadth of the impact of foreign firms will strongly depend on the development of the securities industry overall and the further removal of restrictions on foreign participation. Prospects for this are discussed in the next section.

Concluding remarks

What are the future strategic options and structural opportunities for foreign financial firms in China's securities markets? What will determine whether foreign securities firms will be in a position to make the most out of them? With respect to size and quantitative growth, all prospects and prognoses for the development of China's domestic securities markets remained promising as of late 2004. The stock market alone was estimated to reach approximately 65 per cent of GDP by 2010, at about US$2 trillion (Wilson and Purushothaman, 2003; Hu, 2002). The growth of the total amount of savings feeds an increasing demand for securities and a larger role for collective savings instruments and institutional investors. The boundaries between the banking and the securities industry continue to be demolished, slowly creating a greater flexibility in investment and saving options.[111] The largest boom segments of the securities markets are likely to be the fund industry and the insurance business (interviews). In addition, future reforms that will foster the development of the securities market include social security reforms and the structure of the evolving pension system.[112] With regard to the bond market, the diversification of corporate finance options will increase the supply of domestic corporate bonds while the financing needs for infrastructure projects will keep government bond supply high.

Depending on future reforms, China's economy is also likely to internationalise further, thus creating market opportunities that are especially relevant from the perspective of foreign financial firms in the securities industry. The opportunities that arise in this regard include onshore and offshore business. In China, the increased listing of foreign invested firms would not only be a catalyst for changes in corporate governance, but could also create promising deals for foreign securities companies and their JV partners. With regard to China-related business overseas, the IPOs of major Chinese enterprises have already been mentioned above, including those of the four state-owned commercial banks. The size of the IPOs of ChinaLife and the property insurer PICC, the world's largest IPOs in 2003, give an indication of the enormous size of future deals. Market analysts forecast the world's IPO market to be dominated by Chinese issuers until 2010 (Ernst & Young, 2004). In addition, the massive consolidation in Chinese industry due to 'obvious overcapacity, lack of profitability, and improving regulatory enforcement' (Walter and

Howie, 2003, p. 162) creates new opportunities for foreign firms. Plans by the State Council to create eight to ten national firms by 2006 were announced in 2003 (Green 2003c, p. 94). Have foreign firms participated in this process?

Based on the analysis in this chapter, it can be argued that in the dynamic environment driven by market opportunities, reform and regulation, the structural opportunities for foreign financial firms both to grasp market opportunities and participate in the restructuring depend primarily on the development of the regulatory framework for foreign firms. If the framework is not liberalised further, the quantitative options will still attract foreign participation, but in a much more limited way. Notably, differing from the WTO agreements on commercial banking, for the securities industry there is no set timetable to increase allowed participation over the 49 per cent ownership share in JVs. The implicit consensus that after 2007, foreign firms will be allowed to operate wholly foreign-owned businesses and to gain majority control is only an expectation, not a certain future reality. They thus depend on the policy choices of the CSRC and the evolving direction of the Chinese regulatory regime. There are, however, identifiable incentives for the Chinese side to engage foreign firms further, such as in the development of the QDII scheme that will allow qualified domestic firms to invest in international markets, an area where foreign firms are particularly well positioned to assist the process with their international experience. In order not to overemphasise the relevance of regulation, however, it has also to be kept in mind that *within* the evolving regulatory framework, business prospects of foreign firms depend on the qualitative improvements in the securities markets, such as reduced risks and volatility, a stronger credit culture, better information and improved accounting standards.

The above analysis has highlighted the decisive role of regulation in the development of the Chinese domestic securities markets as well as for the participation of foreign actors in these markets. Until 2001, regulation set a tight frame for foreign participation, almost suffocating onshore business opportunities. A change in regulation after 2001 allowed more market participation but still within restrictive limits. The future development of foreign participation will depend primarily on the evolution of the regulatory framework. In the domestic background of this evolution are troubled markets and a dominance of state-owned and controlled actors on the part of the listed enterprises as well as with regard to market intermediaries.

Comparing the findings with the commercial banking sector, it can be seen that in both cases the incentives and constraints determining market access for foreign financial firms have remained dominated by regulation. However, the degree of restrictiveness varies; the (continuing) channelling of foreign firms' market access through JVs in the case of the securities industry highlights the more restrictive regulatory regime in this area. Yet, in both cases, the emergence of more liberal and cooperative policies has been identified as well. The market entry in the securities business through the QFII scheme, however, also highlighted that capital account liberalisation and currency issues play an important role in the market access of foreign firms to China's financial markets.

5
Foreign Firms Lobbying for Liberalisation

Foreign firms as external actors in the Chinese financial markets have been portrayed in the previous chapters as mere rule-takers, facing a restrictive regulatory framework that heavily restrains their market participation and scope of business. However, commercial players usually do not perceive themselves to be receivers of regulation only, but instead actively influence the process in their interest, both in developed countries and emerging market economies (EMEs) (Hellman, Jones and Kaufmann, 2002a; Rajan and Zingales, 2003a).[113] Interestingly, Hellmann, Jones and Kaufmann found that regulatory capture abroad is over-proportionally pursued by foreign firms offering financial services.[114] This chapter sets out to complement the analysis focused on the business strategies and market conduct of foreign financial firms with an assessment of foreign firms' impact on market development through their lobbying for changes in regulation. In looking at foreign firms from this angle, the chapter acknowledges the role of industry players in regulatory policy-making in China. This chapter investigates the ways in which foreign financial firms identifiably lobby Chinese regulators in their interest and explores the channels and patterns of foreign financial firms' interest representation that have emerged.[115] It then approaches the question of whether foreign firms have been able to impact regulation and whether they have lobbied successfully for market liberalisation. It will be shown that a remarkably diversified organisational structure of foreign firms' interest representation has emerged in China and that foreign firms actively employ strategies of both formal and informal lobbying. New patterns of interaction and semi-institutionalised working relations have thus emerged between regulators and foreign financial firms. Chinese regulators have been responsive to the requests of foreign firms in some cases, but it can not be said that foreign firms have been successful in lobbying for their interests on a large scale, especially not in the case of the broader directional decisions in regulation. Here, domestic interests and priorities have dominated regulatory policy-making and the lobbying of foreign firms has thus had a limited impact on market opening.

Formal and informal lobbying

Based on their limited market position as outsiders, representatives of foreign financial firms interviewed for this study have perceived themselves mostly as comparatively weak players with regard to interest representation. For them, the policy process and the process of regulatory decision-making has remained a black box on the domestic side, although it was widely recognised that the largest domestic industry players are directly represented in the regulatory decision-making process, such as through the position that the heads of the four SOCBs take on certain committees and panels.[116] Overall, representatives of foreign financial firms expected the regulatory bodies, the State Council, and the domestic financial firms to be the main actors in the process, with a smaller and more opaque role assumed for the Communist Party and non-financial SOEs (see Figure 5.1). Even with large state-owned actors losing political clout, the representatives of most foreign financial firms interviewed expected regulators to play a predominately domestically determined game. Based on this rather pessimistic view expressed by the interviewees, it is almost surprising that the foreign firms actively engage in the process at all.

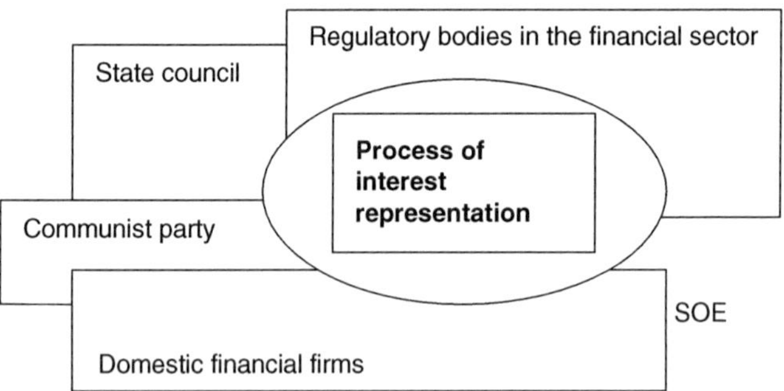

Figure 5.1   The black box of domestic interest representation
Source: Own compilation

Formal organisations of foreign financial firms' interest representation

Processes of collective action and interest representation in the sense of a liberal, pluralistic democracy have officially been de-legitimised in the Chinese political system for a long time, just as the pursuit of regional interests has been. Yet both have driven the reform process to a considerable extent.[117] In the process of the organisational adaptation of the Chinese government to the emerging market structure, new channels of interest representation and inclusion into the political system were built alongside changes in social composition and the reconfiguration of interests, interest groups and their political weight in society and the political system (Zheng, 2004, p. 292; Dickson, 2000). In the economic sphere, semi-autonomous associations of interest representation were set up on an organisational level in form of a (semi-)corporatist model. Numerous business associations were founded, reflecting among others the emergence of private entrepreneurs and foreign invested enterprises as two new groups of players.[118] Additionally, business associations originating in the foreign enterprises' home countries have entered the organisational landscape, helping foreign enterprises to set up business successfully, as well as fostering their members' interests in China. Also with regard to interest representation in the financial markets, two broad categories of organisations can be distinguished – firstly, those that were initiated by the Chinese side and are semi-independent from state agencies and, secondly, those that were initiated by foreign market entrants in the form of business chambers and associations.

Organisations initiated by the Chinese side

The establishment of Chinese business associations in the financial market took place in the overall wave of establishing new industry chambers during the reshuffling of the administration and the outsourcing of industry ministries. Among other aspects, this policy aimed at establishing self-regulatory bodies as a third layer for financial market regulation. In line with its general approach to interest intermediation, the State Council founded diverse associations operating as a transmission belt in the financial markets, helping to implement policies on different administrative levels.[119] Accordingly, in 2004, there was one national banking association, the China Banking Association, as well as 30 associations on the provincial level and 40 on the prefecture level (CBRC, 2005a). Among these, the Shanghai Banking Association (SBA) was most important for foreign banks in Shanghai. However, it was primarily regarded as a mouthpiece of the PBC and CBRC and as having limited potential for genuine interest representation.[120] This was especially the case from the perspective of foreign banks because the SBA bundled the interests of foreign and domestic banks, thus effectively curtailing the representation of interests of foreign banks as a group in themselves.[121] Foreign banks and their representatives are present on the board of directors and are convenors or co-convenors of the SBA working groups.

In the securities industry, likewise, there is the Securities Association of China (SAC).[122] The objectives of the SAC are self-regulation over the securities industry under the government's centralised and comprehensive supervision and management, as well as building bridges between the government and the industry. The SAC provides services to members and – according to its website (www.sac.net.cn) – aims at maintaining a fair competition order in the securities industry, as well as promoting transparency, justice and fairness of the securities market and pushing forward its healthy and steady development.

Sino-foreign JVs in the securities business and international investment banks such as the CICC are members of the SAC alongside wholly domestically owned market participants. The functions of the SAC are primarily on a self-regulatory level and it remains subject to the 'guidance, supervision and administration of the CSRC and the Ministry of Civil Affairs' (CSRC, 2004a). It has an important role in formulating self-regulatory rules, industry standards and business practices, but also in the training and examination of professionals.

Overall, the organisations of interest representation originating from the Chinese side, with their latently corporatist character and their intention to represent whole industries, have been regarded sceptically by foreign financial firms and have been perceived to have limited relevance for their interest representation. Yet, they have engaged and participated in the work of (some of) them.

Organisations initiated by the foreign side

On the side of the foreign-initiated organisations, industrial organisations such as the chambers of commerce have gained a prominent role in organised interest representation. Their primary function is to help foreign firms to set up business in China and offer appropriate services. Most prominent on the level of national chambers of commerce are the US-American AmCham, the Australian AustCham, and the Japanese Chamber of Commerce, as well as the national chambers of commerce of major European countries. On a supranational level there is the European Union Chamber of Commerce in China (EUCCC), representing the

EU member states' commercial interests and bundling their commercial power.[123] This position makes the EUCCC a potentially powerful organisation, as the presence of European financial firms in the Chinese market is strong, especially in the case of European banks.

With regard to the process of interest representation, each chamber of commerce operates on two levels; the first is the general level of thematically unspecific committees that foster contacts and exchange with Chinese government and regulatory bodies in general. The second comprises working groups or forums for specific business areas. AmCham, for instance, has a committee for the appreciation dinner and a Chinese government relations committee, as well as forums 'bringing together members with common interests to share experiences and address industry issues' such as the Forum on Financial Services (AmCham, n.d.). AmCham publishes the AmCham White Paper on a yearly basis, giving an overview of the current situation of US-American business in China as well as industry specific overviews of problems (AmCham, 2004a, 2007). For the financial markets, this paper is divided into banking, capital markets, and insurance, each including policy recommendations. They also publish a WTO implementation report, again structured along the lines of single industries (AmCham, 2003). In this regard AmCham is quite typical as similar structures are found for the EUCCC; it publishes a yearly position paper on European business in China (EUCCC 2004a). The EUCCC has working groups on banking, capital markets and insurance, both in Beijing and Shanghai. They are self-organised sub-organisations under the umbrella of the chambers.[124] The statutes of the EUCCC working groups on finance and banking state that they monitor market environment and regulatory issues for foreign financial firms in China, as well as certain banking products such as consumer finance, derivative and trade financing products, and foreign exchange and interest rate management (EUCCC, 2003, p. 48).

In principle, the groups encourage dialogue with regulatory bodies and provide a platform for it. To that aim, white papers and position papers are sent to the regulatory bodies in China on a yearly basis as well as to ministries and other government agencies. In addition, meetings and seminars with 'key working level Chinese government leaders' are held in order to discuss policy recommendations (AmCham, n.d.).[125] The papers are also sent to relevant organisations and government agencies in the home countries of the firms in order to brief domestic politicians.

Essentially, the working groups follow a double strategy of simultaneously reacting to new regulations that prove detrimental to the business of foreign financial firms or in violation of the spirit of the WTO, as

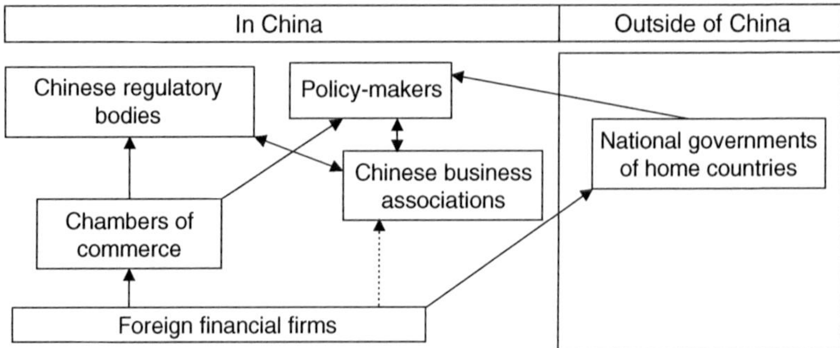

Figure 5.2   Organised interest representation of foreign financial firms: channels and players
Source: Own compilation

well as lobbying in a long-term perspective for broader interests, such as the removal of long-existent regulations and restrictions. While single chambers of commerce cooperate on a case-by-case basis, there is no organised interest representation for all foreign businesses in the financial market in China, despite the geographical clustering of institutionalised interest groups around political decision-makers in Beijing and around the commercial interests that they represent in Shanghai.

As Figure 5.2 above shows, there is also a structure of organisations foreign financial firms can turn to in their home countries, including government agencies and home-country chambers of commerce. For the European countries, there is the EU Commission on a supranational level; although not specialised on financial services, it plays a part in representing foreign firms' interests in China through high-level visits and negotiations by EU commissioners. These visits are well covered in the media and thus also provide an opportunity for public debate and pressure. The home country organisations can be approached from the individual financial firms through letters of complaint as well as through the intermediary structure of bodies such as the EUCCC and the Delegation of the EU in China.[126]

Pitfalls of organised interest representation

As with any collective action, in the case of foreign financial firms' interest representation, the more heterogeneous and the larger an interest group is, the more difficult it is to articulate its interests (Olson, 1965). Foreign banks in China, for example, are diverse in their institutional structure and business strategies. According to their areas of business, scale of operations and strategies, they have different interests and perceptions of problems, and are affected differently by regulations. This makes it harder to effectively act as a joint actor in favour of and actively promoting further financial liberalisation. Banks with a defensive business strategy, for example, might even be interested in conserving existing obstacles because these will not allow their competitors to move on. Some interviewees also stated that they favoured the restrictive regulatory environment and slow opening as it guaranteed the stability of the Chinese financial market. Even where a consensus can be reached on the aim and strategy of lobbying, representing foreign interests is not an easy task in an environment that questions the legitimacy of foreign interests (and their representation). There is as yet no established understanding of industry lobbying organisations in China (Kennedy, 2005). While an institutional framework for the chambers' work is also missing, there are increasingly stable working relations with Chinese regulators, highlighted by frequent talks on an increasingly routine level and two-way channels for initiating discussions (interviews).

However, cultural and language barriers make it hard to find the right tone in negotiating difficult issues and disagreements. In 2003, for example, there was a debate ongoing among foreign financial firms on whether 'foreign faces or local faces' would be more warmly welcomed by the Chinese side with regard to lobbying efforts. While a 'foreign face' might still gain more attention, the willingness to negotiate with 'local faces' was held in higher regard (interviews). Complicating the situation of interest representation even more was the question of whether those foreign firms most active and visible in the collective interest representation process have to fear detrimental effects on their own business interests.[127] Therefore, regarding the formal, organised interest representation described in this section, it can be concluded that although there is a remarkably diversified structure of organisations of interest representation, the internal problems as well as the under-institutionalised and opaque nature of the lobbying processes in China make it a difficult endeavour.

Informal channels of lobbying

In every economy, informal lobbying also is an important part of interest representation. In the case of China – a country with few legitimised and institutionalised channels for interest representation, but a strong perception of the importance of personal relationships and

networking – the role of informal lobbying may even be larger.[128] Therefore, it seems reasonable to expect that foreign financial firms engage in
informal lobbying, in particular due to the limits of organised interest
representation explained above. This subsection thus asks whether there
are indications that foreign financial firms engage in processes of informal lobbying, what their strategies in this regard are and whether foreign
firms have learnt to play the game of informal interest representation in
China successfully. The subsection shows that foreign financial firms
have devoted a considerable amount of energy to building favourable
conditions for their business and have employed multi-faceted strategies
in this regard.

In order to set the stage for more direct attempts of lobbying, foreign firms first of all have tried to position themselves well *vis-à-vis* the
regulatory bodies and political decision-makers. Strategies have included
stressing the historical links of their company with China, as well
as highlighting their pioneer and leading role in the Chinese market.
Rhetorically linking their own fate to China and showing loyalty in
times of distress have also been part of their repertoires (Katz, 1997).[129]
In addition, foreign financial firms have tried hard to behave in a way
that would be perceived as politically correct by Chinese leaders.[130] As
Chen and Thomas (2001, p. 6) have pointed out, the demonstration
of long-term commitment, proven by investments in professional education for the financial industry, are also common. As pointed out by
interviewees, 'giving face' to Chinese leaders was another aspect, in circumstances such as large-scale ceremonies for the closure of deals where
high-ranking firm representatives shake hands with political leaders
(interviews).

Starting from these smoothed relations, foreign financial firms have
in particular tried to respond to the high importance and prestige of
individual leaders, and to the role of *guanxi* networks in China. For
them, learning to play the Chinese way, in the sense of abiding with the
rules of informal lobbying in China, has mainly been aimed at ensuring
leadership access and playing political cards.

Ensuring leadership access

Personal contacts have always been helpful in doing business, and this
is especially so in China. Personal contacts thus were named by a lot
of interviewees as the main approach taken to solving arising problems
and these therefore lay at the core of the foreign financial firms' informal lobbying strategies (interviews). In order to ensure leadership access
and usable *guanxi* networks, foreign financial firms have employed three

approaches to nurture new contacts; firstly, recognising the importance of personal relationships in China, a number of foreign financial firms has increased the time their high-level management and CEOs spend in China, visiting and courting Chinese officials and thus expressing the high relevance China has for their company. This has included developing the notion of 'regular visits' as a sign of deep commitment. Examples include the former head of Goldman Sachs, Hank Paulson, who visited China 68 times between 1992 and 2004, as well as the head of AIG and high-level management staff of Allianz (interviews, Liao, 2004). Visits of complete Boards of Governors, such as in the case of the visit of the HSBC Board under the lead of Sir John Bond in 2004, are also important in this regard (*China Daily*, 2004f). When in China, CEOs of leading foreign financial firms have met with high-ranking Chinese officials, such as the meeting between Jiang Zemin and Citibank CEO Sanford Weill for the 100th anniversary of Citibank in China in 2002, but also for much less public and extraordinary events (*People's Daily*, 2002). One interviewee pointed out that the yearly visits of his company's CEO had opened many doors and had allowed the CEO to establish personal relationships on the Chinese side.

Secondly, foreign financial firms have been active in creating opportunities for interaction through the organisation of seminars and study tours in China or abroad. Examples of this are the yearly Euromoney China conferences sponsored by leading financial firms, whose list of participants and speakers included the most important high-level officials on the Chinese side, including Zhou Xiaochuan, Liu Mingkang and Shang Fulin for 2003 and 2004 (Euromoney, 2004). Through informal interaction, it was perceived, a favourable climate could be fostered and minor concerns could be raised on the side (interview).

Thirdly, the long-term strategy of foreign financial firms to ensure leadership access includes hiring skilled Chinese nationals who have exceptional *guanxi* networks of their own. Mostly trained abroad, these professionals have obtained their *guanxi* either by birth or due to prior high-level work in mainland China. Examples of these professionals that have surfaced in the media include the children of leading Chinese politicians; these include Zhu Yunlai, the son of Zhu Rongji, who worked for CICC, Ren Keying, daughter-in-law of Zhao Ziyang, who worked for Citibank, and the son of the president of the China Construction Bank who worked for HSBC and was expected to help HSBC to secure a role in the listing of CCB (*People's Daily*, 2004b).[131]

Empirically, the leadership access of foreign firms varies greatly, and mostly for historical reasons some firms are better positioned than others from the start.[132] Firms that operate without a partner in China have used informal personal connections in particular, while those with partners have tried to rely on the partners' connections in some cases. Building one's own *guanxi* network or securing access to the partner's *guanxi* therefore is an essential part of foreign financial firms' informal lobbying in China.

Playing political cards

Foreign financial firms have typically made use of their political connections at home, both in the case of conflicts in doing business in China (typically either with an SOE or a regulatory agency) or when trying to close a particularly important deal. In dispute settlement, a first step includes the use of the embassies. Foreign financial firms stated that the official nature of this proceeding increased their leverage over SOEs and that sometimes the embassy staff would be a helpful shield in negotiations. More importantly, however, foreign financial firms also engaged influential home country politicians for their interests. A striking example of this is the way three foreign financial firms each engaged different politicians to close the deal on the underwriting and management of CCB's IPO. When Deutsche Bank, Citibank and JP Morgan Chase were competing in early 2004, each resorted to political backing in fostering its luck; German Chancellor Gerhard Schröder supported the bid of Deutsche Bank and reportedly lobbied Wen Jiabao by writing a letter on the issue, while Robert Rubin and Henry Kissinger tried to leverage their positions in favour of Citibank and JP Morgan respectively (*People's Daily*, 2004b). An even more subtle way of playing political cards is to arrange leadership access abroad for Chinese leaders, something that well-connected financial firms can offer to Chinese officials as a part of 'traditionally well established relationships with the Chinese government', for example, during the WTO negotiations (interview).[133] For an overview of informal channels of interest representation see Figure 5.3.

Clientelism

From the perspective of foreign financial firms, it is rational to employ these strategies of informal lobbying. While informal lobbying occurs in other countries as well, the features of China's political system and regulatory process make it even more important here, as judged by interviewees. Foreign financial firms' market participation was perceived to be driven to a large extent by informal criteria with regard to the question which *individual* foreign firms were chosen for a particular deal.

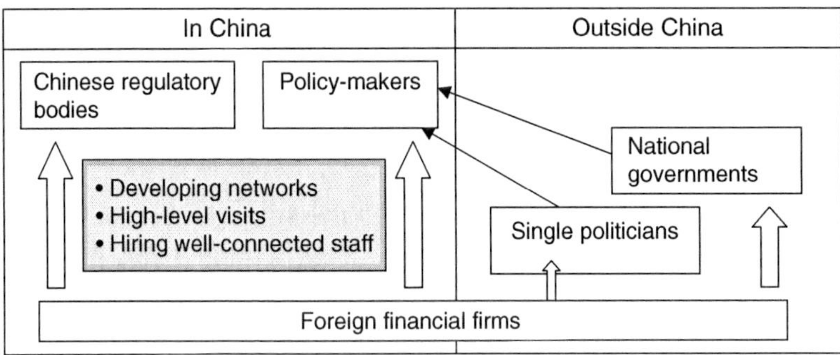

Figure 5.3   Informal channels of interest representation
Source: Own presentation

It is no coincidence that some foreign financial firms are more present than others in the Chinese market; one interviewee explicitly attributed this to successful informal lobbying. While the restrictive formal rules of the game of interest representation in China's financial market thus become softened by informal lobbying on an individual level, this is the case only for some firms and, for this analysis, has little identifiable relation to the overall level of market access for foreign financial firms in general.[134] On the other hand, this informal structure affects the formal level of lobbying. As pointed out by Pearson (1991), informal vertical clientelism generally prevents the strengthening of horizontal ties between market actors and thus hinders powerful broad-level, industry-wide interest representation. As confirmed by the interviews, informal lobbying creates incentives to break out of the formal lobbying process. This tendency was identifiable for foreign financial firms; as long as individual business interests could be fostered in China, incentives for broader initiatives were less attractive (interviews). One interviewee stated that his company was just trying to make the best out of the situation for itself in the hybrid market environment, while broader strategies seemed unpromising (interview).

Informal lobbying was also used to ensure individual benefits for single companies at the expense of the development of broader market opening; this was the case for AIG who had a conflict with the CIRC over the applicability of its (exceptional) licence and fought to enlarge its competitive advantage *vis-à-vis* other foreign insurers rather than fostering a broader level relaxation of market entry restrictions. These observations about the informal lobbying of foreign financial firms should therefore lead to more careful assumptions about the role of foreign financial firms in China's financial market; foreign market players may become part of the clientelist structures rather than active actors in order to break them up, and may thus have less impact in fostering market development. Evidence from other sectors of the Chinese economy confirms that the primary interest of foreign companies (when benefiting from the monopoly position of their JV, for example) may in fact be to preserve an *uneven* playing field.[135] Kalathil (2003) points out that in case of the media sector, there is little evidence that foreign investors 'are inherently opposed to reliance on *guanxi*, or informal personal connections' and that many make the effort to build government ties. That they may use these connections for their own benefit rather than for lobbying for a level playing field may in consequence diminish their beneficial role for market development.

Lobbying for market access in day-to-day business

Reacting to a planned or implemented regulation that opposes the interests of foreign financial firms has been the classical case for organised interest representation in day-to-day business. This section discusses three cases in this regard; the rules on RMB lending quotas, regulation on the withholding tax and the implementation rules of the 'Law on Foreign Financial Institutions'. The cases have in common that they represent smaller changes in the market entry regime for foreign financial firms in China and thus can serve both to illustrate the process of lobbying and to assess the responsiveness of the regulators and accordingly the success and impact of foreign firms' lobbying.

The new rule on RMB lending quotas for foreign and domestic banks was a hot issue during the time the interviews for this research were conducted. What had happened was that not long after WTO entry had assured foreign banks of expanding access to RMB-business, the PBC issued the 'Draft Interim Measures on the Administration of RMB Inter-bank Loans' in 2002 stating that the ratio of any commercial bank's RMB loans that could be refinanced through the inter-bank market was limited to 40 per cent. Thereby the rules seriously limited the refinancing options for all banks. The rules were to be implemented gradually, in order to allow banks to adjust their loan portfolio, and came into full effect in 2006. From the perspective of foreign banks, for whom the refinancing issue had always been the Achilles' heel in China banking, this was an extremely threatening draft rule, as they (given their limited access to RMB deposits) disproportionally depend on the inter-bank market. So while the draft rule applied to all commercial banks in China, it particularly limited the ability of foreign banks to make RMB loans, rendering the market access gained through the WTO concessions 'almost insignificant' (interview). Officially, the rules were intended to slow down the loan growth of younger domestic banks by linking loan growth to the growth of deposits. Foreign banks, however, saw their business interest gravely endangered and started a campaign in order to lobby against the adoption of this rule. The campaign had already started during the summer of 2002 after the *Financial Times* had published a report on the pending issue.[136] In the campaign, efforts were undertaken by the EUCCC and AmCham working groups on banking as well as by foreign banks on their own. Interviewees stated that the protest took the form of letters to the PBC, and later to the CBRC and the State Council, repeatedly stating their point and highlighting the detrimental effects of the draft regulation as well as its violation of the spirit of the WTO entry agreement. Public pressure and silent lobbying behind the scenes were combined (interviews).[137] The EUCCC position paper (2003, pp. 52ff) accordingly pointed out that:

> EU foreign banks do not understand the rationale of such an intended regulation. If implemented, this additional rule would limit foreign banks from funding themselves through wholesale banking avenues, thus impacting negatively on the scope and profitability of any subsequent business they are able to carry out.

In addition, foreign politicians were briefed accordingly and they pressured for a change in the rules; these included the EU Trade Commissioner Pascal Lamy and the German Chancellor Gerhard Schröder, during his visit in late 2003. However, there was no direct reaction on the Chinese side; the 'Draft Measures' stayed in place. Yet foreign banks have been allowed to issue bonds through a separate regulation, thus relieving some of the refinancing pressure from them (*Shanghai Daily*, 2003). The regulation allowing for the bonds' issuance was timed just to be implemented when the WTO commitments allowed foreign banks to conduct RMB-business with Chinese enterprises in December 2003 and was interpreted as a sign of goodwill and accommodation on the side of the CBRC (interviews). Since the refinancing problems of foreign banks were in fact eased considerably by the bond rules, it can be argued that the CBRC displayed some indirect responsiveness to the concerns of foreign banks in this case.

The introduction of a withholding tax on foreign banks' inter-branch and inter-bank borrowing of funds in 1995 is an example of lobbying that produced a more directly attributable response. It was quoted several times during the interviews conducted for this study. Essentially a law made by the tax authorities, it also threatened to hamper the business options of foreign banks severely with regard to refinancing (both in RMB and foreign currency alike) as foreign banks rely to a considerable degree on transferring funds between their operations as well as from branches abroad. Following harsh reactions by foreign bankers through letters and protests in the foreign media, Chinese policy-makers and the PBC became aware of the problem and reportedly Zhu Rongji himself stopped the regulation from being implemented (interview).

The third case discussed here is the promulgation of the new 'Implementing Rules on the Administration of Foreign Financial Firms' by the CBRC in 2004. This case highlights that besides an ad-hoc responsiveness of the Chinese regulators (displayed in the first two cases), a more systematic responsiveness towards the 'requests' of foreign banks can also be identified. The case also gives indications of the relevance of the position papers discussed above. Both rules that are compared in this regard, the 'Implementation Rules for the Regulations on the Administration of Foreign-invested Financial Institutions', promulgated in 2002, and those promulgated in August 2004, are post-WTO-entry interpretations of the 'Law on the Administration of Foreign Financial Institutions in China', promulgated in 1994, and thus transferred WTO commitments into national regulation. Figure 5.4 illustrates a comparison of the old and the new implementation rules together with the recommendations of the interest representation bodies.

From the perspective of interest representation, it is remarkable that some of the major requests made by foreign financial firms in 2003 in the position papers found their way into the revised rules of 2004. However, it remains hard to assess the extent to which the changes in the implementation rules, considered to be a great step forward in opening the banking sector to foreign banks, have been motivated or fostered by these lobbying and interest representation efforts (Chuan, 2004). Two scenarios are possible in this regard; in the first scenario, the 2002 regulations represent the cautious approach of the PBC just after WTO entry and therefore primarily reflect fears of the policy-makers, as well as attempts to restrict and control the opening process. After two years, the fears on the Chinese side could have diminished (in part possibly by seeing domestic banking reform progressing according to plan), and the

Topic	2002 implementation rules	EUCCC 2003 position paper	AmCham 2003 white paper	2004 implementation rules
Working capital requirements	RMB 400 million for corporate and RMB 600 million for retail banking per branch	Regarded as excessive, recommended to lift		Reduced to RMB 300 million for corporate and RMB 500 million for retail banking
Calculation of capital adequacy	Non consolidated (=per branch) calculation of CAR	Regarded as unjustified, recommended to lift	Regarded as 'unreasonable and unrealistic', recommended to lift	Unchanged
Limit on branch opening	Limited to one branch a year	Recommended to lift	Recommended to lift	Lifted

Figure 5.4 Development of the regulatory framework of foreign banks' market participation
Source: 'Implementation Rules' 2002, 2004, EUCCC position paper, AmCham White Paper: Banking, 2003c

changes in the implementation rules thus are a mere continuation of the Chinese policies that more or less would have occurred with or without the pronounced lobbying of foreign financial firms.[138]

In the second scenario, only the persistent lobbying of foreign financial firms led to the change; this would reflect a strikingly increased bargaining power for foreign financial firms in 2004 compared to 2002. Here, only the lobbying and amount of protest among foreign financial firms would have led the CBRC to make concessions (and implement WTO commitments fully) and to aim at a level playing field among foreign and domestic firms. In this scenario, however, the remaining restrictions are hard to explain and are not backed by the interviewees' view. Conclusions about the actual success of foreign banks in lobbying for their interests and in impacting the regulations should therefore remain cautious.

These three cases illustrate some aspects of the lobbying process and give an indication of the existent but limited responsiveness of the PBC and the CBRC. With regard to the way foreign firms and Chinese regulators in the financial markets interact in the day-to-day mode, the newly emerging habit of Chinese financial market regulators to invite domestic and foreign financial firms alike to comment on and review pending draft regulations before their enactment is particularly noteworthy. An example of this new kind of working relation is the 'Implementing Rule for the Administrative Measures on Foreign Invested Insurance Companies', issued on 31 July 2003. Here, foreign insurance companies were asked for their opinion before enactment. However, as the AmCham White Paper: Insurance pointed out:

> We applaud the CIRC's request for public comment that accompanies recent draft regulations issued in July and August of 2003. However, in the first instance (Draft Trial Implementing Rules on the Regulations of the PRC on the Administration of Foreign Invested Insurance Companies, issued July 31, 2003), interested parties were given just 15 days to comment and in the second instance (Draft Revision of Insurance Company Administrative Measures, issued August 18, 2003), just under 30 days to comment (2003, p. 2).

At the same time, AmCham also found fault with the fact that the invitation for comments did not go so far as to set up more institutionalised channels of interest representation: 'While the CIRC often confers with foreign insurers on a selected ad hoc basis, it does not allow for broad industry representation' (p. 2).

Still, the emerging ability to (routinely) comment on pending regulations offered a new channel for the participation of foreign firms. At the same time, it highlighted a stronger participation by industry players in general in the process of regulatory policy-making that followed the previous top-down approach.

However, the relative success of the lobbying of foreign firms has to be balanced against noting that there have also been examples of Chinese regulators closing and further restricting foreign firms' market participation. Examples of harsh policies towards foreign financial firms' interests (and complaints) can be found in the case of the collapse of GITIC and other TICs, where foreign borrowers were caught in an insecure legal position and lost considerable amounts of money during what was regarded as a clean-up by the central government. A more recent example was the 'Regulation on the Foreign Debt of Foreign Banks' promulgated in May 2004. This regulation curtails the foreign-exchange liquidity of foreign banks, which is after all the most important line of business of foreign banks in China, in order to control overall foreign debt exposure. The regulation triggered a wave of complaints among foreign bankers, comparable to the case discussed above. While reactions of the State Administration of Foreign Exchange (SAFE) vice-president were reported in the press (and were directly linked to the complaints of foreign players), according to the interviews the rules remained problematic for foreign banks despite an adaptation in June 2004.[139]

A more restrictive picture also emerges from the securities industry. Although less concentrated on the domestic side, the lobbying efforts and demands for opening from securities companies in general have been less fruitful. Participation is still largely restricted to JVs and even though requests for increased predictability for future liberalisation by foreign investors have been made, there was limited response on the side of the CSRC. The provision of a schedule for greater liberalisation regarding both the level of ownership and scope of business was, for example, repeatedly requested by both EUCCC and AmCham. With regard to broader issues that foreign financial firms also lobbied for, such as the liberalisation of interest rates in the fixed income market and a reintroduction of broader financial futures, the CSRC remained largely inactive.

The day-to-day lobbying of foreign firms therefore shows that increasingly stable patterns of interaction emerged along the organisational lines discussed earlier in this section and that some general responsiveness towards the concerns of foreign financial firms can be identified. Protests of foreign financial firms through international media or organisations of interest representation in China gradually became (more) legitimate measures and some concessions on the operational level were achieved through long-term lobbying. With regard to the rules of day-to-day interest representation, the position papers emerged as a viable channel of communication and were supplemented by newly emerging invitations from the Chinese side to comment on regulatory issues and draft legislations. The emerging pattern of communication was based on the understanding that Chinese regulators were not ignorant of the requests of foreign financial firms but that at the same time the responses to those requests could have been indirect and delayed (interviews). With regard to the effectiveness of foreign firms in pushing for their interests, though, it has to be noted that the changes in the regulation remained largely driven by the regulators and their priorities and no evidence emerges for a strong influence from foreign firms. Given the evidence collected here, responsiveness has only been observable where the requests were in line with the overall priorities of regulatory bodies in market reform. Broader issues have been much harder to accomplish. While foreign firms thus emerged as routine players in the process of day-to-day lobbying in China, their success and impact on regulation and market development remained limited.

Lobbying for market access in times of strategic reorientation

This subsection turns to the role of foreign firms and their lobbying in relation to more extraordinary decisions in China's financial market opening. It asks if foreign firms emerged as important players in initiating fundamental directional changes in China's financial market opening and whether the changes that occurred can be attributed to their lobbying. In order to answer these questions, three strategic decisions on the direction of financial market opening and liberalisation are discussed here; the introduction of RMB-business for foreign banks in 1996, the WTO entry in 2001 and the introduction of the QFII scheme in 2003. This allows an implicit comparison of the role of foreign financial firms in international and national-level negotiations, in negotiation in the banking and securities sector, as well as in earlier and later stages of financial market development.

Granting RMB-business licences for foreign banks

Prior to 1996, foreign banks in China were allowed only to conduct business in foreign currency and no timetable was set for them to enter

RMB-business. Most of the customers of foreign banks at that time, however, also required RMB loans and there was a strong incentive at least for some foreign banks to be able to offer these services to their clients. The introduction of RMB-business was regarded as the eventual opening of the domestic currency market for foreign banks, and thus was a significant step forward for their market access.

Shanghai was starting to emerge as a regional centre during the early 1990s and foreign direct investment and the presence of foreign invested companies made it a natural regional cluster for foreign banks. Foreign banks in Shanghai therefore had been lobbying for RMB licences for some time without success. When relevant regulations were put through in late 1996, in the form of the 'Tentative Procedures on the Administration of the Pilot Operation of Renminbi Business by Foreign Financial Institutions in Pudong', promulgated by the PBC on 2 December 1996, this was regarded as a significantly successful outcome of their lobbying, which had aimed to convince the PBC to grant some concessions.[140]

However, a second look reveals that it was only within the context of the State Council's and the PBC's strategy to build Pudong's Lujiazhui area into an international financial centre that their concerns were listened to. The 'Tentative Procedures' conceived RMB-business licences on an experimental basis, allowing RMB lending to only foreigners and foreign-invested companies and stipulating that foreign banks had to have a commercial presence in Pudong in order to be eligible for the RMB licence. They were careful regulations that were revocable and had the side-effect that the foreign banks who wished to obtain a licence had to move their branches to Pudong, something, it can be reasonably argued, that they would have been reluctant to do on their own as at that time only very few international companies were located there.[141] The PBC on the other hand had a strong incentive to have them move there. After all, how could one build an international financial centre in Pudong without foreign financial firms?

Since all the foreign bank branches at that time were concentrated in Puxi, the old commercial centre of town, and there was no foreign bank branch in Pudong in 1996, the new regulation indeed led to a reallocation of branches across the Huangpu river. Citibank was the first foreign bank to move its Shanghai branch from Puxi to Pudong in February 1997. The first banks that received a RMB licence for Pudong in 1997 included Citibank, Bank of East Asia and HSBC, all of whom were by that time present in their new business locations. For Lujiazhui, in order to develop into a true financial and high-tech development zone and grow into the financial heart of Shanghai, the new regulation therefore was crucial; it made it the home of the most active foreign banks in Shanghai, a position that linked up nicely with it hosting both the first banks allowed to conduct RMB business and the new stock exchange building.

While it is hard to say whether it was the lobbying success of foreign financial firms or the alliance of interests between foreign financial firms and the State Council and the PBC that was responsible for this situation, it is important to note that the special circumstances of the overall financial market development strategy very likely played an important role in the decision and the conduct of the introduction of RMB-business; a window of opportunity opened up due to the impetus of developing the Lujiazui area,[142] and foreign financial firms took it.

The case of the introduction of RMB-business thus highlights the *domestic* impetus for liberalisation rather than the lobbying success of foreign firms. Their bargaining position only increased temporarily, when their requests fitted in with the interests and priorities of the PBC. However, in normal instances where this is not the case, they have found it much harder to lobby successfully for their interests. After all, they had been lobbying to be allowed to conduct RMB-business for a number of years. And even when the interests of foreign financial firms and the PBC were compatible, liberalisation remained limited, experimental in nature and requiring concessions from the foreign banks, such as moving their branches to Pudong. Additionally, it can be argued that it was only because the international prestige and reputation of Shanghai as a developing international financial centre in Asia was at stake that concessions on the Chinese side were made in the first place. This is even more striking because the market share of foreign banks is larger in Shanghai than anywhere else in China and their commercial weight there could have led to an expectation of greater political influence.

Foreign financial firms and the WTO-entry negotiations

Without doubt, from the perspective of foreign financial firms, China's entry into the WTO and the related financial market commitments have been the largest single step in opening the domestic financial market. The WTO-entry concessions constitute the first firm commitment by the Chinese government to open its financial markets to a considerable degree and they for the first time provided a timetable for single opening measures. Furthermore, the commitments were made on an international level, thus increasing their credibility and binding character. One can also say that prior to WTO entry, the first genuine negotiations in an institutionalised manner between foreign market players, their interest representation organisations and Chinese policy-makers took place. The long process of bilaterally conducted WTO-entry negotiations was accompanied by large-scale lobbying activities, particularly by American and European organisations of interest representation. In this regard, both organisations in China and channels of lobbying in the foreign financial firms' home markets were used.

In general, during the negotiating process, European firms were perceived to have much more clearly articulated interests in opening Chinese financial markets, whereas American firms were perceived to be comparatively reluctant to push issues, a tendency that may have been due to the booming market in the US at the time of negotiation as well as a stronger perception of risks in EMEs in the aftermath of the Asian financial crisis.[143] What was achieved in the negotiations? First of all, the far-reaching nature of the WTO agreement has to be emphasised, especially considering the limited existing level of opening. In the banking sector, the concessions on the Chinese side were extensive, although with a long phasing-in period and some built-in clauses delaying the market access of foreign banks, such as the requirement to operate for three years in China and for an additional two years of profitable business before being able to apply for a RMB licence. In the securities industry, which had been even more restricted before WTO entry, fewer concessions were reached; this led to a maximum being set for minority positions that foreign market participants could reach in Sino-foreign fund management and securities JVs. Interestingly, negotiations were particularly heated with respect to the insurance sector, which was regarded as the most restricted area of the Chinese financial market (interview). The important role of European companies and the EUCCC Insurance Working Group predecessor were reflected in fierce bargaining in this area; some concessions were reached, but did not include allowing majority positions in life insurance JVs.

Additionally, there were successes in some niches of the financial market, such as the automotive financing sector that was opened through the WTO agreement for foreign financial firms. This was interpreted as a success primarily for the American government and AmCham lobbying. It is systematically interesting because the commitment opened a new market segment and led to the proliferation of hybrid financial service companies in China, something the PBC had tried to avoid (interview). In addition, some opening commitments in narrower areas were included in the agreement, most likely resulting from fierce bargaining by specific EU interest groups. Examples of this were the opening of the local banking market in Zhuhai, the insurance market in Foshan and the granting of immediate licences to a set number of EU financial firms upon accession (Laprès, 2000; WTO, 2001b).

The emerging pattern of WTO commitments thus showed some broad concessions as well as some in niche areas. Are these primarily the achievement of foreign firms' lobbying and thus a sign of their strong position in the negotiations? Or are these commitments better understood in the context of the changing financial market policies of the Chinese government and regulators just before and during the peak of the WTO negotiations in 1999 and 2000? It shall be argued here that it is only in the context of the financial market policies pursued after the Asian financial crisis that the lobbying successes in the WTO negotiations can meaningfully be understood. The single most important event leading to a major readjustment in financial market policies in China was the Asian financial crisis of 1997–8. It resulted in a reassessment of risks inherent in the Chinese financial markets, highlighted the dangers of organisationally weak banks and thus significantly reduced the bargaining power of the four SOCBs. Starting from a crucial Working Conference of the State Council in 1997, the priorities of financial market policies were consequently readjusted towards the reform of the SOCBs, the development of the bond market and an overall more comprehensive reform strategy. These major shifts in financial market policies created the framework for the more proactive strategies on financial market opening that were observable already before WTO entry in 2001, as well as in policies unrelated to the WTO entry, such as the significant concession of the geographic opening of Jiangsu and Zhejiang to foreign banks in 1999. The main point is that it was a mix of changes in domestic regulatory priorities and the lobbying of foreign firms that led to the far-reaching WTO commitments; it was only due to the changed priorities in regulatory policies that the historic opportunity for WTO entry emerged.

WTO entry thus has to be seen in the context of the gradual change of regulatory policies on market opening. The fact that the concessions made in the WTO-entry agreement were considerably greater than before was due to changes in domestic regulatory priorities and actor constellations. The WTO commitments were in fact a more pronounced continuation of the *gradual* opening policy and thus did not indicate such a striking deviation from earlier policies as has been often perceived. In their gradual nature, they can be understood as a part of the emerging strategy of the CBRC and CSRC to exploit the resources of foreign financial firms to modernise, reform and recapitalise the banking sector, as well as 'building up the institutional investor industry and internationalising China's securities markets' (Harner, 2001, p. 29). The fact that the phase-in was extremely careful, as highlighted by the above discussion of the 2002 'Implementation Rules on the Administration of Foreign Financial Firms', emphasises that the commitments were made to fit in with overall strategies. The domestic impetus thus remained key. Therefore, the WTO commitments in the financial market would not have occurred without the domestic impetus to reform the financial market that drastically increased after the Asian financial crisis. More important than the lobbying of foreign firms was the fact that the WTO negotiations took place in a time in history when the trends in the domestic financial market were shifting due to unrelated international events.

Introducing Qualified Foreign Institutional Investors

With regard to financial market opening, 2002 was a busy year; WTO commitments were transferred into national regulation and in addition, the 'Provisional Measures on Qualified Foreign Institutional Investors (QFII)' were promulgated on 5 November 2002, opening the previously closed market of RMB-denominated securities to foreign investors. The QFII scheme was regarded as an extremely important step in the opening the domestic securities markets, not only because it allowed foreigners to make portfolio investments in Chinese securities, but also because it was understood to lead the way to the complementary Qualified Domestic Institutional Investor scheme (QDII), which allowed domestic investors to invest in international markets in the future. In both regards, the interests of foreign financial firms were pronounced; investing in RMB-denominated securities had been on the wish-list of foreign financial firms for a long time, as it would essentially allow them to offer a wider range of services and China-related products to their international clients. The QDII scheme on the other hand – pending regulatory details – allowed foreign financial firms to use their competitive advantage in international markets and sell their services to (increasingly liquid) Chinese investors (*People's Daily*, 2004d). Systematically, QFII and QDII are closely related in particular with respect to RMB revaluation pressures. They have opposite effects on the demand for RMB and foreign currency respectively; therefore it is no surprise that the first experimental QDII transactions were implemented at a time when QFII money was regarded to increase the revaluation pressure on the RMB (*China Business Weekly*, 2004).

But was it primarily the lobbying of foreign financial firms that led to the introduction of the QFII scheme in the end of 2002? Most interviewees stated that although they were in favour of the scheme in general, it had long been clear that it would be implemented when the Chinese government and the CSRC had concluded their lengthy preparations and saw it fit their plans. They originally had expected it to be introduced some time in 2005. Therefore, the early introduction of the scheme in 2002 was a surprise to many in the industry. It shall be argued here again that looking at the domestic Chinese stock market at that time explains the timing more than lobbying efforts do. In 2001, attempts to reduce the state shares via the stock market had encountered severe problems (Naughton, 2002). In order to restore confidence in the troubled market and ensure a favourable development of the share prices, a stable demand was needed, and QFII was a convenient way to achieve just that. Additionally, the introduction can been seen in line with overall attempts to develop securities markets further and foster the development of the institutional investors industry, a process in which the CSRC has assigned a strategic role to foreign market participants. The pending review of the fund and the securities law in order to increase the market attractiveness from the perspective of institutional investors, foreign and domestic alike, can also be seen in this context.

The introduction of the QFII scheme, though regarded as an important step in opening the financial markets thus has to be interpreted primarily as a policy tool to foster the development of the *domestic* securities markets with the help of foreign money and foreign financial firms' reputation and expertise. The careful structuring of the QFII scheme, which allows the fine-tuning of the process and an ability to react to potential problems, reflects the gradual approach and makes it fit with overall principles of CSRC policies. The strong domestic impetus for this regulation also explains the limited influence of foreign financial firms on the proceedings and timing. In this interpretation, the QFII scheme also fitted well with new regulations on foreign equity investments in Chinese financial firms in 2003.[144] On the grounds of this interpretation, it was expected that foreign financial firms would be invited to provide expertise to domestic firms that will become QDIIs. With regard to interest representation, the QFII case confirms the picture that emerged from the introduction of the RMB-business and the WTO negotiations; domestic regulatory priorities and considerations are key to understanding regulators' moves towards more financial market liberalisation and directional change in regulation. The lobbying of foreign firms has been of limited importance in this regard.

Looking at foreign financial firms' lobbying in the day-to-day business mode shows that some general responsiveness of Chinese policy-makers and regulators towards the concerns of foreign financial firms can be identified, but that regulation and regulatory change have remained largely driven by the priorities of the PBC, CBRC and CSRC. Moreover, with regard to the directional decisions concerning financial market opening, the cases above showed that events that seemed to be large lobbying successes for foreign financial firms have to be placed in the context of domestic regulatory priorities and the changes therein. Based on the limited access to detailed information on the actual decision-making process, it is hard to fully assess the effectiveness of lobbying efforts. It can be concluded, however, that because empirically lobbying efforts have been responded to primarily if, when and where they fitted in with Chinese regulators' domestic priorities, the ability of foreign firms to effect genuine changes in regulation remained limited. Their lobbying thus had only a limited impact on regulation, financial market liberalisation and financial market development. It is only due to favourable domestic policies that foreign financial firms have been able to extend their market participation, but foreign firms have not been able to initiate changes in regulation on a significant scale. The opening process of the Chinese financial market was thus not driven by foreign financial firms.

Yet, the position of foreign financial firms *vis-à-vis* the regulators has become stronger since they have been identified as strategic actors to develop, modernise and internationalise the domestic financial market. In this process, the PBC, CBRC and CSRC have become more responsive to the needs of foreign firms. At the same time, regulators in general have been in the comfortable position that foreign financial firms' interest in the Chinese market was so great that the regulators needed to make only limited concessions in order to achieve their priorities; the bargaining power of foreign firms so far therefore has remained limited.

However, the success of lobbying should not be judged based merely on whether single decisions have been pushed through by lobbying groups or not. On a systemic level, the lobbying of foreign firms might have enabled Chinese regulators to access more information and make decisions on a broader basis. It should therefore be kept in mind that indirect effects on the financial market may have been larger than the direct impact assessed here. Overall, foreign financial firms have emerged as proactive actors in financial market development with regard to their lobbying, but have not been able to affect new regulations to a large extent. Priorities of the regulators have been more important. Reform and regulation have thus remained domestically determined.

Concluding remarks

This chapter has identified and analysed the formal and informal channels of interest representation by foreign financial firms in China. It has pointed out that interest representation is conducted actively through both channels with varying degrees of success. Formal interest representation is significant and has contributed to changes in regulation with regard to the operational level, while clear causal relationships between protests against pending regulations and change in them remain hard to establish. On an individual level, securing leadership access and building *guanxi* networks informally as well as utilising political support from home countries has helped some foreign financial firms more than others. Still, both formal and informal interest representation and lobbying are limited in scale and scope, not least because foreign financial firms' interests are diverse and thus hard to coordinate. Based on the evidence presented on day-to-day lobbying and lobbying for directional change, it can be said that the impact of foreign firms' lobbying on regulation has remained limited and that the process of regulation has remained domestically determined.

On a broader level, this chapter has highlighted two aspects; firstly, the fact that (foreign) industry players have been participating on an increasing and more institutionalised level in the process of regulatory policy-making highlights overall changes in patterns and structures of lobbying and interest representation in China's financial markets (on this issue see also Naughton, 2002). While consultation is still conducted in an *ad hoc* and arbitrary way, these trends are nonetheless represent a significant change from former modes of interaction and regulatory policy-making. If continued, further developed and institutionalised, this trend will have important implications not only for foreign financial firms in China, but for the structures of interest representation and the interaction between industry players and regulators in general.

Secondly, the new strategies of regulators to incorporate foreign firms as active players into the process of financial market reform increase the necessity to cooperate with them. As Chinese regulators try to develop and liberalise the Chinese financial markets more actively, they increasingly depend on foreign financial firms' presence, as well as on their knowledge and expertise. Making these sources accessible requires regulators to actively build new channels of interaction with these firms in their own interest. An early indication of new patterns of interaction is the invitation for comments on draft regulations. Consulting with foreign financial firms on regulations gives foreign firms not only an opportunity to voice their interests, but also lets them share their expertise. While limited so far, this trend thus indicates perspectives for a larger participation of foreign firms in the process of regulatory policy-making in the future, especially where sophisticated financial products are concerned. The transfer of knowledge to regulatory bodies in a mode of consultation is therefore likely to emerge as the most important channel of influence for foreign financial firms, mirroring the market-level attempts of Chinese regulators to use them as strategic actors in modernising and internationalising China's financial markets.

Part III
Domestic Actors in an Internationalising Context

6
Internationalising the Regulators

As a new and distinct type of actors in the organisational landscape of Chinese government agencies, regulatory bodies have been set up over the later years of the economic reform process in China and have gained much public attention since their founding. In particular, the PBC's position in the Chinese emerging market economy has been widely discussed with regard both to its role in financial market regulation and as an independent central bank (Holz, 1992; BIS, 1999) before the regulation of commercial banks was transferred to the CBRC in 2003. The securities market regulator CSRC has been described as a professional and enlightened government organ and is perceived to be the only regulatory body in China actually facing a market environment (Walter and Howie, 2003, p. 70). Undoubtedly, each of the regulatory bodies has played a major role in shaping the emerging Chinese financial markets. By shifting the focus of this analysis to the domestic side of internationalisation, this chapter looks at the evolving regulatory regime of China's financial markets and investigates how the regulatory bodies in China's financial markets themselves have been internationalised. The chapter then goes on to enquire as to how far international concepts of markets and regulation, as well as international standards, are reflected in the new regulatory policies that have emerged within this internationalised framework. To approach these questions, the chapter is split into four sections. The first section focuses on the emergence of the regulators for China's financial markets and the organisational structure of the regulatory regime. The second section analyses the established international links and the channels thus created for international exchange, cooperation and the influx of new ideas and concepts in regulation. Then, focusing on the personnel strategies employed by Chinese regulators, the third section discusses the hiring of internationally experienced and trained staff by Chinese regulatory bodies and its consequences for changes in the regulatory regime. Section four analyses new rules and regulations made in this context of internationalisation and asks both whether they are in line with international standards and how regulators dealt with the challenge of increasing market internationalisation. Here, since establishing clear cause-effect chains remains difficult with respect to the impact of internationalisation, the chapter primarily looks at observable changes in single rules and through them the development of broader principles in the regulation of China's financial markets.

Throughout, the analysis is based on the distinction between the organisational structure of regulatory bodies (regime organisation) and the orientation of these regulatory bodies (regime orientation), shaped by the 'beliefs about the proper scope, goals, and methods of government intervention in the economy' (Vogel, 1998, p. 20). Changes in regime organisation and in the beliefs of regulators – also called *ideas* by Vogel – are thus highly relevant for understanding the future development of any regulatory regime. In this context, the aim of this chapter is to trace the international influences on the emergence, development and change of the regulatory regime in China's financial markets. However, while identifying some important channels of influences and *de facto* changes in regulation, this chapter does not intend to say that international influences have *dominated* the process of regulatory evolution in China. To be sure, financial market reform and the emergence of the regulatory regime have largely been driven by a domestic power-play of ministries, government agencies and political factions.[145] This chapter does challenge the notion, however, that these processes have remained sealed off from international influences and that the international context in which they took place has not had a significant impact on the outcome. Highlighting both the changing organisational structure and the changes in beliefs of regulators during the process of opening up, this chapter draws attention to the relevance of the international framework for the domestic process.

Evolving regime orientation and organisation in an international context

The process of economic reforms, economic liberalisation and the transition from a command to a market economy led to a decrease of state actors' direct role in the Chinese economy, but at the same time created new responsibilities for the government to regulate and supervise the emerging market economy. Regulatory bodies, created to provide the organisational framework for this regulation and supervision, emerged in parallel to the changing mode of economic regulation itself, as command-economy-style contents and methods such as quotas, credit plans and administrative controls were replaced by more market-oriented approaches and means of regulation. The organisational adaptation of government bodies has been an important component of China's economic opening and integration into international markets.[146] With regard to the financial markets, the process of differentiation and specialisation of regulatory bodies started with the separation of the PBC from the Ministry of Finance (MOF) in 1976 and the transformation of the PBC into China's central bank in 1983. This section does not re-draw the organisational history of the PBC and the CSRC in total, but is intended to highlight both the relevance of overall economic internationalisation to this process and the direct international influences on the current organisational shape of regulatory bodies in China's financial markets (regime organisation).[147] Inherent in the ongoing process of financial market reform in China, the regulatory structure remains in flux and is still 'work in progress'.

The People's Bank of China: creating China's central bank

At the beginning of the reform course in China, creating a central bank and separating it organisationally from the MOF was one of the most important steps in moving towards the institutional and organisational foundation of a market economy. However, the new PBC largely lacked the theoretical and practical skills for reacting to newly emerging challenges in the emerging dual-track economy, in particular with regard to monetary policy. As a consequence of this lack, inherited from the bureaucratic subordination to the Ministry of Finance, the PBC had limited power, independence and decision-making capacity during the 1980s (Lardy, 1998, pp. 172ff). How did PBC officials gain an idea of how monetary policy needed to be conducted in a market economy in this context? How did they learn to deal with the emerging challenges in price reform and liberalisation? How have they been able to strengthen the position and power of the PBC?

It has been widely noted that international experiences helped in building the necessary skills within the PBC and provided orientation in manoeuvring through this new terrain. In a process of opening to new economic concepts and theories, the influence of the IMF, the key international actor in offering generous advice on solving monetary problems, increased in Chinese policy-making because it offered a stability-oriented transfer of skills and policies (Jacobson and Oksenberg, 1990).[148] At the same time, IMF advice guided the whole Chinese system into the direction of the typical organisational setup of a market economy. In this context, Liu Hongru, then vice-governor of the PBC, emerged as a key promoter of Western-style reform of the monetary policy system during the 1980s (Holz, 1992, p. 153). International advice and role models have guided the emerging regime in monetary policy since, notwithstanding the systematic contradictions between the predominant Western concept of an independent central bank and the (initially) subordinate position of the PBC (Holz, 1992, pp. 151ff). Further aligning the position of the PBC with international practices, the PBC was freed from functioning as a cashier for the central government in 1994, when its financing of government debt was ended under the then central bank governor Zhu Rongji.

An important step in shaping the regime and clarifying the position of the PBC was the promulgation of the 'Central Bank Law' in 1995 that stipulated the position of the PBC in monetary policy, with regard to the RMB exchange rate and in respect to financial supervision and control.[149] It modelled the role and responsibilities of the PBC on the US Federal Reserve (EIU, 2003, p. 8).[150] The US model of the Federal Reserve also seems to have partly inspired the subsequent PBC restructuring in 1998 along regional lines, increasing its independence from local and provincial government levels (Mo, 1999). International influences have thus been important in the ongoing incremental process of enlarging and consolidating the powers of the PBC as well as in shaping its position in monetary policy. More recently, monetary issues were further developed and clarified in the 2003 revision of the 'Central Bank Law'. After the revision, the monetary policy committee of the PBC, a key panel in the policy process based on Article 12 of the law, became a direct copy of the US Federal Open Market Committee (EIU, 2003).

With regard to the PBC's position in financial market regulation (an area where the PBC actually lost most of its original powers over the course of financial market and regulatory diversification), international models have also served as guides. The subsequent separation of responsibilities for the securities and insurance markets away from the PBC to specialised regulatory bodies between 1992 and 1998 was continued and further completed by the establishment of the CBRC in 2003, a step that international advisers had been advocating and that is in line with the emerging international trend to separate banking supervision and monetary policy.[151] The establishment of the CBRC in April 2003 was also explicitly related to the provisions of the Basel Committee's 'Core Principles of Effective Banking Regulation' for the structure of financial supervision and management.[152] On the other hand, in setting up three independent regulatory bodies for the segments of the Chinese financial markets, Chinese decision-makers did not follow the international trend to create a single regulatory authority, such as the UK Financial Services Authority (FSA) or the German Bundesanstalt für Finanzdienstleistungsaufsicht (BaFin) (Dai, 1999). Yet this option has been subject to great debate in China and abroad, and it is noteworthy that the current structure of three single regulatory bodies is widely regarded as a preliminary step. For the future, a unification of the regulatory agencies has been envisioned.[153]

However, this is not to argue that Western ideas dominated the emerging central bank regime. The PBC remained under tight control of the State Council with regard to monetary policy as well as banking regulation and supervision, a structure that has also been identified to be one of the cornerstones of politically influenced credit allocation (for example, see Lau, 1999, p. 79). Still, international ideas and concepts of a (market-economy-style) central bank were influential in the process of shaping the PBC with regard to its organisational structure and the regulatory instruments available to it. Both structure and instruments have been moving into the direction of the internationally accepted 'Core Principles for Effective Banking Supervision', a development that is highly noteworthy when keeping in mind the organisational history of the PBC and its nature as a post-Leninist government agency.

The CSRC: the emerging securities markets' regulator

The role of international influences on the organisational side of the regulatory regime in China's securities markets has also been considerable, just as the international influences were in the emergence of the securities markets themselves. Green (2004b, p. 65) explicitly identifies an informal stock market promotion group, encompassing internationally trained and experienced experts who were key in the early years of experiments with stocks and shares in China, highlighting the fact that international influences were crucial in the birth of the securities markets. Heilmann (2001, p. 13) identifies the role-model function of the American and Hong Kong stock exchanges respectively for the stock exchanges in Shanghai and Shenzhen in the early 1990s. Hertz (1998) identifies the critical role of international influence and assistance in the early years of stock market development. Pointing out the frequent visits of international experts, she notes that the 'Chinese government's decision to create stock markets was guided by its comparative study of American, western European, and east Asian economic systems' (p. 5). During the interviews conducted for this study, it was pointed out that

	1993	1994	1995	1996	1997	1998	Subtotal
Number of companies	6	11	2	6	17	1	43
Total capital raised (in million US$)	10.49	22.34	3.796	12.125	46.869	4.57	100.19

Figure 6.1   Capital raised annually by overseas-listed companies between 1993 and 1998
Source: CSRC (2001)

the American Wall Street model was very important as a reference system in guiding the overall stock market policies (interview).

Several studies have also shown that the CSRC has emerged in the context of strong organisational rivalries and overlapping regulatory powers in a domestically dominated process (Heilmann, 2001; Green, 2004b; Walter and Howie, 2003). However, long before achieving a well-established position as the securities market regulator, the CSRC also started to develop international ties that were very important for its power consolidation in this process; Walter and Howie (2003) state that the CSRC in fact established its regulatory power first with regard to overseas listings. Here, the CSRC could operate without the interference of other domestic regulatory bodies. Overseas listings therefore became a key component of the work of the CSRC after 1993 (see Figure 6.1).[154]

Despite the organisational rivalries, international models of stock market regulation were an important input for shaping the organisational structure of the regulatory regime in China, and international events were crucial in its formation. The establishment of the CSRC was finalised by the promulgation of the 'Securities Law' that centralised the powers of the CSRC and provided a long-needed and more profound legal basis for the stock market in general. The promulgation of the law, however, was greatly influenced by the impressions caused and fears raised by the Asian financial crisis in 1997; this highlighted the importance of the external shock for the domestic process of emerging regime organisation.[155] With regard to the nature of the regime organisation, it was repeatedly pointed out during the interviews that the CSRC was on the way to becoming the Chinese version of the US Securities and Exchange Commission (SEC).[156] As pointed out by Lo (1999) the role of the CSRC according to the 'Securities Law' conforms with the five main principles for regulators stated in the IOSCO 'Principles of Effective Securities Market Supervision' and thus reflects the greater acceptance of these long-established principles by the Chinese after the Asian financial crisis, as well as the influence of international standards on the national securities legislation.[157] The 'Securities Law' in fact implements the international norms with regard to the position, legal backing and responsibilities of the CSRC.

Overall, it can therefore be concluded that the organisational framework for regulating China's financial markets (the regime organisation) has been moving towards an internationally accepted configuration of regulatory bodies and has been influenced by international norms, standards and principles of regulation. This process has been fostered by the pivotal role of 'new technocrats' on the leadership level – such as Zhu Rongji and later Liu Mingkang and Zhou Xiaochuan – who have themselves been described as internationalised and under whose power and influence the organisation of the regulatory regime emerged.

However, this is not to say that there are no problems remaining, in particular with regard to implementation, nor that there are no specific institutional characteristics that differentiate China from other countries with regard to the organisational setup of financial market regulation. Most notably among these are the remaining political channels of influence, the incorporation of regulatory personnel into the cadre and political control system, and the lack of genuine organisational independence, a point that has also been made with regard to monetary policy. In Chinese regulatory bodies, there is a coexistence and overlapping of cadre controls and new management techniques because the control and disciplinary structures of the Communist party coexist with newly emerging internal structures, new recruitment and remuneration as well as an increased transparency and more public discourse on controversial issues. As Pearson (2003) has argued, the independence of the Chinese regulators is last but not least compromised by the lack of separation and insulation from policy-making bodies, a lack of sufficient authority and the nature of state ownership of the industry that they regulate. On this basis, financial market regulatory bodies in China have been used and abused for government priorities in industrial policies, international influences notwithstanding. They have been used as instruments of recentralisation policies, and have been subject to conflicting double mandates in regulation, for example in the case of the CSRC with regard to the listing process, the quota system and administrative pricing (Green, 2003c, pp. 160ff). *Vis-à-vis* the State Council, they still have limited genuine power and constitutional security and they face constant conflict with ministries and commissions.[158] International influences on the regime organisation have thus coexisted with significant organisational particularities. It is in the context of these hybrid organisational structures that channels of international exchange and cooperation have been established, which the next section looks at.

Expanding channels for international exchange and cooperation

This section turns to the impact of internationalisation on the *orientation* of the regulatory regime in China's financial markets. Since the change of beliefs, ideas and accepted theories of regulatory organisations is a complex and opaque process, in a first step this section analyses the channels of international exchange and cooperation that have emerged since the 1980s, thus highlighting the increasingly international context that Chinese regulatory bodies operate in. The analysis starts from the observation that the willingness of regulators such as the PBC, CBRC and CSRC to learn from others and to study other countries' lessons has been a remarkable feature of the economic reform process in China and that in the process of building adequate knowledge and transferring market-oriented techniques to regulatory bodies, a number of channels for international exchange and cooperation have been established. They are reflected organisationally in the departments for international cooperation that have been set up and that were originally intended to be the exclusive windows of these organisations to the outside world. However, besides the international cooperation departments, other departments and sections have established strong international connections of their own as well. Since the beginning of the reform process, the following other channels have emerged.

Study groups and international research seminars

The most evident early channels of informational exchange and China's learning from the experiences of other countries have been loosely organised study groups and international research seminars. However, the organisation and degree of institutionalisation of the study groups has varied greatly, from one-time study group trips abroad to yearly tours that cover several countries, and some of them have been important parts of the bilateral and multilateral (development) cooperation projects described below. In principle, the concept of a study group allowed Chinese regulators to explore new ideas as well as policies and solutions for challenges considering other countries as an example on an informal level. Visiting more than one country often allowed a comparison between different experiences and enabled discussion of the benefits and hazards of particular rules and policies. With regard to financial market regulation, important early study groups were sent, for example, to

Hong Kong to look at stock market regulation and a potential cooperation in overseas listings of Chinese enterprises. The main output of study
groups usually was written reports to superiors.

The organisation of conferences, often closely linked to study groups,
was a second important part of the exchange of ideas and communication by regulatory bodies. Often set up with some organisational linkage
to international financial institutions, they were a condensed form of
studying the experiences of other countries and discussing options for
China with international experts in China or abroad. Examples of this
were the joint PBC/BIS conference on 'Strengthening the Chinese Banking Sector' in 1999 or the 'World Bank Conference on the Development
of Institutional Investors in China's Financial System' in 2003. Some
conferences were also held on a yearly basis; these included the China
Development Forum (CDF), organised by the Development Research
Centre of the State Council. The CDF brought together high-level
Chinese and foreign officials as well as members of international financial institutions and the business community. It offered a forum to
discuss economic reform issues and policy options, and also allowed for
informal talks between experts and high-ranking regulators and politicians. These kinds of international conferences contributed greatly not
only to the exchange of information, but also to the increase in the
'international exposure' of Chinese regulators and their international
orientation (interviews).

Membership in international regulatory organisations

With regard to the more formalised channels of interaction and communication, Chinese regulatory bodies became members of all major
international regulatory organisations for financial markets during the
course of reform. As these international regulatory organisations actively
promote the convergence of regulatory practices and the introduction of
international standards in all member states, and as Chinese regulatory
bodies have been eager to cooperate and gain access to information, the
interaction with these organisations created an important channel for
the influx of new ideas and concepts into the regulatory bodies of China's
financial markets. China became a member of the Bank for International
Settlements in Basel in 1996, the same year it joined the Institute of International Finance in Washington. The CSRC became an ordinary member
of the International Organisation of Securities Commissions (IOSCO) in
1995 and a member of IOSCO's Executive Committee in 1998. It is a
also a member of the Asia Pacific Regional Committee and the Emerging

Markets Committee within the IOSCO structure. CIRC is a member of the International Association of Insurance Supervisors (IAIS). The membership in these international organisations has been important particularly due to the role of international agreements in the introduction of new regulatory standards into the Chinese markets. The two most prominent examples of this, the Basel Accord and the IOSCO principles of securities regulation, are discussed in detail below.

Bilateral cooperation

Additionally, Chinese regulatory bodies cooperated bilaterally with foreign central banks and other regulatory bodies, as well as overseas stock exchanges and industry associations. Bilateral agreements of understanding and cooperation, the Memoranda of Understanding (MOU), not only laid the foundation for Chinese financial firms operating abroad and foreign financial firms entering the financial markets in China, but also formed important channels of communication and cooperation. The CSRC, for example, had signed 24 MOUs with securities regulatory authorities from 22 jurisdictions by the end of December 2003. A report by the CSRC (2004a) states: 'The MOUs facilitate information exchange, investigative assistance, and dialogue about policies and regulation. The MOUs establish channels of communications that improve mutual understanding, regulatory co-operation and technology transfer.'

Bilateral cooperation between regulatory bodies was accompanied by bilateral development assistance projects targeted at financial market development.[159] Primarily designed as technical assistance, these cooperation projects aimed at institution building in the financial markets.

Cooperation with international financial institutions

Chinese regulatory bodies' interaction and cooperation with international financial institutions, most notably the World Bank, the IMF and the ADB, was part of the overall engagement of China in these organisations. China's participation in the IMF and the World Bank started as early as 1980, and since then, both organisations have accompanied most of the Chinese reform process with their consultation and advice. Particularly with regard to macroeconomic policies and problems, both organisations had significant influence on the reform process during the 1980s (Jacobson and Oksenberg, 1990), as Chinese authorities, and particularly the PBC, needed to react quickly to newly arising challenges of macroeconomic imbalances such as fiscal deficits and rising inflation. From the perspective of the PBC, cooperation in these years offered access to information on international finance and economics that has been crucial in designing the reform course (Jacobson and Oksenberg, 1990, p. 70).

Organisationally, the MOF was the designated counterpart of the World Bank and the PBC the counterpart of the IMF, yet in practice, World Bank and IMF officials regularly worked with all relevant government bodies, and projects were often linked to the agencies concerned so that, for example, the CSRC was the partner of a project relating to stock market development. Inside the PBC, a department was established in order to manage the relationship with the IMF.

The work of international financial institutions in general consisted primarily of advisory services and projects, study tours, as well as (limited) loans for technical assistance and training components for Chinese regulators in China and abroad.[160] The relevance of advisory services increased as China moved from direct to indirect methods of governing and regulating the reformed economy. The cooperation was, however, not limited to the regulatory level as it also included a broad range of policy dialogues and policy-oriented advice. Sector studies of the World Bank, mostly from a comparative prospective, were a key input in these debates. The annual consultations between China and the IMF became a forum for intense dialogue through which important concepts for governing a market economy were introduced both in general and with special focus on the financial markets.[161] However, restrictions due to 'political will' applied, and sensitive issues, such as government control over state-owned banks and political interference in lending decisions, were mostly discussed off the official record if at all.

Examples of cooperation on a day-to-day basis were the projects and missions of the Financial Sector Development Department at the World Bank, as well as newer initiatives of the Financial Stability Forum, both targeted directly at the regulatory bodies. Projects of the IMF generally focused more on the management of monetary and exchange rate policies. International financial institutions were also active in setting up internationally funded training institutes (primarily for short-term education of officials and executives) such as the Shanghai Institute of International Economic Management and the Central Financial Institute in Beijing, both funded by the UNDP.

Among international financial institutions, the International Finance Corporation (IFC), as a part of the World Bank Group, was particularly active and has became an investor in numerous smaller Chinese banks and other financial firms. Its equity participation, linked to technical assistance provision and active contributions to the management of these firms, was intended to precede and induce broader private sector investments. It thus became a catalyst for strategic investment in Chinese financial firms in general. For the actual investment, the focus of the IFC's work was more on soft skills than on money, and on making valuable contributions to the organisational development of the firm (Slater, 2004).

The impact of cooperation within the context of development assistance is hard to measure. It can be said, however, that it generated additional support for the overall economic reform policies, and led to a 'convergence of views' on some issues in the development and transition process (Jacobson and Oksenberg, 1990, p. 140) as well as fostering processes of benchmarking and the introduction of international standards.[162] The importance and urgency of meeting international standards, such as those set forth in the Financial Stability Assessment Programme of the World Bank and the IMF, an international response to the problems highlighted by the Asian financial crisis, increased after the crisis and added more pressure for compliance and cooperation, although no coercion was applied to these standards.

International agreements and contracts

The single most important international agreement with an impact on the development and opening of the Chinese financial markets was the WTO-entry agreement. With regard to the financial markets, the WTO agreement set forth a detailed timetable for the future opening of the financial markets. There were two noteworthy aspects of China's WTO-entry commitments; firstly, the commitments were a concentrated effort to align China's financial markets with international standards of national treatment of foreign banks (WTO, 2001a). Secondly, while not a channel for international exchange and cooperation in itself, the agreement was accompanied and fostered on a project level as well, for example by the EU-China Financial Services Co-operation Project, which focused on WTO implementation and compliance in the financial markets. The project's approach included the three divisions of banking, securities and insurance, focusing on developing a training regime and the implementation of a standardised training programme and examination.[163] The project was part of a larger programme with regard to China's WTO entry, coordinated by the German Development Cooperation Agency (GTZ). On a practical level, it employed educational methods of distance learning, as well as a pool of experts available to take part in workshops and seminars in China. It thus provided help with implementing the WTO commitments effectively.

The emerging network of international advisers

Advisory boards are a recent phenomenon in the organisational history of Chinese regulatory bodies and within the domestic context. They have in general reinforced the linkages between the PBC and the largest Chinese banks rather than contributing to the regulators' (or banks') independence (Lardy, 1998, pp. 174ff). The establishment of the CBRC Council of International Advisers, consisting of six high-profile Anglo-American regulators, therefore was a remarkable move in establishing and securing a new channel for continuous exchange between the CBRC and international experts. The Council held its 'First Conference of the Council of International Advisers' in November 2003 in Beijing and has henceforth been consulted on several prominent issues in banking sector reform. It is intended to work as a two-way exchange:

> The establishment of the Council of International Advisers aims at, on the one hand, opening a window for the CBRC to learn from international experiences and to widen the policy-making visions, and on the other hand serving as one of the important channels for the newly built CBRC to 'walk out' and to set up a good international image so as to enhance the international cooperation in banking supervision (CBRC, 2003b).

Its members included Andrew Sheng, the chairman of the Hong Kong Securities and Futures Commission, Andrew Crockett, chairman of the Financial Stability Forum and former general manager of the Bank for International Settlements, Sir Edward George, Governor of the Bank of England, Sir Howard Davies, former chairman of the UK Financial Services Authority, Gerald Corrigan, former president of the Federal Reserve Bank of New York, and David Carse, former deputy chief executive of the Hong Kong Monetary Authority.[164] Although no public statements on the role of the international advisers were made either from the Chinese or the international side, it was pointed out during the interviews that their role was primarily seen as giving detailed and specific technical advice on the implementation of confined regulatory measures as well as providing general judgments on broader issues on an informational basis.[165]

The securities markets regulator CSRC has a longer tradition of international advisers than the CBRC. The most prominent appointment in this regard was that of the chief advisor Anthony Neoh, the former chairman of the Hong Kong Securities and Futures Commission, who resigned in 1998 after informally advising the CSRC during most of the 1990s. He is credited with implementing important changes in China's securities markets in line with international best practice as well as in regard to the opening of the stock market. A Council of International Advisers was also set up at the CSRS, with its first meeting held in October 2004. Its members included Laura Cha, president of the council, Alan Cameron, formerly of IOSCO, Sir Howard Davies, who thus served on both the council of the CBRC and of the CSRC, Linin Day, of the Taiwan securities regulatory body, Stanley Fisher of Citigroup, Gary G. Lynch of the US SEC, Anthony Neoh, Luigi Spaventa, an MOF and securities regulator from Italy, John Thornton of Qinghua University and Goldman Sachs, and Georg Wittich, a securities regulator from Germany. As international advisers remain a considerably new development in the internationalisation of Chinese regulatory bodies, it seems too early to reach conclusions on their role. Their setup, however, created a new channel for the exchange of international ideas. In this structure, they had the institutional foundation and continuity to develop a meaningful dialogue with Chinese regulators and policy-makers that none of the other channels achieved.

It can be said that a number of important channels for international exchange and communication were established and used by Chinese regulatory bodies that allowed for the influx of international ideas as well as for increased and substantial interaction with international experts in the field. Both go hand in hand with the increased interaction with foreign financial firms present in Chinese markets and with their lobbying strategies, as surveyed in Part II. Together, this highlights the changing operational mode and organisational context of the regulatory bodies. However, the increased exchange and cooperation have hardly been a way of *implanting* international regulatory standards into Chinese financial markets. Instead they have led to a broadening of the ideas that dominate the regulatory process and to an alignment of perceived policy options with international discourse, as shown below. In effect, new perspectives and options have been offered to Chinese regulatory bodies in the form of scientifically based advice. Before assessing the impact of these channels in more detail, the next section turns to the hiring of internationally trained and experienced personnel by Chinese regulatory bodies that emerged as an important part of the personnel policies and that formed another important channel for the internationalisation of regulatory bodies in China.

Internationalised staff as a key source of regulatory regime change

The new regulatory bodies for the Chinese financial markets emerged in the context of overall staff modernisation, professionalisation and increased outward orientation. Building new institutions for the financial markets required in particular to find new, adequately trained and qualified regulatory staff who were not available within China. As shown below, Chinese regulatory bodies therefore changed their personnel policies from the traditional mechanisms of cadre recruitment towards hiring increasing numbers of internationally trained returning Chinese nationals as well as overseas Chinese. Both groups have contributed significantly to the internationalisation of the Chinese regulatory bodies and have complemented the channels for international cooperation and exchange that were analysed in the last section. Here, the position and role of internationalised staff members are discussed as an additional aspect of the internationalisation of regulatory bodies in China's financial markets, in particular since this process is most deeply connected to the orientation of the regulatory regime.[166] After presenting the changes in personnel strategies, implications of the increasingly internationalised staff are discussed by using the concept of an emerging regulatory community. This allows a focus on the impact of internationalisation on the actor constellation and interaction among regulatory bodies in the financial markets.

Hiring internationally trained and experienced staff

How have the new skills and techniques needed to regulate the newly emerging financial markets been developed? How have regulatory bodies managed to adjust their capacities to the new challenges that emerged during the transition to a market economy? It has been noted widely that an important component of the personnel policies of the PBC and the CSRC in particular was to hire internationally trained and experienced staff in order to increase regulatory capacity (Green, 2003c; Naughton, 2004b). During the interviews conducted for this chapter, it was pointed out repeatedly that the gap in knowledge, skills and techniques in financial market regulation could in fact hardly have been overcome within an acceptable timeframe *without* the transfer of internationally trained returnees into the regulatory bodies, in particular because market development constantly necessitated more sophisticated regulation.[167]

In principle, the increasing quantitative and qualitative importance of returnees (*haiguipai*) was also observed for other sectors of the Chinese economy, a tendency that was further fostered by the official strategy of 'Strengthening China through Human Capital' ('*rencai qiangguo zhanlue*') (Li, 2004). For the regulatory bodies in the financial markets, two broad patterns emerged; the first group of returnees typically studied overseas (most likely in the US) and has then worked in the American financial markets for a number of years, gaining first-hand 'Wall Street experience'. The second group included staff who had originally worked for the Chinese government or a Chinese state-owned bank and had then been transferred to an overseas post, thus gaining international experience for a number of years, before returning to a higher-ranking post in China.[168] Both groups of returnees-turned-internationalised-regulators were often posted to key positions inside the Chinese regulatory bodies, for example, as heads of operational departments or in strategic and research departments, and thus to positions in which they could have a considerable impact on the future shape of Chinese financial markets. In these positions, the returnees not only applied and disseminated their internationally gained knowledge and expertise but also pressured for and initiated reforms along the lines of internationally accepted financial market practices and regulation (interviews). They tried to align Chinese markets with international standards and lobbied for the provision of a legal framework for the introduction of new products (interviews with regulators). In this, they complemented the international orientation and experience of top regulators on an operational level and helped to build an 'international culture' in regulatory bodies.[169] Well-known US-trained professionals in the PBC included Dr Yi Gang, assistant governor of the PBC. Gao Xiqing was a similar example in the case of the CSRC.[170]

Overseas returnees were recruited through direct contacts and personal networks as well as through more anonymous job advertisements of the regulatory bodies on both their own websites and on special websites for the returnee community. After settling back in China, these returnees were paid more than other government officials. However, hiring internationally trained operational staff was only one part of a multi-faceted new personnel policy in Chinese regulatory bodies that also included training one's own personnel overseas and recruiting non-mainland Chinese internationally experienced staff from abroad, including Hong Kong citizens and overseas Chinese.

Recruiting in Hong Kong

The most prominent case of hiring regulatory personnel from Hong Kong was that of Laura Cha (Shi Mei-Lun). As a former deputy chairman and executive director of the Hong Kong Securities and Futures Commission, she became vice-president of the CSRC in 2001 on a three-year contract. She resigned from her post in 2004, due to a 'personal health condition', but continued to serve as head of the newly established CSRC Council of International Advisers (Yu and Kang, 2004). She was the first non-mainland Chinese national to work on a vice-minister level inside China's bureaucracy and her role in the CSRC was controversial. Accused by some of imposing policies on the Chinese market that did not suit Chinese circumstances, she was praised by others for initiating important and long-awaited changes in the Chinese securities markets. Most prominently, she actively (and publicly) fought for an internationally oriented approach to regulation (Hu, Wei and Niu, 2002). Other Hong Kong Chinese have subsequently been hired to occupy less prominent positions in Chinese regulatory bodies.

Recruiting overseas Chinese

The CSRC has also recruited overseas Chinese scholars and professionals. An announcement on the website of the CSRC in summer 2004 invited overseas Chinese to apply in the current round of CSRC hiring (*haiwai rencai geren jianlibiao*) in an attempt to make the overseas Chinese community important contributors in the process of economic reform and modernisation (CSRC, 2004b).[171] The downloadable personal history questionnaire for the application required applicants to state their citizenship and their involvement in party or 'group' activities, but neither was a formal prerequisite for the application, although actual choices may have been influenced by that.[172] However, for the PBC and CIRC, similarly open recruitment procedures have not been established. In order to participate in the PBC entry exams, candidates do have to have a mainland Chinese citizenship (People's Bank of China, 2004e).

Overall, by 2001, about 50 overseas returnees worked in the CSRC (Naughton, 2003a). Most departments of the CSRC were headed by internationally experienced staff; these included the Strategic Committee on Planning and Research that is key for policy suggestions (interview). Representatives of foreign financial firms who had been in contact with these regulators confirmed this and interviewees regarded the CSRC as the most internationalised regulatory organisation because of its practice of hiring internationally trained and experienced staff. The PBC and the CBRC were encouraged to display a lesser degree of internationalisation and the CIRC was generally acknowledged to be the most closed regulatory body in China's financial market (interviews).[173] The degree of organisational internationalisation among the regulatory bodies in China thus varied considerably.

The new personnel strategy was not without its problems and the hiring of internationalised staff caused some frictions as the views and approaches of the new staff members could not easily be integrated into the regulatory bodies; returnees were seen as arrogant and were accused of having lost their Chineseness (Hu, Wei and Niu, 2002). Green (2003c) points out that in the case of the stock market, *haiguipais* were blamed for the market downturn and were accused of not supporting Chinese interests. Frequently cited problems included the charge that their approach may have conflicted with the governance structure and with the political leadership.[174] Despite these issues, the hiring of internationally trained and experienced staff was an important new trend in the personnel strategies of Chinese regulatory bodies. It can be identified as an additional channel for the large-scale transfer of know-how and skills into the Chinese regulatory organisations and a contributor to change in personnel structures in regulatory bodies in China. It was also an important component in changing the intellectual foundations, the beliefs and ideas of the regulators; that is, in Vogel's term, the *orientation* of the regulatory regime. After all, the professional staff carried the new orientation into regulatory bodies. Following the findings of Green (2003c, pp. 172ff), it is along these lines that internationalisation can be seen as one of the sources of institutional change in China's financial markets.

The emerging transnational regulatory community

On the basis of the increasingly internationalised regulatory staff and the increased international interaction of Chinese regulatory bodies, can the above analysis be developed further into identifying a newly emerging internationalised community of regulators in China? The basic idea of regulatory (or, as they are also called, epistemic) communities is that their members carry common ideas about regulation, and share the same *orientation*, as well as a regulatory culture, and become – as a group – change agents in the process of regulating the development of financial markets. Regulatory communities are characterised by (national and transnational) horizontal linkages between regulatory actors as well as a common concern and common expertise. They are an analytical concept that allows focus on the level of individual actors. Are Chinese regulators becoming part of a transnational regulatory community? Is there a group of regulators emerging who carry internationally inspired ideas within the Chinese financial markets?

It is argued here that, based on the channels of internationalisation and international cooperation of Chinese regulatory bodies, there is indeed a group of internationalised regulators emerging in China that can be understood as part of a transnational regulatory community. The members of this community include internationalised parts of the regulatory agencies in China, such as the heads of departments and research staff that are internationalised themselves or engage directly in interaction with regulatory agencies from abroad, but also the key regulators on the leadership level, as well as research institutes, internationally connected advising economists and government agencies related to the policy consultation process.[175] They are people who interact frequently with each other at (international) conferences and through the dialogue between regulators. The key members of this community have been trained internationally, have spent time abroad and are intimately familiar with the international discourse on financial market regulation. They have learnt to 'blend in with their international peers' professionally and personally, as several interviewees pointed out. At the top level, regulators such as Liu Mingkang and Zhou Xiaochuan, who have impressed international experts with their professionalism, cosmopolitanism and international orientation, are role models and figureheads for this group.[176]

The concept of a transnational regulatory community is used here as a means to highlight three points; firstly, the perspective of an emerging transnational regulatory community in China highlights the *international dimension* of the changing regime orientation in China's financial market regulation. Members of the transnational regulatory community are characterised by their international exposure and interaction. With their ensuing higher positions due to these characteristics, they have become important actors in the process of financial market development. They have increasingly aligned the choices available to political decision-makers with international concepts and have in general added a more objective and theory-based foundation to domestic power- and interest-driven financial market reform.[177] They have thus contributed to shifting the debate towards international orientation and international standards, directing it more strongly towards a market-oriented system. By providing drafts for policy decisions, they have translated their international exposure into paradigm shifts in financial market regulation and reform.

Secondly, the concept of a transnational community highlights the emergence of a *group of connected actors* within and among the regulatory bodies, who share their international outlook and principles in regulation and who have the power to translate their ideas into new regulatory principles and practices. On a national level, this unites them across the organisational boundaries of single ministries, government agencies and regulatory bodies. On an international level, they have important international alliances with other regulatory authorities. It can be argued that this has important consequences for the self-perception of these regulatory bodies as they might perceive themselves as cosmopolitan agents rather than planned economy regulators. Moreover, their international exposure potentially stands in stark contrast to the administrative imperative and also to their incorporation into party structures at home.

Thirdly, the broad definition of this community highlights the blurred boundaries of the regulatory process that now incorporates new actors across borders and across the divide between regulatory actors and firms. The international influence on the process as well as the increasing connections between government bodies are new phenomena in the Chinese process of regulation and the political system as a whole. Regulators and firms cooperate on an increasingly changing basis and in new modes of interaction at a face-to-face level, highlighting the increasing functional differentiation among regulatory actors and financial firms. This mode of interaction between government bodies and firms has last but not least been conveyed through the international sphere and by the practices of regulatory bodies abroad. Overall, this again highlights the hybrid nature of the regulatory process and organisations in China between cadre control and discipline, and international integration.

Consequences of internationalisation: new rules and regulations

Internationalisation has led to a change in the structures of regulatory bodies (regime organisation), and it can be argued that it has also had a significant influence on regime orientation through the established channels for international exchange and cooperation and the hiring of internationally experienced staff. Can an effect of this be confirmed empirically by looking at changes in regulation? Have new regulations reflected international standards and norms?[178] How have regulators, based on the changed regime organisation and influences on regime orientation, dealt with the challenge of increasing market internationalisation? Has there been a newly emerging pattern in financial market regulation and a gradual change in the direction of regulations that can be attributed to a change in the regulatory regime? This section looks at these questions by discussing some regulations for the domestic financial market and their alignment with international standards. In addition, it takes up some points made in Part II and analyses the reactions of the regulators to the challenges of financial market internationalisation on the basis of the internationalised context of the regulators themselves.

The domestic level

With regard to the reflection of international standards and norms in the new regulations made to govern China's domestic financial markets, two examples are considered here; firstly, the new developments in the regulatory framework for domestic banks and secondly the regulations on the risk management of domestic securities firms.

Establishing a regulatory framework for domestic banks

The Chinese regulatory framework for domestic banks is now centred around the concepts of corporate governance, risk management and equity capital. This section shows that within the complex structure of domestic regulation, each of these parts is in line with international standards. The new concepts are a clear reflection of international influences. As regulation in the banking sector in China is closely and inseparably connected to the reform of banks, both aspects are looked at here.

To this end, with regard to corporate governance, a number of regulations have been important in setting out the new framework, most comprehensively the 'Commercial Bank Law' revision in 2003. First of all, however, the fact that the concept of corporate governance emerged as a dominant concept in the reform of domestic banks is itself remarkable as it marks a clear shift away from the previous focus on reducing NPL ratios. This shift in itself is in line with the 'Core Principles on Effective Banking Supervision', published by the Basel Committee on Banking Regulation, and can thus be interpreted as an example of the transfer of internationally accepted standards into the Chinese regulatory regime. On an operational level, the concept of corporate governance as an important tool in the reform process and as a means of regulation in China emerged first in the 'Guidance on the Internal Control System of Banks', promulgated on 18 September 2002. Here, the corporate governance system of commercial banks is defined as comprising the

> organisation structure with the main bodies of shareholder's meeting, the board of directors, the board of supervisors, and the high-ranking

management, the systems to guarantee the independent operation and effective mutual check of all departments, and the scientific and high efficient decision making, incentive and restraint mechanism (Article 2)

Based on this definition, the most important provisions of the guidelines include the establishment of a new board of independent directors and the institutionalisation of external supervision for domestic banks. The concept of corporate governance then became a key element in the reform of the two pilot banks, as described by the 'Guidelines on Corporate Governance Reforms and Supervision of Bank of China and Construction Bank of China' (CBRC 2004c). Explicitly referring to the Basel Committee guidance paper on 'Enhancing Corporate Governance for Banking Organizations' (Basel Committee on Banking Supervision, 1999), Liu Mingkang said in a speech at the Beijing International Financial Forum in 2004 that: 'In light of our understanding of governance issues and international experience we stress that creation of sound corporate governance is a key element of the state-owned banking reform' (Liu, 2004b).

In the internal structure of domestic banks, boards have been introduced as well as an audit, and risk management and compensation and remuneration committees. Interestingly, with regard to the management personnel of domestic banks, the import of foreign talent became an explicit aim, and Liu Mingkang stated that '[i]t would be preferred that some committees are chaired by high-calibre professionals from developed markets' (Liu, 2004a).

Overall, the change in the corporate governance system of commercial banks in China has been characterised by the introduction of a more risk-oriented framework, the second point this section discusses. Again, the importance of international principles in the reformulation of regulations in this regard stands out and BIS standards have been a point of orientation. Schüller (2002, p. 19) points out that soon after the Asian financial crisis commercial banks in China were urged by the PBC to implement BIS standards for credit management. This is also reflected in the 'Guidelines on Commercial Banks' Due Diligence in Credit Business' that cover the whole credit process, including information collection, approval and decision-making procedures and standards for risk identification. A statement on the CBRC website at the time asserts that these draw on the 'supervisory philosophies advocated by the Basel Committee on Banking Supervision as well as the sound supervisory practices of other countries' (CBRC, 2004e).

In this context, market risks of commercial banks have also become a new focus of regulation due to the increased trading activities of commercial banks. This is reflected in the 'Guidelines on Market Risk Management of Commercial Banks' whose introduction was based on a discussion that closely related to the 'Amendment to the Basel Capital Accord to Incorporate Market Risk', as reflected in CBRC comments (CBRC, 2005b; Basel Committee on Banking Supervision, 1996). A CBRC official interviewed stated that the 'CBRC has embraced the basic risk management concepts widely accepted by the international banking community in drafting the guidelines' and explicitly referred to the active management of inevitable risks in business and the balancing of risks and returns. The CBRC has accepted the principle of allowing the design of individual risk management systems with autonomy and flexibility and has claimed – in line with international trends in banking regulation – to increasingly rely on the banks' ability to judge their own risks within a framework of regulation rather than micromanaging the risk management system of banks.

With regard to equity capital provisions of domestic banks, arguably the most important part of the new regulatory framework, the clearest shift towards the implementation of international standards can be identified in the introduction of new capital adequacy rules for domestic banks, as implemented through the 'Law on Capital Adequacy of Commercial Banks' that became effective on 1 April 2004.[179] The rules required Chinese banks to have a capital adequacy ratio of 8 per cent by 1 January 2007 thus in fact implementing the capital adequacy norm of the Basel Accord for the Chinese banking sector.[180] Related to this shift in regulatory principles towards the risk-weighted equity capital of commercial banks is the 'Rule on the Issuance of Subordinated Bonds', promulgated on 17 June 2004 in order to allow commercial banks to replenish their capital base.[181] As pointed out by Harner (2004), both rules together highlight the significant 'change of the rules of the game' away from deposit collection and NPL reduction to risk orientation. Asset growth of domestic banks under this regime will depend on their capital base as well as on risk inherent in their loan portfolio, rather than merely on their ability to collect deposits. As all banks in China need to be adequately capitalised under these rules, this also marks an important intellectual shift away from the perception that the SOCBs are agencies of the state and do not need capital on their own as they do not carry significant risks because of government bail-outs. With regard to regulatory principles, it marks the shift to quality of loans and away from loan growth. With regard to international orientation, the new capital adequacy rules' intention explicitly was 'bringing the Chinese banks into conformity with global standards that have prevailed since the mid 1980s' (Harner, 2004, p. 43).[182]

In addition, benchmarks for the performance of domestic banks have increasingly been set in line with international standards, such as in the case of the two pilot banks for which benchmarks were set with regard to capital adequacy, ROE, ROA and cost-to-income ratios relative to the top 100 largest banks (Liu, 2004a). International influences can furthermore be identified in the new disclosure rules on capital ratios that are explicitly intended to increase transparency and market discipline (CBRC, 2004d). Overall, it is therefore justified to say that the regulatory framework for domestic banks has been influenced by and oriented towards international standards and benchmarks to a significant degree. Regulatory principles have increasingly been in line with international best practice.

Risk management and the direction of securities market regulation

The IOSCO 'Objectives of Securities Regulation' state three main aims of securities regulation; firstly, the protection of investors, secondly, ensuring that markets are fair, efficient and transparent, and thirdly, the reduction of systemic risks (IOSCO, 2003, p. 5). In general, the CSRC has used its powers, enshrined in the 1998 'Securities Law', to gradually bring the Chinese securities markets more in line with these internationally accepted standards. This has in particular been the case with regard to new rules implemented during the shift in securities markets regulation in China after the Asian financial crisis (Heilmann, 2001, p. 15). Here, two aspects of the broad IOSCO framework are significant; the regulation of market intermediaries (securities firms) and the regulation of securities investment funds. What have been the emerging principles in their regulation, particularly with regard to risk management? Have international standards been an important influence in this regard as well?

With regard to the securities houses as the predominant market intermediaries, the IOSCO objectives call for the regulation of capital requirements as well as implementation of standards of internal organisation and operational conduct (IOSCO, 2003, pp. 31ff). In this regard, the CSRC set regulatory standards through the 'Securities Law' of 1999 that were further specified by the 'Rules on the Administration of Securities Houses' in 2001, and the 'Guidelines on the Internal Control System of Securities Houses' in 2003. The 'Securities Law' specifies minimum capital requirements for different types of securities houses (brokerages or comprehensive securities houses) as well as conditions for those who administer the securities house's business. A sound management system, separating the business on the own account and brokerage, is called for in Article 121. In the 'Rules on Administration', procedures and requirements for the establishment of a securities firm are specified, as are provisions for its closure (Articles 4-19). In part IV, measures for internal control and risk management are set out, including minimum capital requirements. The 'Guidelines', however, lay out the most comprehensive framework for internal control with regard to capital as well as single lines of business such as brokerage, transactions on the own account, investment banking services, and research services, but also areas such as human resource management and incentive systems, therefore setting standards for internal organisation and operational conduct. In addition, a codex for the corporate governance of securities firms was issued by the CSRC in December 2003 (CSRC and SETC, 2001). The regulation of Chinese securities houses has thus moved significantly in the direction of international standards and has incorporated IOSCO principles as well as broadly accepted concepts such as corporate governance systems.

Interestingly, the formation of these rules highlights the process of international exchange and influence as well. In the preparation of the 2003 rules and guidelines, there was a conference on risk management in securities regulation, cosponsored by the World Bank and PriceWaterhouseCoopers in September 2003.[183] The involvement of international advisers in the evolution of securities regulation has also been strong in the case of the revision of the securities law. The FIRST Initiative, a high-level development assistance platform, provides technical assistance in order to create 'risk-sensitive capital adequacy guidelines for securities firms and indicators for a capital adequacy monitoring system', thus displaying the regulators' intention to move the capital adequacy regime of securities firms more into the direction of internationally accepted standards.[184]

With regard to the administration of securities investment funds, the IOSCO objectives set out four principles for the regulation of collective investment schemes, including standards and regulations for those who set up funds, the legal form and structure of funds, segregation of assets, disclosure of information, and rules for asset valuation. These principles are well reflected in the provisions of the CSRC for regulating and administering securities fund management companies in China. The 'Securities Investment Fund Law', promulgated on 6 January 2004, provides the overall framework for the establishment of securities investment funds 'in order to protect the legal rights and interests of investors' (Article 1). It sets rules for the segregation of client assets (Article 6), conditions for fund managers (Articles 12ff), as well as rules for fundraising, trading, the purchase and redemption of shares, and information disclosure (Articles 57ff). The 'Information Disclosure Rules on Securities Investment Funds', promulgated on 8 June 2004, set out rules for publishing information in nationwide newspapers and on internet websites, and set out what information to disclose (Article 5) as well as what information not to disclose (Article 6). Rules for the special disclosure for fundraising and operation, as well as for the establishment of an administrative system to manage the disclosure, are provided. The 'Measures for the Administration of Securities Investment Fund Management Companies', promulgated on 16 September 2004, set out rules for the establishment of fund management companies, as well as its alteration and dissolution.[185] The Chinese regulatory framework thus provides comprehensive rules that reflect international standards of the IOSCO.

The regulation of securities investment funds has also evolved under the active advice of international agencies, such as in the FIRST Initiative that ran a project on the revision of the 'Provisional Measures on the Supervision of Securities Investment Funds' issued in 1997, and the further development of the 'Securities Investment Fund Law'. The aim here was to improve the distribution channels for securities investment funds and their regulation (FIRST, 2004b). Both have become important components of the strategy for capital development that was set out at a comprehensive level in the 'Nine Articles' on securities market development in 2004. The 'Nine Articles' in general also reflect the increasing alignment of regulatory aims, principles and norms with international standards; they reflect a comprehensive approach to a better regulated market and highlight, incorporate and frame new initiatives to further develop the bond market, an area of increased international attention. They also lay out a framework for the future development of institutional investors in China's capital markets.[186] In addition, two points can be pointed out; firstly, the CSRC published a corporate governance code for listed Chinese companies in which it implemented internationally accepted norms in corporate governance in 2002 (Pißler, 2002). Secondly, CSRC stepped up an initiative on anti-money laundering and has issued relevant rules for the Chinese financial industry in line with the international regime ('Provisions on Anti-Money Laundering in Financial Institutions', promulgated 1 March 2003). This also aimed to lead to increased transparency of specific transactions and in addition highlighted the cooperation of the Chinese regulatory bodies in other processes of international standard-setting and common efforts.

Summing up, it can be said that the domestic regulation of both the banking sector and the securities markets have been moving increasingly towards international standards and can thus be interpreted as being influenced and guided by international norms. In the case of the 'Capital Adequacy Rules' for domestic banks, the national regulation was in fact an implementation of international standards. It was an explicit aim of the new regulations to narrow the gap with international practices, again in particular with regard to capital adequacy but as well with regard to other aspects of risk management (CBRC, 2004d). It can therefore be argued that internationalisation has had an important impact on the regulation of the domestic financial markets and that it has changed the orientation of the regulatory regime towards more internationally accepted standards, norms and procedures.

Reacting to the challenges of financial market internationalisation

Not only have Chinese regulators provided a new framework for the domestic financial market, they have also reacted to challenges posed to them by the process of financial market internationalisation; the market entry of foreign firms brought along new products, and foreign firms themselves had to be regulated as new market participants. In taking up some of the aspects discussed in Part II, this section analyses how regulators have responded to these challenges on the basis of their international integration. The section analyses the evolving regulation of new products and then moves on to the reactions to the different organisational structure of foreign financial firms. Here, the impetus of regulations to structure competition (and make domestic firms internationally competitive) is highlighted. A third aspect looked at are the problems that have emerged in regulating foreign firms alongside domestic firms. This allows a focus on some specific features of regulatory means in China, particularly with regard to informal channels of control, as well on some indications on the underlying principles of regulation. Are regulations overall based on the idea of a liberal market or on a more interventionist approach? The last two aspects are of particular significance as they further specify the findings of the preceding section. Even though international standards have increasingly been influential in the evolving regulations, this does not mean that the regulators in China will necessarily stick to creating level playing fields in the domestic market. Also, it does not imply that the regulatory approach is necessarily aiming at a liberal market.

Providing a regulatory framework for developing financial products

New products have necessitated the development of new regulations, and many examples of this process can be found in the area of consumer banking. The new products are not necessarily brought into the market by foreign financial firms alone, but they have often been fostered by them and have been important to foreign firms' business development. Here, four examples are highlighted in which the new regulations of products that are important to foreign firms have increasingly been aligned with international standards. Firstly, in the case of online banking, the 'Regulation on Online Banking Services', promulgated on 23 April 2002, provides a legal framework for the market entry of suppliers of online banking services and respective risk management, thus permitting legal clarity and comprehensive business development. The regulation is in line with the 'Electronic Banking Group Initiatives and White Papers' and the 'Risk Management Principles for Electronic Banking' published by the Committee on Banking Supervision in 2000 and 2003 respectively (Basel Committee on Banking Supervision, 2000, 2003). Secondly, credit cards can be issued by locally incorporated foreign banks as well as Chinese-foreign JV banks, as long as prudential regulation standards are met. The same is true for RMB-business. These rules came into effect in December 2006. Between 2004 and 2006, foreign banks could issue credit cards through a local partner only. The new rules (2006) imply that a foreign bank branch (without local incorporation) still cannot issue credit cards and can only engage in limited RMB-business (time deposits for non-private customers, or very large time deposits that limits them from entering the mass market), but every foreign bank may apply for local incorporation.

Thirdly, in the automobile financing sector, regulation evolved quickly with the 2004 promulgation of the 'Administrative Rules for Automotive Loans', replacing the 1998 'Administrative Rules for Automotive Consumer Loans'. These rules opened the sector to a broader range of loan providers, including foreign companies, and have a strong risk control and risk management impetus that reflects the increasing alignment of the rules with international trends of risk-based regulation (CBRC, 2003a). Fourthly, the best example for the regulatory bodies implementing new rules in this risk-oriented fashion, as well as a case reflecting the response of the regulatory regime to the market access of foreign firms, is derivatives trading; the 'Interim Rules on Derivatives Business of Financial Firms', which became effective on 1 March 2004, follow closely the Joint Report by the Basel Committee on Banking Supervision and the Technical Committee of IOSCO on a 'Supervisory Information

Framework for Derivatives and Trading Activities', issued in September 1998 (Basel Committee on Banking Supervision and IOSCO TC, 1998). They make detailed provisions for the qualification requirements and required procedures for financial firms in hedging risks or providing brokerage in derivatives for clients. The derivatives market in China is dominated by foreign firms and the new rules have provided a better legal framework for these products.

Another area where foreign firms have been active in fostering the making of new regulations (highlighting that this has not been restricted to consumer banking) is the issuance of specialised funds with regard to fund composition, such as money market funds and bond funds. New regulation on money market funds was provided by the 'Provisional Measures on the Money Market Fund Management', issued by CSRC and PBC on 16 August 2004; this highlighted the move of the system into the direction of allowing more diversified fund composition and allowing some deposit money to move into funds, as is the case with money market funds (Li, 2003).

These examples highlight the successful making of new rules in order to allow for the further development of the industry and regulate the behaviour of new market entrants. They are increasingly in line with international standards. Thus, the rule-making of the regulatory regime can largely be described as responsive, proactive and in line with international standards.

Reacting to the organisational structures of foreign financial firms

Foreign financial firms have not only introduced and fostered new products in the domestic market, but they have pursued a different organisational structure from their domestic competitors. Typically, foreign financial firms are large and complexly structured corporations encompassing subsidiaries in different segments of financial markets, such as commercial banking, investment banking and insurance business (see Figure 6.2). Chinese financial firms' business, on the other hand, is divided along the lines of commercial banking and securities business and the formation of financial holdings and conglomerates is not routinely possible.[187] In discussing the challenges that the differing organisational structures pose for regulatory bodies in China's financial markets, this section highlights three points; firstly, in the discussion about universal banking and financial holding companies in China, the organisational structure of foreign market entrants has been a key factor. Foreign firms' market entry has initiated and fostered the discussion. Secondly, there are indications that the Chinese regulations will increasingly

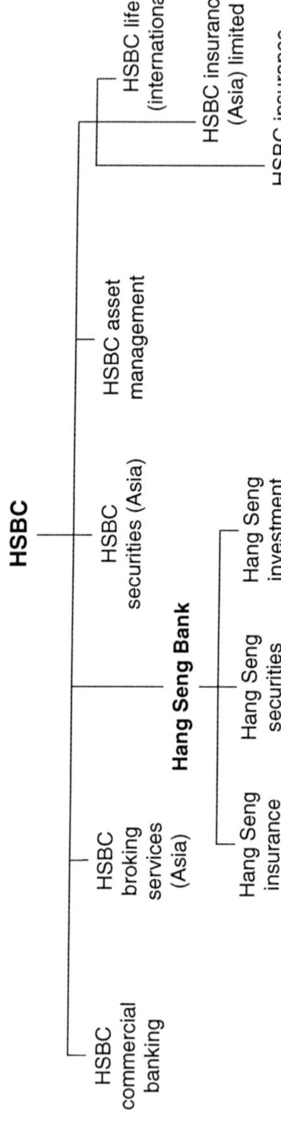

Figure 6.2 Organisational structure of HSBC in China
Source: HSBC (2007)

allow for a blurred division of lines between businesses and will thus move towards the internationally dominant model of universal banking. Thirdly, in this move, there is a strong impetus by Chinese regulatory bodies to make domestic financial firms internationally competitive. The section thus highlights how Chinese regulators (mainly PBC and CBRC) have reacted to the challenge posed by the market entry of foreign firms.

Based on their complex organisational structure, foreign financial firms have broadened the spectrum of services they offer in China; HSBC, for example, moved into banking and insurance services, but also formed an investment fund JV, and Deutsche Bank, in general focused on corporate banking, has also formed an underwriting JV in the securities business. In this regard, foreign firms challenged Chinese firms with their different internal structure and the advantages it offered in terms of cost management, streamlining of business and offering a comprehensive brand, because most Chinese financial firms have to adhere to the separation of commercial and investment banking. In 2004, only three privileged domestic financial firms were exempt from this separation of commercial banking and securities business through a holding construction; the Bank of China, the China Construction Bank and the CITIC.[188] Yet, industrial corporations also moved into different segments of the financial markets at the same time, of which Haier Group, originally a households durables producer and China's most popular brand in 2004, is an example.[189]

Given this overall imbalance in organisational structure, the establishment of financial conglomerates and financial holding companies has been discussed by Chinese policy-makers and regulators. In 2001, a first draft for a potential regulation in this regard was made by Xia Bin, then director of the non-bank financial institution regulatory department at the PBC, later director of the Financial Research Institute at the Development Research Centre of the State Council. He, as a pivotal figure in the discussions, repeatedly pointed out the cost and strategic advantages of foreign banks' universal business approach, and their nature as 'comprehensive financial conglomerates':

> [Foreign banks] have greater scope of business to expand their capital and deploy their funds. They have high concentrations of professional personnel, and the cost reduction and various overall advantages from this [...] If [domestic firms] compete with foreign firms on the basis of 'national treatment', [they] will be at a definite disadvantage. Hence, given the special conditions of the entry of WTO, China's

three dominant regulatory bodies (PBC, CSRC and CIRC) must, on the basis of the overall Chinese industry, diligently study organisational factors for boosting the competitiveness of China's banking, securities and insurance industries (Xia, 2001).

In the discussion, the international guidelines published jointly by the Basel Committee, IOSCO and IAIS on the 'Supervision of Financial Conglomerates' have been a strong guiding force (Xia, 2001; Basel Committee on Banking Supervision, IOSCO and IAIS, 1999). However, no regulation had been promulgated on the issue by 2004. Article 43 of the 'Commercial Banking Law' allowed exceptions only from the central principle of separation of investment and commercial banking. Still, in addition to the market entry of foreign firms and the resulting competitive pressure, the increasing numbers of cross-border mergers and acquisitions (through foreign strategic investments) and the reorganisation of the Chinese financial industry were thought likely to lead to more complex financial conglomerates (Shanghai Jingji Daxue Jinrong Xueyuan, 2003). It has therefore been argued by Chinese experts that eventually, retail banks and securities companies will be allowed to be linked and commercial banks will be allowed to move into the securities business (Hu, Li and Yu, 2002). In 2004, the first indications of this trend emerged and the setup of funds was expected to be allowed soon for Chinese commercial banks.[190]

In this discussion, an important aim was to increase the competitiveness of Chinese financial firms domestically and internationally. Another important aspect was the competitiveness of domestic commercial banks specifically *vis-à-vis* their foreign competitors in the domestic market. As the domestic commercial banks have wide branch networks and are well positioned for wealth management services, including investment banking, the provision of fund management services would allow them to better use this competitive edge in relation to foreign commercial banks and securities firms. The move has thus been interpreted to signify an active policy in structuring competition (in favour of domestic commercial banks) rather than creating a level playing field in the financial industry.[191]

Related to the question of introducing universal banking and financial holdings was the question of establishing one single regulator for the financial markets, thus touching on the question of regime organisation (Sun, 2004). This question has already been discussed briefly above. In relation to the question of financial holdings, a comprehensive approach and an umbrella mode of regulation was also explicitly suggested

(Shanghai Jingji Daxue Jinrong Xueyuan, 2003). In late 2004, however, the understanding was that the division into three single regulators would remain for the nearer future, a position that was implicitly confirmed by a joint memorandum of the CBRC, CSRC and CIRC on the division of supervisory responsibilities with regard to holdings, issued in June 2004 ('Rule on the Regulation of Holdings', promulgated 28 June 2004).

The case of financial holding companies thus highlights that Chinese regulatory bodies reacted in a proactive way to the challenges provided by the organisational differences between foreign and domestic banks and tried to increase the competitiveness of domestic banks *vis-à-vis* foreign banks. In this, their main aim was not primarily to create a level playing field, but rather to structure competition, giving a first rough indication of the interventionist impetus that can be suspected behind regulations. Overall, however, it can be said that the market entry of foreign firms had a converging impact on the discussion of regulations.

Incorporating foreign financial firms into the regulatory framework

The initial system of regulating foreign financial firms as separate entities through specific regulations, evident in the development of the regulatory framework starting from the regulation of foreign banks in Shanghai in 1990, has already been discussed in Part II. More recently, up to 2004, a trend to regulate them alongside domestic banks instead of having independent regulations emerged. This is also the idea behind the national treatment of foreign banks that was envisioned for 2007 in the WTO agreement. But foreign financial firms differ from their domestic peers in their incorporation into the regulatory regime, as has been highlighted in Part II, since they are organisationally, financially and politically independent firms. They are not state-close or state-owned actors, and are neither incorporated into structures of party committees or political control over personnel decisions. Politicians and regulators have thus a much lesser direct grasp on foreign firms, especially in relation to administrative means of regulation and informal pressures. Besides their different organisational structure, foreign financial firms have therefore been a challenge to the Chinese regulatory regime because they are positioned outside most of the informal channels used to regulate and control domestic financial firms.

The impact and meaning of this, as well as the reaction of the Chinese regulators, can be illustrated using the case of the macroeconomic re-control campaign of 2004.[192] The aim of this campaign was to achieve a soft landing of the Chinese economy and a cooling down of the overall growth rate (in the context of a perceived overheating of single sectors in the Chinese economy) by reducing the loan flow, in particular to the overheated sectors.[193] As pointed out by Lu Zhongyuan, director of the macroeconomic research department under the Development Research Centre of the State Council (DRC), this was not to be achieved by 'one-size-fits-all measures that simply drag down the growth rate, but flexible mechanisms that optimize investment growth and resources allocation' (Lu, 2004).

The key tool used by Chinese policy makers to achieve this was the banking sector. The reserve rate for commercial banks was therefore increased in three steps after August 2003. As this did not produce the desired results, more drastic (and less market-oriented) measures were sought. While the true course of events in this regard remain opaque (highlighting the informal nature of the process), experts argue that the CBRC resorted to an outright suspension of new loans in the last days of April 2004, and informally pressured domestic banks to delay loans until after the May holiday.[194] The CBRC actually denied the suspension or any related directive on 29 April 2004, for the first time responding to 'rumour' in an official statement (CBRC, 2004f). However, the 'Guidance to Commercial Banks Regarding Loan Management' was issued soon afterwards, inducing a drastic reaction by JSCBs that accounted for much of the loan growth around that time.[195]

While this process highlights the relevance of informal means and channels of regulation, it also indicates the administrative nature of the control measures. In this time of threatened macroeconomic stability, regulators resorted to administrative means rather than market-oriented regulation. Naughton (2004a) states that 'the instruments chosen bear the brunt of macroeconomic recontrol and were clearly administrative measures, familiar from the era of planned economies.' The limited use of market-oriented tools, such as interest rates, has also been discussed by Hu (2004), highlighting the limited effectiveness of market-oriented instruments in China; in a system that does not respond to interest rate changes, the only options, she argues, are essentially strategies marked by government approvals, loan curbs and administrative penalties. Later statements of the CBRC and especially Liu Mingkang highlighted the emerging connection of the reform of the banking sector to the issue of macroeconomic control (CBRC, 2004a).

Where did foreign banks stand on that issue? First of all, it has to be pointed out that they were hardly contributors to the problem (as the loan growth ratios of foreign banks were significantly lower than those of JSCBs), but that in principle, they would have been harder to pressure in an informal way, at least through the personnel structures and related sanctions that most likely were used in the case of the domestic JSCBs.[196] The example thus highlights the systematically different position of foreign banks, as they are not part of the informal, administrative mode of regulation. This systematic contradiction is likely to increase in significance when foreign firms expand their market share (in certain market segments) or alter the informal control that regulators have over the domestic firms that foreign firms have invested in.

How did regulators react to that position? With regard to the inflow of foreign funds that were equally a concern at that time (partly based on RMB revaluation speculation), foreign banks themselves faced a reimposition of administrative control measures on their foreign exchange loan business in China. In May 2004, the 'Rule of the Foreign Debt of Foreign Banks' was promulgated, limiting the foreign exchange import by foreign banks to previously set quotas. This essentially limited the credit expansion of foreign banks in China, subjecting them to regulatory approval of quotas. It can be seen as an additional step in the process to re-establish macroeconomic control because it effectively limited the loan growth potential of foreign banks whose main line of business was foreign exchange loans. In the case of the macroeconomic recontrol campaign, the problem of foreign banks' foreign currency loan growth was thus comparatively easy to solve and not a pivotal problem to begin with. Still, the overall systemic contradictions between informal control measures and independent foreign firms are also evident.

The following observations can be recapitulated; the hypothesised change in the regulatory regime orientation due to internationalisation could be confirmed by the observable changes in *de facto* regulations made by the PBC, CBRC and CSRC. Regulations increasingly were aligned with international standards in both domestic market regulation and in responding to the challenges posed by foreign firms' market entry. However, there was also a significant variation in the degree to which regulations reflected international norms, ranging from vaguely being influenced by them to actually being implementations of international standards. The regulatory regime responded effectively to the challenges posed to it with regard to regulating new products, reacting to the different organisational structure of foreign firms and reacting to the challenge these posed for informal means of regulation, although in this, the measures were not necessarily fully in line with a liberal, market-oriented approach. Rather than creating a level playing field among domestic actors and between domestic and foreign ones, indications are that the CBRC tried to structure competition. The new regulatory regime in China thus not only reflected a shift towards international standards but also displayed some interventionist, opaque, micro-regulating and control-oriented features that were particularly highlighted by the macroeconomic recontrol campaign. It is in this context that the emerging cooperative mode *vis-à-vis* foreign financial firms identified in previous chapters should be understood.

Coming back to the original question posed at the beginning of this section, however, there are strong indications of the impact of international ideas and processes of internationalisation on the orientation of the regulatory regime. While no clear cause-effect relationships can be established between these effects and the channels of exchange, the assumed transfer of know-how and input into specific regulations could be substantiated by highlighting, for example, how World Bank projects on risk management standards in securities firms contributed to specific regulations. The implementation of the Basel standards in the new capital adequacy rules for domestic Chinese banks was another case in point. In addition, explicit references to international standards can be found in Chinese laws, regulations and statements by regulatory authorities. As a consequence the regulatory regime overall became more aligned with international norms. It can reasonably be argued that internationalisation had an effect on the regulatory regime, both on its orientation and its organisation.

Concluding remarks

Turning to the domestic side of financial market internationalisation, this chapter has shown that the process of internationalisation has been broader than the mere market entry of external actors, and that internationalisation had a profound impact on the regulatory regime in the Chinese financial markets. Both with regard to regime organisation and orientation, the channels of international influence, such as the exchange of ideas, interaction on a professional level and international role models had a significant impact on the new regulations in the Chinese financial markets. For regime orientation, the changing personnel structures were particularly important. In this context, the rules and regulations made by the regulatory bodies increasingly were in line with international standards, and in some cases were a full implementation of them.

This process has two important implications for regulatory rule-setting and policy-making; firstly, on the basis of increasingly internationalised regulators, the strengthened position of regulatory bodies can be identified. Even without constitutional protection and the power to formally appoint top personnel (which remains with the CCP Disciplinary Commission), the regulatory bodies emerged as strong and professional organisations. The PBC, though not an independent central bank by international standards, is one of the most influential bodies in economic affairs on the ministry level in China (Liew, 2004, pp. 50ff). It has made a significant transformation towards a central bank in a market economy. The CSRC has accomplished much in establishing more regulated securities markets. And both have played an important role in policy-making, as regulatory agencies can influence the (perceived) menu of options that are available to political leaders, even if the top-level policy decisions thereafter remain opaque.

Secondly, the findings highlight the international dimension of the regulatory regime change in China's financial markets, thus challenging the notion that these processes remain merely domestic. The international framework has instead been increasingly important to the domestic process. Most importantly, however, the emergence of new types of regulatory agencies contributed to a changing *modus operandi* on the level of day-to-day regulation that was important for the general redefinition of borders and relations between commercial and regulatory actors. Overall, the changes in the regulatory regime led to the increased importance of rules and regulations for the governance of business transactions and state-economy relations in the financial markets, as well as to increased transparency and accountability.

7
Domestic Firms Undergoing Internationalisation

With the market entry of foreign firms that led to both increased competition and cooperation and an increasingly international market for financial services itself, internationalisation has significantly changed the business environment and the incentive structures domestic firms face in China's financial markets. How have domestic financial firms reacted to these changes? How have they positioned themselves as actors in an increasingly international market environment? Have they aimed at becoming more competitive and internationally present firms? To what extent has their nature as predominantly publicly owned firms had an impact on this process? Shifting the focus of this analysis from regulators to domestic firms, this chapter looks at the impact financial market internationalisation has had on domestic commercial players as well as their reactions to the changing incentive structures they face. After recapitulating the changes in the market environment due to internationalisation, the chapter considers a number of strategies domestic financial firms have developed in reaction to arising challenges. Here, partnership arrangements and the introduction of foreign strategic investment are discussed as well as international IPOs. Human resource policies in domestic financial firms and the internationalisation of domestic financial firms' staff are then analysed.

Looking at the implications of changed business strategies and the increasing internationalisation of staff, this chapter presents two main findings; firstly, internationalisation has induced a differentiation among the predominantly state-owned and state-controlled domestic commercial players, some of which have started to internationalise aggressively and thus have tended to become market-oriented actors of change in the domestic setting. The increased commercial strength and decrease of vulnerability of these domestic firms has been a *conditio-sine-qua-non* for this process. Secondly, there has been a significant change in the professional foundation of China's financial markets that will likely provide the basis for new business ethics and practices. Both of these processes have led to a significant change in the position of domestic actors *vis-à-vis* regulatory bodies. Responding to new incentives in the changed market environment based on a stronger institutional basis, some domestic firms have started to increasingly favour and request a more rules-based system and a stronger enforcement of rules, as well as less direct government interference in their business. They have thus started to emerge as actors in favour of institutional change and at the same time as a potential counterweight to regulatory actors. This chapter thus identifies a new group of actors that has been fostered by internationalisation and that emerged during the differentiation of domestic financial firms; newly emerging, internationalised, institutionally strengthened and more market-oriented domestic financial firms.

The changing market environment

As was pointed out in Part II, the quantitative importance of the business of foreign financial firms is still limited and even in the foreseeable future, foreign financial firms will most probably play a subordinate and complementary role in China's financial markets. Yet, foreign financial firms' market access in China and the broader process of financial market internationalisation as well as the increasingly internationalised regulatory framework have had a significant impact on the market environment *domestic* players face. As these effects can hardly be separated from either the overall ongoing reforms in Chinese financial markets or from the ongoing process of overall economic internationalisation, instead of differentiating between domestic and transnational influences and processes, those aspects that have been aggravated and intensified through internationalisation shall be highlighted here.

First of all, it is important to note that the opening of the domestic Chinese market to foreign firms has been accompanied by the reverse process of gradually opening international markets for Chinese financial firms to go abroad and expand their business. Chinese banks, for example, have borrowed money extensively from international banks in offshore centres (Katz, 1997). Lardy (1999) points out that these international operations as well as international bond offers of (selected) domestic financial firms significantly increased their international presence. New business opportunities have thus become available to domestic firms in international markets and the Chinese regulatory system has increasingly allowed approved firms to expand on an international level. On the domestic side, financial firms have faced increased competition and a shift in demand towards international services. As was pointed out in Part II, Chinese financial markets have increasingly been opened to international competition, in particular since 2001. While some restrictions remain for foreign financial firms' market access, and the competition of foreign firms has often been overemphasised by regulatory bodies as a way of increasing the pressure on domestic firms through rhetorical means, competition has *de facto* increased significantly in some market segments. For example, there has been a significant increase in the competition domestic players face in the business with foreign-invested enterprises and large SOEs, and particularly so in the foreign currency business. As a prospective trend for the future, this is also likely to be the case in consumer finance. While most of this competition has not been price competition in a strict sense, as interest rates remain administratively controlled, the domestic players have been challenged with regard to their customer orientation in financial service provision as well as the quality of services and the introduction of new products, especially in the commercial banking sector. Most importantly, however, foreign competitors have a strong position with regard to internationally oriented services, which increased the need for domestic firms to improve their respective services and increase their own international orientation.

Competitive pressures have further increased due to the fact that customers of financial firms in China have become more sophisticated, internationally experienced and internationally oriented on a private and corporate level over the course of reform. Due to the large amounts of FDI that China has been receiving, the international contacts and financial requirements of domestic firms and JVs have increased on a large scale and a growing number of foreign firms have entered the market. Chinese businesses have additionally started to go international and operate abroad on a growing scale. The need to provide cross-border and foreign-currency services has greatly increased for domestic financial firms over the course of the economic reform and opening process. In consumer banking, international services have become more important, just as they have in corporate banking, such as with regard to international trade finance. The same has been true for investment banking services with regard to international IPOs, bond offerings and QFII services. Domestic financial firms thus needed to expand their international orientation due to increased demand.

In addition to increased competition and the international orientation of services, the introduction of international benchmarks and the implementation of international standards by regulatory actors have had a large impact on domestic financial firms' business. This has been true for the capital adequacy rules based on the Basel Accord, but also with respect to the design and pricing of new financial instruments and products. Regulatory bodies have also fostered the use of international cooperation in the reform and restructuring of domestic financial firms, which has increased the incentives for domestic firms to develop their own strategies in this direction. The changes in the market environment thus have gone hand in hand with the new regulations and regulatory efforts to reform domestic financial firms. Overall, the deeper international integration of Chinese financial markets has led to a changed market environment and thus has changed the incentives and constraints faced by domestic financial firms considerably.

Internal reforms and cooperation with international partners

In order to respond to the arising challenges in the business environment strategies of domestic financial firms have been driven by domestic and international factors simultaneously. They have thus responded both to regulatory changes and changes in the market environment as well as to the processes of marketisation and internationalisation (Keng, 2004). In the context of restructuring, internationalisation and the strengthening of competitiveness, the aims of single strategies may overlap and the relationship between aim and means may be blurred. For example, internal restructuring of a domestic financial firm is often intended to boost international competitiveness, and many firms may try to achieve both through cooperating with international partners. Domestic firms position themselves in the triangle of organisational (internal) restructuring, internationalisation (outward orientation) and strengthening competitiveness.

In the context of internationalising market conditions, different response strategies of domestic financial firms have emerged. The most prominent ways to proactively respond to the changed commercial environment have been internal reforms, such as organisational reforms of the governance structure, and reforms with regard to products and services offered (Hu and Zhang, 2004). The repositioning with regard to product and business lines, however, has been the most clearly observable change in the market behaviour of domestic financial firms; in the case of domestic banks, they have tried to get access to new revenue sources by expanding business into areas that are more lucrative than

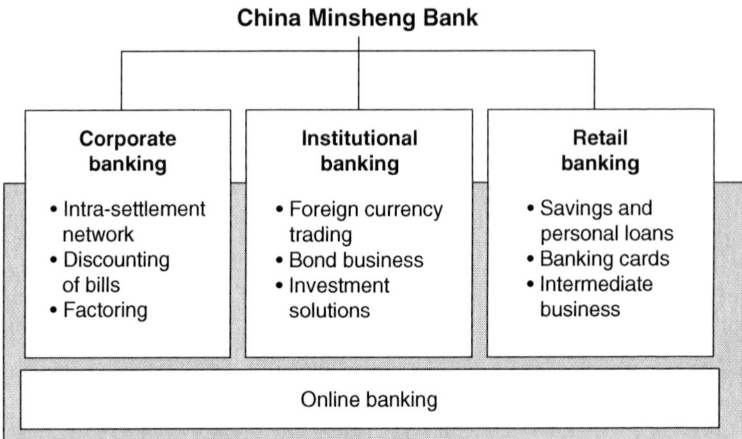

Figure 7.1   Product range of China Minsheng Bank
Source: China Minsheng Bank website: www.cmsb.com.cn

their traditional narrow SOE-oriented credit business and accordingly have diversified their business lines. From their position, the SOE business has been a major obstacle to them becoming more competitive and they have tried to balance it with stronger product lines. With a focus on international orientation, both domestic banks and securities firms have broadened their product range to meet the demand for internationally available products, such as in the case of factoring, and to provide internationally oriented services, such as in the case of QFII brokerage (Wang, 2002a). The product range of China Minsheng Bank (Figure 7.1) reflects an international orientation and the addition of product lines that are both new, internationally oriented and facing high competition.

On an organisational level, changes in strategy have included changing the structure and number of branches and the numbers of employees, but also reforms of the internal governance mechanisms and management techniques of the domestic financial firms. ICBC, for example, reduced branches at the outset of its reform path from 28,345 to 25,960 and employees from 429,709 to 400,558 between 2001 and 2002 alone. It refocused its commercial presence to more lucrative urban areas (ACFB, 2003, p. 611). With regard to the internal structure of domestic firms, internal management and incentive systems have been particularly important. For example, as highlighted during an interview given by the president of CITIC published in *Caijing* in 2002, in the reform of the incentive system of CITIC, employee pay became linked to profits (Hu, Li and Yu, 2002). The most prominent example in this regard, however, is the Bank of China employee system that has been reformed as a part of the overall reform strategy (Bei, 2004a). In this process, all staff of the BOC had to reapply for their jobs and had to show that their skills met the upgraded job descriptions. They also lost the lifetime employment security they enjoyed before (also see McGregor, 2004a). Another important aspect of internal reforms were the new capital adequacy rules that were designed to have a significant impact on the perception of risk within domestic firms and were aimed at forcing the banks to increase equity until 2007 (Harner, 2004).

The reform of China Construction Bank (CCB) can be used as an example to highlight the components of the strategies of domestic financial firms with regard to internal structure, governance and management. In the process of restructuring, a subsidiary company was set up, non-banking assets were hived off and market-oriented management mechanisms were introduced (Ling, 2004a). However, the case of the CCB also highlights the ambivalent nature of the reforms in the area between regulatory and firm-level initiatives, as the CCB is one of the two pilot banks earmarked early in the reform phase by the PBC and CBRC. Detailed plans for reform were laid out by the CBRC, including benchmarks for key financial data (CBRC, 2004c; Tang, 2004). Internal reforms were thus prescribed by regulators in the case of CCB. This was also the case for the other large SOCBs and it also encompassed the internationalisation of these banks, as will be shown below.

Domestic firms have also responded to the changed market environment through increased access to international markets. They have expanded their international commercial presence and have both offered and bought financial products on international markets. With regard to the loan business of domestic banks, Katz (1997, p. 100) noted:

> The extensive involvement of Chinese banks and ITICs in the international loan markets has had a strong effect on their lending practices within China. Officially, these Chinese institutions are still subject to the credit plan and to interest rate prescriptions in their RMB business. Unofficially, they are applying foreign banking practices to an increasing degree in their highly regulated home market.

This has allowed them to gain considerable international market experience. Banks at the forefront of this process include the Bank of China, with the broadest network of overseas branches among Chinese banks and an evolving complex organisational structure that includes BOC Hong Kong (BOCHK), a subsidiary that is owned by BOC and listed on the Hong Kong stock exchange.[197] Both through the establishment of branches and the general participation of Chinese financial firms in international markets, domestic firms have exploited new business opportunities and have increasingly learnt to operate smoothly under international conditions, a process that has had important repercussions for their business in China.[198]

Within the realm of internal reforms, the explicit (contractual) cooperation with international partners has been a major building block. Domestic firms sought the cooperation, advice and capital of international partners in restructuring themselves and in reforming their product lines. This was reflected in domestic banks hiring international consultants but also in the increasing number of Sino-foreign cooperation projects and JVs between Chinese financial firms and international ones. Here, internationalisation actively played an enabling role in the process of domestic financial restructuring and organisational internationalisation, while the degree of institutionalisation of this cooperation varied from loose agreements to formal arrangements.[199] Partnership agreements were one of the earliest versions of cooperation between a domestic financial firm and an international partner. Most of the agreements have been of limited scope, and many have only encompassed one topic, such as international settlement cooperation. Partnership agreements have been a limited way of linking domestic and international partners and have often been sought by the international partner in order to overcome regulatory restrictions. From the perspective of the domestic bank, this brought about an early exposure to the banking practices of foreign banks.

With regard to the formation of JVs, the securities business has been the main testing ground because regulations have made the formation of JVs attractive both for domestic and for foreign partners. Here, securities firms and fund management firms have to be distinguished. In the fund management business, numerous JVs have emerged between local and foreign firms. Prominent examples included Guotai Jun'an Allianz and Fortis Haitong Asset Management. At the end of August 2006, there were 20 Sino-foreign joint venture fund management companies in operation (see Figure 7.2).

Due to the high competition in the fund management business, the pressure on these firms to differentiate themselves is comparatively high. As a consequence, a trend of domestic fund management companies to enter JVs and to 'internationalise aggressively' in cooperating as much

Fund management companies	Foreign partner	Local partner	Foreign equity (%)
Harvest	Deutsche Asset	Zhongcheng Trust	19.50
Fullgoal	Bank of Montreal	Fullgoal	27.78
ABN AMRO Xiangcai	ABN AMRO	Northern Investment Trust	49
China Merchants	ING	China Merchants	30
Fortune SGAM	SGAM	Fortune Trust	33
INVESCO Great Wall	INVESCO	Great Wall	49
Fortis Haitong	Fortis	Haitong	49
Guotai Jun'an Allianz	Allianz	Guotai Jun'an	33
SW BNP Paribas	BNP Paribas	SW	33
China International	JP Morgan Fleming	Shanghai ITIC	49
UBS SDIC Hongtai	UBS	SDIC	49
Everbright-Pramerica	Pramerica	Everbright	33
BOC International	Merrill Lynch	BOCI	16.50
Franklin Templeton Sealand	Franklin Templeton	Sealand	49
AIG Huatai	AIG	Huatai	49
BoComm Schroders	Schroders	BoComm	30
CCB Principal	Principal	CCB	25
ICBC Credit Suisse	Credit Suisse	ICBC	25
CITIC Prudential	Prudential plc	CITIC Trust	33
HSBC Jintrust	HSBC	Shanxi Trust	49

Figure 7.2   Sino-foreign joint venture fund management companies (as of August 2006)

Source: PriceWaterhouseCoopers (2006)

as possible with their international partner, learning as much as possible and giving control to the foreign partner, has emerged (interviews with representatives of fund management JVs).[200] On the back of the reputation and brand name of the foreign partner as well as know-how, skill and management transfer, these fund management JVs have aimed both to increase their domestic competitiveness and their international orientation. Since not all domestic fund management companies have followed this strategy and not all of those willing to set up a JV have found a foreign JV partner, this emerging strategy of some firms has led to a considerable differentiation among domestic fund management firms. As noted by a study by PriceWaterhouseCoopers (2006), the JV companies are beginning to challenge the purely domestic fund management companies on this basis.

For securities firms, the interviews indicated similar results, but on a more limited scale due to the limited number of JV securities firms that were established in 2004. The newly founded securities firm JVs were clearly seen to be internationalising as rapidly as possible, in particular with regard to offering internationally oriented services to domestic customers. Interestingly, CICC, the first JV securities firm in China, was regarded as the dominant firm in this respect and thus the main competitor to other JVs, but it was also portrayed more like a flagship in the market, fostered by political support and preferential regulatory treatment. It was thus not perceived as an institutionally strengthened and more independent domestic financial firm. This can, on the other hand, be explained by the special historical circumstances and the exceptional character CICC had after its founding in 1995. Other JV securities firms have played an active role in the market, but have faced restrictions on their business scope, as pointed out in Chapter 4.

One aspect to be kept in mind is that in the process of internal reform and increased cooperation with international partners, the organisational structures of domestic financial firms have changed remarkably and have increasingly displayed both international linkages and a higher degree of complexity due to their international cooperation and their orientation towards international customers. An example of this is the case of XiangCai Securities, the seventh-largest broker among Chinese securities companies. XiangCai Securities, originally a securities company from Hunan, was founded in 1993 and became the first nationwide comprehensive securities firm in 1999. It then entered a JV with CLSA in 2002 and a fund management JV with ABN AMRO in 2003. In addition, it opened a representative office in Hong Kong, offered comprehensive financial and investment services to domestic and international clients, and established a significant QFII department in which it employs international staff.[201] It thus displays a comprehensive international orientation in its products and its organisational structure and highlights the organisational consequences of the internationalisation strategies of domestic financial firms.

Introducing foreign strategic investment and going public internationally

Other than forming JVs, the most prominent way of domestic financial firms' internationalisation was the introduction of a foreign strategic investor. Most of these investments were introduced by commercial banks.[202] Some investments were also made in the insurance business. However, allowing foreign strategic investment in domestic financial firms was a relatively late trend in China's financial market reform.

In assessing the introduction of foreign strategic investment by Chinese banks, it needs to be pointed out that this was a mix and match of regulatory decisions and the incentives of the domestic banks. While it can be argued that introducing foreign strategic investment was the most visible action of domestic commercial banks in order to internationalise themselves, it had become CBRC policy to advocate foreign strategic investments as long as they matched explicit conditions and to instrumentalise foreign strategic investments for the reform of domestic banks by 2006; according CBRC Vice Chairman Tang Shuangning, the CBRC explicitly wanted to create a win-win situation for Chinese and foreign banks through foreign strategic investments. In this endeavour, the CBRC curtailed the scope and design of foreign strategic investment deals in order to ensure that they do not introduce only capital, but also technology and not just shareholding, but also business development. According to the CBRC, Chinese banks' association with foreign banks should be voluntary and for mutual benefit, with major foreign financial firms offering their domestic partners advanced management experience and an improved corporate structure. By 2006, the CBRC had developed five principles in respect of long-term foreign strategic investment, and these principles seemed to govern the right of entry for foreign banks. They were:

1. A 5 per cent minimum holding by a foreign strategic investor.
2. A three-year minimum holding period.
3. Board membership by the foreign strategic investor, and development of good corporate governance.
4. Restricting the foreign strategic investor to owning no more than two stakes in the banking sector, in order to avoid potential conflicts of interest.
5. The provision of technical support in respect of control and risk management, product management, human resource incentives and discipline, and other processes by the foreign strategic investor to its partner.

These conditions further specified the legal basis for foreign strategic investments that was clarified in December 2003 when the CBRC published the 'Administrative Rules Governing the Equity Investment in Chinese Financial Institutions by Overseas Financial Institutions'. These rules set out broad mandatory qualifications for overseas investors and the limits of investments. As of the end of 2006, foreign strategic investment in Chinese commercial banks was limited to under 20 per cent of the domestic bank's capital for an individual foreign investor and to under 25 per cent of the domestic bank's capital for all foreign investors in total (see Figure 7.3).

On the basis of preferential regulatory policies, the amount of capital invested in Chinese financial institutions surged significantly in 2005 (Achhorner et al., 2006). However, it has to be kept in mind that numerous deals were concluded earlier and that about 80 per cent of the investment volume went to the large SOCBs (including BoComm).

In assessing foreign strategic investments for the perspective of the domestic banks, it shall be noted that for the large banks, the link

Phase 1: 1996–1999	Phase 2: 2000–2002	Phase 3: 2003 onwards
• First investments made by development finance institutions, such as the ADB and IFC. • ADB's 3% investment in China Everbright Bank in 1996 as the kick-off. However, these were passive financial investments with a technical assistance component. • IFC made numerous investments from 1998 onwards.	• Broadening scale for foreign investors who assume more active roles. • Foreign investors have a clear focus on single market segments with potential for increased cooperation such as the credit card market. • Board seats secured for foreign investors.	• Significant increase of foreign investments after the model cases of the AIG investment in PICC (2003) and HSBC in BoComm (2004, 19.90%) landmark cases. • Large-scale investments with significant management rights for the foreign investor, broad cooperation agreements. • Opening the doors for numerous deals in 2005–6, including three of the large SOCBs.

Figure 7.3   Phases of foreign strategic investments 1996–2006
Source: Hope and Hu (2006), own compilation

between regulation and market orientation has been very pronounced. The regulatory plan for restructuring three of the large SOCBs foresaw foreign strategic investment, as well as an international IPO, as a prerequisite. Smaller banks had more room to make independent decisions, while also facing different market conditions and investor interest. While the SOCBs' offer assumed state guarantees, but also a reduced likelihood to see full privatisation or private control, in particular by foreigners, JSCBs and large CCBs can in many cases offered a better credit portfolio, more diversified and possibly more fragmented ownership structures, less political attention and better adaptability to internal reforms. With the need to position themselves in the increased domestic competition and with their reduced closeness to both state owners and regulators, these banks were active in attracting foreign strategic investment as a part of their own restructuring and reform plans. To some degree, this was also the case for smaller CCBs and some reforming rural or urban credit cooperatives or cooperative banks.[203] However, CCBs often faced problems created by geographic limitation of their distribution network and poor asset quality. A special case among the Chinese banks introducing foreign strategic investment was the Bohai Bank, which was a greenfield investment by Standard Chartered (HK) Ltd made in December 2005, setting up a newly established bank in a banking licence transfer.

In each case, introducing foreign strategic investment requires a match to be made between the needs and interests of the foreign and of the domestic partner. On the side of the foreign partners, different types of financial firms have been engaged, ranging from global universal and commercial banks, to banks focusing on one segment of the market only, as well as specialised finance companies such as credit card firms (American Express) and insurance companies. In addition, a number of financial institutions such as IFC, ADB or the German DEG have invested in smaller banks outside the coastal cities (see Figure 7.4).

The introduction of foreign strategic investment was thus a common strategy for domestic banks to foster their internal reforms and to internationalise themselves. As is the case with JVs in the fund management industry, this led domestic banks to differentiate themselves and to strengthen their commercial backbones. It changed the landscape of commercial banks in China considerably. With regard to foreign strategic investments, from the perspective of domestic firms, not only equity capital, but also active management participation and support in internal restructuring made a crucial contribution to the process of internal

Domestic bank	Foreign investors	Shareholding (%)	Time of investment	Investment volume (US$100 million)
ICBC	Goldman Sachs Group Allianz Group American Express	6.05 2.36 0.47	Mar 2006	25.822 10 2
BoC	Royal Bank of Scotland UBS Asian Development Bank Asia Financial Holdings Pte Ltd	10 1.61 0.24 5	Dec 2005	30.478 4.916 0.737 15.239
CCB	Bank of America Asia Financial Holdings Pte Ltd	8.515 5.878	Aug 2005	25 5 14.66 10
BoCom	HSBC	19.90	Aug 2004	17.47
Huaxia Bank	Deutsche Bank AG Deutsche Bank Luxembourg SA Sal. Oppenheim jr. & Cie KgaA	7.02 2.88 4.08	Mar 2006	0.1656 0.679 0.961
China Minsheng Bank	Asia Financial Holdings Pte Ltd IFC	4.55 1.22	Nov 2004 Mar 2003	1.07 0.235
Industrial Bank	Hang Seng Bank Limited IFC Government of Singapore Investment Corporation Pte Ltd	15.98 4 5	Mar 2004	2.08 0.52 0.65
Shenzhen Development Bank Co Ltd	Newbridge Capital Ltd	17.89	Sep 2004	1.5

Shanghai Pudong Development Bank	Citibank	5.00	Dec 2002	0.6753
China Everbright Bank	Asian Development Bank	3	Oct 1996	0.2
Bohai Bank	Standard Chartered Bank (HK) Ltd	19.99	Dec 2005	1.2346
Bank of Shanghai	IFC	5	Aug 1998	0.2561
	IFC	Up 2 (from 5 to 7)	Dec 2001	0.2467
	HSBC	8		0.6257
	Shanghai Commercial Bank Ltd.	3		0.2347
Ji'nan CCB	Commonwealth Bank of Australia	11	Nov 2004	0.1735
Xi'an CCB	IFC	2.50	Jun 2004	0.032
	Scotiabank	2.50		0.032
Bank of Beijing	ING	19.90	Mar 2005	0.235
	IFC	5	Mar 2005	0.59
Nanjing CCB	IFC	5	Nov 2001	0.0882
	BNP Paribas	19.20	Dec 2005	0.8732
Hangzhou CCB	Commonwealth Bank of Australia	19.92	Mar 2005	0.77
Nanchong CCB	DEG	10	Jul 2005	0.036
	SIDT	3.30		0.12
Tianjin CCB	ANZ	20.00	May 2006	1.10
Ningbo CCB	OCBC Bank	12.20	May 2006	0.71

Figure 7.4 Foreign strategic investments in Chinese commercial banks to the end of June 2006
Source: Based on CBRC statistics, media reports

restructuring (interviews). In particular for the smaller city commercial banks, foreign strategic investments, although typically of limited scale (around 5 per cent), drastically increased the access to foreign know-how and management techniques. Foreign partners, seeing their investment as a long-term commitment, contributed significantly to the restructuring and repositioning of domestic firms both internally and with regard to products. For the domestic partner, teaming up internationally was also an important signal towards customers and further (domestic) investors. As pointed out during the interviews conducted for this research, city commercial banks' options for repositioning, for example, were comparatively limited, and foreign strategic investments were a key opportunity in the process. In two prominent early cases, Bank of Shanghai and Shanghai Pudong Development Bank, in which HSBC and Citibank respectively took 5 per cent stakes in 2003, the foreign strategic investment resulted in a strategic reorientation with regard to products, but the cooperation between the partners was not limited to this aspect (interviews). For larger banks, such as BoComm, the strong participation of HSBC in the introduction of risk management techniques sped up the process of internal restructuring considerably. Here, the international listing on the horizon created strong incentives for the domestic financial firm to adopt new standards of operation, as an international IPO offers capital, an international reputation and access to international markets.

In fact, it can be argued that most Chinese banks welcomed a foreign strategic investor in order to increase their capital base and improve management techniques without losing significant areas of control. The professional prudence of foreign investors, on the other hand, ensured that only those domestic banks genuinely willing to reform themselves and whose organisational and financial foundations made such an endeavour promising were able to find international partners for this cooperation. Through the transfer of skills and capital and the streamlining of business objectives, foreign strategic investments led to a financial and organisational strengthening and increased market orientation of those domestic financial firms with foreign investments.[204] This led to a differentiation among the domestic firms, in particular banks, where most of the foreign strategic investments have been made.

The benefits of introducing a strategic investor from the perspective of a domestic bank bestows positive effects on the restructuring of the bank, including the redefinition of business strategy, and a new assessment of assets and liabilities, and of risks and opportunities for the bank's business. In detail, they also include effects on the following areas (interviews):

- Capital and capital adequacy. The foreign strategic investment leads to an inflow of capital that allows the domestic banks to meet CAR and that enables future growth.
- Introduction of new products. Foreign banks as business partners contribute to developing new products with joint distribution efforts.
- Know-how and expertise transfer. Staff exchange, training and human resource strategies in parallel to the introduction of new technology lead to an increase in marketing and risk management skills, as well as an improved design of management information systems.
- Corporate governance reforms. Foreign strategic investors enhance and foster the transfer and implementation of improved corporate governance structures, such as reporting requirements, committee structures, functions and meetings, in particular regarding the position of the internal audit committee. It also includes the composition and role of the board of directors, the selection and professional background of the top management as well as instruments to create appropriate incentives for management and staff to perform in the interest of the shareholders of the bank.[205]
- Definition of explicit goals and targets, such as asset quality, efficiency and capital adequacy.

However, foreign strategic investments have not been limited to banks. In parallel, non-bank domestic financial firms have also started to secure foreign strategic investment, most prominently in the insurance sector. In the securities market, foreign strategic investments have been less common. Here, fund management companies and securities companies have mainly engaged in JVs, as detailed above. An exception to this is the case of Beijing Securities, in which UBS made an investment.

International IPOs of Chinese financial firms

The international IPO of Chinese domestic financial firms is a component of the internal restructuring of domestic banks in China that has often been related to the introduction of foreign strategic investment. The first prominent example of a Chinese domestic financial firm going public at an international stock exchange was the dual listing of China Life in Hong Kong and New York in 2003 (Li and Kang, 2003). Another example was the IPO of the Chinese insurer PICC P&C in Hong Kong in 2003, in which the American insurance firm AIG had taken a strategic share. These international IPOs of Chinese financial firms after the introduction of a foreign strategic investor created much attention and have been regarded as showcases for other firms and future international IPOs (interviews with insurance firms). In the commercial banking segment, the international IPOs of BoComm, CCB, BOC and ICBC attracted considerable international attention.

Further positive effects include changes in the corporate governance structure. Early research on the international listing of the BOC subsidiary BOCHK, for example, showed that the international IPO contributed to the import of better corporate governance standards. In the pre-IPO phase of restructuring, capital and governance structures, procedures for managerial appointments, and the business strategy were adapted while transparency, accountability and financial strength were improved (Sun and Tobin, 2003; Lin and Wang, 2001). Therefore, internal reforms prior to an overseas listing contribute in particular to the introduction of better governance standards as well as the clarification of ownership structures.[206] Wang Xianzhang, chairman and president of China Life, explicitly told *Caijing Magazine* when asked why China Life insisted on listing in the US as well as in Hong Kong that the American firm's strict supervision over corporate governance and information disclosure would be conducive to China Life's reform and reputation (Li and Kang, 2003). In the interviews conducted for this research, however, the most important impact of international IPOs was said to be the change in the mindset of the management when facing the then imposed market discipline and stronger regulation.[207]

The long-term effects of both foreign strategic investments and international IPOs will have to be accounted for in the future. As of the end of 2006 it can be stated, however, that both have strengthened the commercial foundation of Chinese domestic firms considerably and have fostered a considerable differentiation among the actors in the commercial banking market.

New human resource management

In addition to the strategies analysed above, one of the most significant components of the restructuring and internationalisation strategies of domestic financial firms has been change in their personnel policies. Because in any financial market, it is ultimately the professional staff of financial firms that conducts the day-to-day business and makes the relevant decisions, the human resources of financial firms are not only key for the firms themselves but also for the financial markets on a systemic level. Professional financial firms' staff need to be adequately trained, experienced in the respective field of business and directed through adequate incentive systems and guiding principles, something that regulation can influence only to a limited extent. Focusing on the changing personnel structures and policies in domestic financial firms thus permits us to add two important aspects to the above analysis. Firstly, it allows a focus on the deep structure both of the process of internationalisation and its impact on the development of the Chinese financial markets on an individual level. Secondly, it allows in particular a stress on the significance of internationalisation for the (professional) foundations of the Chinese financial markets and hence its relevance where the limits of regulation in market development are most pronounced; the development of a strong personnel basis on which to ground strong financial firms. This section thus asks; in what ways have the newly emerging strategies of restructuring and internationalisation of domestic financial firms trickled down to the level of personnel policies, such as the recruitment, hiring and remuneration of staff? What can be said about the personnel structures and the role of personnel policies in the process of internal reform and internationalisation strategies? What can be said about the effects of the new personnel policies and the changing structure of personnel in domestic financial firms on financial market development?

The training and qualification of professional staff in domestic financial firms as well as the incentive and corporate governance systems they operate in have long been identified as key points in the modernisation of the Chinese financial markets (BIS, 1999). The need for change in this regard has been particularly pronounced because the institutional legacy of the command economy has been severe with regard to the personnel structures of domestic financial firms; as most Chinese financial firms have been (and still are) state-owned or controlled, originally the professional staff in these firms were quasi-government employees in predominately bureaucratic structures.[208] This had two important consequences. Firstly, on the top level, bankers and other financial market managers essentially were cadres, which implied that candidates for these management positions had accordingly been selected and promoted through the cadre management and disciplinary system of the CCP, based on a mixture of political criteria and commercial performance.[209] Due to this appointment mechanism, managers were (and still are in some cases) primarily responsible *vis-à-vis* their political principals rather than being exclusively focused on the performance of the financial firm.[210] Secondly, on the operational level of staff, the command economy left the emerging market economy with a severe underprovision of financial skills and techniques while the firms at the same time were burdened by overstaffing and resulting high wage costs.

Significant reforms, including the streamlining and partial reduction of staff, have been achieved with regard to the second problem. Additionally, the incentive systems of domestic financial firms have been changed, based on international role models; payment schemes that link wages or wage components to profits have been introduced and individual responsibilities in loan decisions, for example, have been increased (Harner, 2004; Bei, 2004a). However, important aims of the newly emerging personnel strategies have also related to the professionalisation and internationalisation of the staff of domestic financial firms. Hence, new personnel were hired who were younger and had better training and technical qualifications; this was reflected by the increase in degrees among the staff of domestic financial firms. Talent was also imported through the hiring of returnees and overseas Chinese.

Hiring returnees

Domestic financial firms have increasingly employed returning Chinese nationals (*haiguipai*) who have received training and gained expertise in financial firms abroad. In parallel to the hiring of returnees by regulatory bodies, this has become a major source of talent import and knowledge transfer into Chinese domestic financial firms. Yet, because there are many more financial firms with open positions than regulatory bodies, the quantitative impact of the hiring of internationalised staff by firms rather than regulators is likely to be significantly higher. While exact industry-wide numbers on the extent of this hiring have not been available, anecdotal evidence suggests that the proportion of all returnees working in the financial services industry has been significant.[211]

As in regulatory bodies, the *haiguipai* have become an important part of the new personnel policies and a major channel to improve the skill level and professionalisation in Chinese domestic financial firms. The most important contribution of *haiguipai* is their transfer of knowledge, experience and business culture into the operations of domestic financial firms. Outstandingly, returnee venture capitalists have to be mentioned; these have been highly relevant for the Chinese VC industry and for shaping the Chinese VC culture (interviews). To a lesser extent, due to the larger size of the financial firms they work in, returnees in banks and securities houses have also contributed to changing the business culture (interviews).

However, problems have also arisen in relation to returnees, most pronouncedly along two lines. Firstly, although trained overseas and endowed with some work experience, they typically did not have long careers in financial services abroad. This implies that while they may have been better qualified than domestically trained peers, they were not necessarily experienced enough for the higher-level positions they were often assigned to and may thus have caused new risks. Secondly, substantial frictions arose between local staff and returnees in some cases. This complicated internal management processes and reduced team spirit among staff. In addition, a perceived trade-off between foreign training and local knowledge has been noted, indicating that foreign training and experience has to be balanced adequately both with a deep understanding of the financial industry in China – something returnees often lack – and personal *guanxi* (interviews).[212]

Hiring overseas and Hong Kong Chinese

The hiring of overseas Chinese and particularly Hong Kong Chinese personnel has also been an important component of the new personnel strategies of domestic financial firms, aiming at bringing in more talent and skills on an internationally competitive level. The Close Economic Partnership Agreement (CEPA) allows Hong Kong Chinese professionals to work in the mainland financial market, which essentially turns Hong Kong into a large source of professional personnel for the Chinese mainland's financial market (Slater, 2003a; Wong, 2004). The idea behind this is to bring in skilled professionals who know the local culture and have some advantages regarding the Chinese language.[213] However, while being a successful and broadly adopted strategy, problems have been reported arising from the co-working of mainland and Hong Kong Chinese, and many Hong Kong Chinese have been perceived as being unwilling to go to the mainland (interviews).

Hiring foreign managers and personnel

The hiring of foreign staff has been another component of the personnel strategies of Chinese domestic financial firms. While regulatory bodies have largely refrained from this option, for domestic financial firms it has been an attractive choice, albeit carried out on a very limited scale due to the high costs. Most foreigners have been assigned consultancy positions (interviews). Examples of domestic firms hiring foreign personnel include the Bank of China as well as local securities houses, where in some cases heads of the international or QFII departments have been foreigners. However, the foreign staff do not only fill high-level positions for personnel with long-term experience in large and well-known international financial firms but also some positions on lower levels for comparatively junior staff. In this respect, the main aim of the strategy that could be identified in the interviews conducted for this research was to give the domestic firm an international face in its international relations with investors and customers. While this has worked without problems in some cases, there is also anecdotal evidence about the frustration, setbacks and frequent changes in the positions of these international employees of domestic financial firms, just as in the case of foreign managers in Chinese SOEs.

All three components of the hiring of internationalised personnel have to be seen in the greater framework of internal reforms that have changed the incentive systems of employees with regard to job responsibilities, remuneration and promotion. Internationalised staff in particular have actively introduced a new financial culture, and have thus contributed to the introduction of new reference systems as well as new ways of looking at problems in financial firms and the financial market in China.

New standards for training and professionalism

Besides the changes in the incentive systems and the hiring of internationalised staff, the training of domestic staff in the financial industry has also been deeply affected by internationalisation. Following the entry of the first foreign financial firms into Chinese markets, there has been an international impetus for building new facilities and educational institutions for domestic professional personnel. And while originally driven by the personnel needs of foreign financial firms that were confronted with a lack of trained and skilled personnel when opening their businesses in China, the scope of these institutions has expanded significantly. Foreign financial firms, as well as development cooperation projects, were key to building new structures for educating and training domestic staff for the financial services industry. They have been followed by commercially oriented educational institutions that offer degree programmes in China. Examples of this process include: the China Europe International Business School (CEIBS), a JV between the Shanghai Jiaotong University and the European Foundation for Management Development; the Shanghai International Banking and Finance Institute (SIBFI), a cooperation between the International Finance Cooperation (IFC), the German DEG and the Shanghai University of Finance and Economics; and the Chinese-German Hochschulkolleg (CDHK) at Tongji University in Shanghai, where leading German financial firms sponsor (national and international) chairs in their respective academic fields.[214] In parallel to the rising standards of purely domestic educational institutions, these internationally connected institutions have impacted the development of professional education and have led to the increasingly international orientation of young financial market professionals in China.

In addition to increasing the educational level of domestic professional staff, international actors have also contributed to the reformulation of professional standards, and of certification and examination procedures. For example, the implementation of new professional standards and the introduction of new certificates in the three Chinese market segments of banking, securities and insurance in order to secure an adequate level of skill and qualification has been fostered and guided by the EU-China Financial Services Cooperation Project.[215] The domestic trend for the internationalisation and standardisation of educational backgrounds has thus been accompanied by a process of internationalisation of professional standards.

The effects of internationalised training and licensing are particularly important on a quantitative level as they reach the operational staff of domestic financial firms on a much broader scale than does the hiring of returnees or foreign staff. They thus ultimately change the professional foundation of the Chinese financial firms. Under internationally attuned training and examination, a new professional elite with new techniques, concepts about markets and how to operate in them, and new reference systems, aligned in their ideas and concepts with international business practices, has thus started to emerge (interviews). Members share skills, outlook, perception of market problems, and – notwithstanding the particularities of the Chinese financial markets – have started to develop different work ethics and a different professional culture (interviews). They have also developed a strong outward orientation and international connections. It can be argued, therefore, that this emerging professional elite – carrying an emerging internationally inspired financial market culture – increasingly becomes part of a transnational professional elite and financial industry community.

All these aspects of the new personnel strategies have changed the micro-foundations of domestic financial firms; the substantial change of personnel with regard to training, age and outlook, the introduction of international elements in skills and training, the hiring of returnees, and the introduction of internationally acknowledged practices in staff management, remuneration and the design of incentive systems. These new personnel strategies shape and create the new professional elites that are a key constituent of the newly emerging business community in the financial market. Looking at these strategies thus emphasises both the significance of personnel policies and changing staff structures in financial market development and the importance of internationalisation in areas where regulatory efforts will not be likely to succeed.

Differentiation among domestic financial firms and the new business culture

Domestic financial firms have employed elements of all of the strategies outlined above at the same time, but they have not always been fully proactive towards internationalisation and restructuring. In parallel to proactive strategies, firms have resisted, protracted, slowed down and obstructed reform. Not all domestic firms have moved onto the proactive modernisation and internationalisation track, and not all have done so completely. There have been numerous passive, resisting or circumventing strategies by domestic financial firms as they cope with the changing environment. Some domestic financial firms have tried to escape the (market and regulatory) pressures for change. Some domestic financial firms have simply done nothing and have maintained their operations just as before while at the same time increasing their lobbying for protection.[216] It can reasonably be assumed that they have tried to utilise their closeness to the political and regulatory actors, but detailed information on this process was not readily available.[217] Most likely, the strategies of domestic financial firms were a combination of both proactive and passive elements.[218] Overall, though, the change in the regulatory regime and the stronger impetus towards more active reform of domestic firms diminished the leverage of the financially weak domestic financial firms when they sought protection (interviews with regulators).

The most notable consequence of the different strategies of domestic financial firms towards restructuring and internationalisation, as well as of their changed involvement in international cooperation and orientation in the process, has thus been the differentiation among the domestic firms in China's financial markets. For those firms that chose active reform and internationalisation, international cooperation has contributed to enabling them to successfully reform themselves and has led to their organisational and financial strengthening – an effect in stark contrast to the widely expected weakening of domestic firms through international competition. Most important in this regard has been organisational reform, financial strengthening and the stronger market orientation of the firms, which is also likely to have positive effects on their commercial behaviour and success. In an international comparison, Crystal, Dages and Goldberg (2001) found that firms with investment from abroad behaved more prudently than domestically owned counterparts. It can also be argued that the increased strength of the domestic firms is likely to increase their political leverage on the domestic level as it helps them to break out of their weak position *vis-à-vis* the regulators, a position that has been reinforced by their weak commercial position. Up to the end of 2006, manifestations of the strengthening of domestic financial firms in China could be found not only in the improved capital adequacy ratios of domestic banks announced by the CBRC and the expansion of successful securities houses, but also their increasingly successful competition with international participants in the domestic market (interviews).

Among the domestic firms, stronger ones with international participation and cooperation have thus started to emerge. These firms have differentiated themselves from weaker ones and have also operated increasingly according to market and profit considerations. They have in fact only become stronger *because* they operate successfully in this regard. Based on the evidence collected for this chapter, it can also be pointed out that these firms stand in opposition to government interference in their business and financial markets in general, as well as being seen to call for the stronger implementation of rules and better regulation (interviews with domestic firms). This has been more clearly observable in the case of firms in the securities business and less clearly pronounced in the banking industry, a differentiation that can be attributed to the continuing reform peak in the banking sector at the time that the interviews were conducted for this book. While more research with a longer-term perspective remains to be done on this process, it can nevertheless be stated that there are indications that these firms have started to emerge as important actors in fostering and demanding institutional change in China's financial market.[219]

The strategies of 'aggressive internationalisation' of some of the domestic firms and their stronger organisational position has led to a change in the driving forces of the reform process in China's financial markets. Domestic commercial actors are now able to exert an important impetus for reform themselves in a process that had previously been dominated by regulatory bodies and priorities. While many of the organisational reforms up to now have been initiated by regulatory actors and even the increased international orientation and cooperation of domestic firms with international partners has been suggested, fostered and favoured by the regulatory actors, in the medium to long term stronger, more market-oriented and internationally connected domestic financial firms are likely to have a stronger and more independent position *vis-à-vis* the regulators. Exactly the same process that regulators try to utilise for the reform of the financial market therefore might not only lead to a (desired) differentiation between domestic firms but might also increase the strength of firms in relation to the regulatory actors. Overall, internationalisation of the financial markets has led to an increased commercialisation and outward-looking orientation among domestic financial firms, as well as their gradual internationalisation. Most importantly, it has fostered a change in the actor constellation by differentiating domestic financial firms and strengthening some of them, a change that has led to changing power relations between regulatory actors and firms.

There has been a long search for newly emerging independent actors in Chinese financial markets. In other sectors of the economy, a lot of hopes in this regard have been placed on the emergence of private entrepreneurs (Dickson, 2003; Heberer, 2001; Meyer-Clement, 2004). In the financial markets, however, the emergence of private domestic financial firms has been very limited and politically severely restricted. Foreign financial firms, on the other hand, as shown in Part II, have also been disappointing in this respect as they have emerged as powerful independent actors only on a very limited scale. In this context, what will be the consequences of the differentiation between domestic financial firms in China? What will be the implication of this for the financial markets?

In a system whose single most significant feature is the lack of transfer of control either to domestic private financial firms or to international financial firms, the emergence of strong and more independent domestic actors highlights a crucial change in the actor constellation. For those domestic firms that try to internationalise themselves aggressively, it has been argued, based largely on anecdotal evidence collected in the interviews, that (political) interference in personnel and business decisions has started to become an increasing obstacle to organisational reform and market orientation; in fact it has become a *competitive disadvantage* from the perspective of domestic financial firms (also see He, 2004). For the Bank of China, most advanced with regard to restructuring, an additional decreasing influence of party organs has been observed (Bei, 2004b). On this basis, resistance to (political) interference in business operations is likely to increase. Based on the interviews, there is evidence for this, especially in the securities market. In addition, the introduction of the accountability measures required for international cooperation and overseas listings may lead to genuine corporate governance reforms that may further weaken the CCP-based mechanisms of organisational control; internationally accepted principles of corporate governance conflict with the notion of CCP-based personnel appointments and internal CCP committees (Sun and Tobin, 2003). The mode of interaction between firms and the CCP thus has to change. At the same time, the leverage of financial firms *vis-à-vis* the government increases during the course of internationalisation, as domestic financial firms become organisationally, financially and in human resources terms stronger and less dependent on government protection. Both aspects combined may lead to more leeway in day-to-day business operations (the 'normal mode' of operations) and a consequent increase in the centrifugal tendencies among publicly owned players.

However, this is not necessarily observable in the reform peaks that constitute the 'crisis mode' of Chinese politics. The strong position of regulatory actors in the reform of the SOCBs and the limited leeway granted to domestic financial firms during the restrictive, administratively implemented policies to control credit growth in 2003–4 (the macroeconomic recontrol campaign discussed in the previous chapter) highlighted that so far the control of the CCP, the State Council and regulatory bodies over domestic financial firms remained effective in such a crisis mode. In reform peaks, therefore, the old mechanisms of control as well as non-market-oriented administrative measures still work effectively, indicating that the change in the actor constellation and the increased independence of domestic financial firms have not yet reached an effective level. The distinctive differences between day-to-day operations and concentrated reform campaigns have also been confirmed by the findings of the interviews.

Overall, the trend of differentiation among domestic players therefore has led to a change in the normal mode of operation of financial markets. In this, internationalising domestic financial firms have become more powerful actors in fostering financial market development. There are, however, two important caveats; firstly, since domestic players in China's financial markets have often been very well connected politically, they remain likely to use their political connections for their (economic) benefit, while opposing interference from the outside. After all, they still operate in volatile and hybrid financial markets. More powerful financial firms in these markets therefore have to be balanced by more forceful market-oriented regulation, in order to avoid the emergence of a financial oligarchy. Secondly, in the long run, the decreasing political control may diminish the government's capability to act effectively in the case of crisis, as the politically important, stability guaranteeing crisis mode crucially depends on the CCP-based channels of command over domestic financial firms. It is therefore essential to build up new and more market-compatible ways of control. In combination with stronger domestic commercial players and a reduction of the role of regulators in financial market development this would induce a productive creative tension in the financial market between regulators and financial firms.

The change in the normal mode of financial market operations has also been fostered by increased skills in domestic firms resulting from changes in personnel policies under internationalisation. In fact, the impact of increased skills on the day-to-day business of domestic financial firms can not be emphasised enough; for example, in the NPL problem, one of the largest crises of China's financial markets, at least part of the solution has to occur on the level of day-to-day-business decisions, as the problem loans emerged on a continuous basis and are rooted in poor credit decisions as well as political interference. It can also be argued that with increased professional skills and under the right schemes of incentives set by corporate governance reform, resistance to politically motivated credit decisions can increase on the operational level. It may thus very well be the change in the underlying professional structures of China's financial markets that turns out to be the most significant contribution of internationalisation.

To what degree do the members of this new professional elite emerge as a second layer of agents for institutional change? If their training prevails, new-type professionals are more attached to the ideas of a market economy and acknowledge the benefits of establishing one. Just like the employees of foreign-invested companies, the professional personnel in the financial industry thus has the potential of becoming a strong force in pressing for and initiating the further formalisation of state-business relations.[220] On the other hand, it is important to note that their interests might not be primarily political ones, and that Chinese managers in foreign enterprises, for example, have not generally been interested in changing the political system. It is important to recognise that these people are, in fact, a group that has benefited greatly from the past reforms and that stands to gain even more in the future.

Essentially, two different changes resulting from financial market internationalisation can be identified; the differentiation among domestic financial firms and the emergence of a new professional elite playing a supportive role in financial market development. Both trends are mutually reinforcing and, remarkably, both originate within the state-owned and controlled realm, thus continuing the phenomenon of state-owned actors being overwhelmingly important for the economic reform process in China so far. Most importantly, however, this chapter has highlighted the relevance of domestic financial firms – regardless of their ownership structure – in the process of market development and internationalisation. It has shown that, in contrast to Pearson (2003) and Vogel (1998), who looked exclusively at the regulatory actors and the regulatory regime, looking at the *firms* themselves contributes significantly to understanding the dynamic of market development. By highlighting the impact of internationalisation on the domestic firms in China's financial markets, this chapter has thus extended the state-actor-centred view of the regulatory regime in China, stressing that commercial market players as new actors who initiate institutional change and shape markets are important. Regulation can not create vibrant markets alone and the focus on regulatory organisation and orientation can thus not explain the whole process of market development and the resulting market structure. Firms need to make the markets work and need to balance the power of the regulatory authorities in claiming their own rights. It is in this creative tension between rules, rule-setting and economic action that strong and viable markets emerge. In the case of China, internationalisation has contributed considerably to the strengthening and differentiation of these firms. This is the most important finding of this chapter.

Concluding remarks

Two arguments have been made in this chapter. Firstly, in the context of financial market internationalisation, domestic commercial players – while still predominately publicly owned or controlled – have started to differentiate themselves in their business strategies and commercial behaviour. Secondly, a number of new strategies pursued by some domestic financial institutions, including foreign strategic investments and changes in personnel strategies and the introduction of new professional standards, have led to an increased level of skills, professional sophistication and a newly emerging business culture in Chinese financial firms; they have thus led to the emergence of a new professional elite and changed the foundations of China's financial markets. These findings are remarkable as they highlight that one of the most significant groups of 'actors of change' in China's financial markets may well generate itself from within the state-dominated realm of domestic financial firms – a finding that contradicts the commonly accepted notion in institutional economics that it is private actors that lead institutional change.

Part IV
Conclusions

8
Financial Market Internationalisation and Institutional Change

Internationalisation has been one of the main driving forces of financial market development in China and gained increasing importance in the years up to 2007. While numerous foreign financial firms have entered China in this process, internationalisation has developed its most significant impact on the side of domestic actors, including regulators and domestic state-owned financial firms that have actively started to internationalise. In this process, most notably through significant foreign strategic investment in domestic firms, but also through proactive internationalisation strategies by Chinese banks, the boundaries between domestic and foreign firms have begun to blur. BoComm, for example, is an internationally listed Chinese bank in which HSBC owns almost 20 per cent with an option to increase its share to 40 per cent should regulatory restrictions permit it to do so. This has contributed to a new actor constellation in which new agents of change can be identified on the sides both of public and private actors. Institutional change in China's financial markets has thus been initiated and promoted by state and state-owned actors as well as domestic and international private ones. In turn, internationalising China's financial markets and integrating China into international markets and regulatory regimes does change the domestic actor structure significantly and through this the economic foundations of the political balance of power.

This chapter offers three things: firstly, it presents a brief summary of the main findings regarding the changes in actor structure and constellation in China's financial markets that were induced by internationalisation; secondly, it offers a brief discussion of their economic and political implications; and thirdly, it sketches out three scenarios for the future prospects of financial market development and internationalisation in China.

Key promoters of institutional change in China's financial markets

Foreign financial firms as unique market actors

Foreign financial firms have had a significant impact on financial market development in China as they are unique actors in these markets in two ways; firstly, as international players, they are in a position to offer and introduce new products, technologies and operational structures as well as management expertise to China that all match the international banking benchmark. They have thus fostered the introduction of international products, management and information standards in China. Secondly, they are themselves unique actors as they are commercially strong and independent, operating on the basis of purely commercial principles. In this capacity, they have increased competition, particularly in profitable top-end market segments, as well as fostering cooperation with domestic banks. Foreign firms are distinct commercial actors in China with regard to their organisational structure and strength because they are market-experienced, professional, well capitalised and solely profit-oriented actors.

The analysis in this book has also shown that foreign financial firms entering the Chinese markets have faced a highly complex and dynamic institutional framework. Regulatory restrictions, market opportunities in relation to their comparative advantages and specific operational problems they face when operating in the Chinese markets as foreign actors have all determined their perception of the market environment and thus the incentives and constraints they face for market entry. These factors have shaped their market entry strategies as well as their actual participation in the market, which has remained limited with regard to scale. While the single most important reason for this has been restrictive regulation, market conditions such as a lack of credible customers have also been important disincentives to market entry. This is an important finding as it demystifies the image of 'the large Chinese market' with its abundant market opportunities for foreign financial firms. Foreign firms are therefore most likely going to be niche players in China. Only a few players are prepared and willing to operate in the Chinese market on a significant scale. Since the commercial activity of foreign firms in China is thus limited, the firms have only been able to utilise their unique position in the market and their comparative advantages *vis-à-vis* domestic banks to a limited extent. In this regard, they have failed to fulfil hopes that were placed on them because they have not become decisive external actors in financial market development in China (as yet). In day-to-day business, they operate as outsiders in distorted and immature financial markets and they do so on an unequal footing, because domestic regulation often favours state-owned enterprises and state-owned financial firms. They have thus not been able to fully utilise their potential for fostering institutional change in China's financial markets, and while their overall qualitative impact has exceeded their quantitative market presence, they have not exerted a strong influence on the overall modes of resource allocation in China's financial markets.

Lobbying of foreign financial firms and the changing priorities in market regulation

Based on their limited market share, foreign financial firms have also remained in a relatively weak position *vis-à-vis* regulators when lobbying for their interests in China. However, even with their limited bargaining power as foreign actors, they have actively engaged in interest representation activities using surprisingly diversified organisational structures. In formal interest representation, foreign firms as actors in the Chinese lobbying process have been weak due to their position as outsiders, their limited knowledge of the domestic process, and their heterogeneous structure, in contrast to the more concentrated structure of domestic firms, especially in the banking sector. Some trends in the institutionalisation of foreign financial firms' participation in the regulatory process, however, indicate a potential future change in this situation. In addition, they have learnt to play along with the logic of discretionary Chinese regulatory decision-making and accordingly engage in numerous (opaque) informal high-level lobbying activities. With regard to informal lobbying, some foreign financial firms have learnt to operate successfully in the Chinese game of interest representation and have thus been able to foster their respective individual interests. This indicates that foreign financial firms might just as well become part of an uneven playing field and try to exploit the advantages of the hybrid market environment, rather than foster broad market-oriented regulatory change. It is therefore important not to overestimate the impetus of foreign financial firms in fighting for level market conditions.

However, with regard to their overall success in lobbying and further market opening, it has been found that it is only in day-to-day lobbying that they have had a considerable impact. Overall, it is only where, when and to what extent foreign firms' requests have been concordant with regulators' priorities that they have been able to assert their interests. The overall directional changes in regulation with regard to market opening analysed in this book can only be explained by domestically initiated changes in regulatory priorities. In relation to lobbying, foreign firms thus seem to have had a limited impact on rule-setting for market opening so far. Financial market internationalisation has not been driven by their lobbying. Instead, the developmental dynamic of China's financial markets has been determined by domestic regulators and priorities; this has, however, not impeded further market opening. In this process, foreign financial firms have in part been coopted by Chinese regulators in service of the latter's regulatory aims.

Stronger domestic actors in an increasingly international context

Financial market internationalisation has forced domestic actors to operate in an increasingly open and competitive context. Regulators and domestic financial firms have faced new constraints, incentives and opportunities and have increasingly interacted and cooperated with transnational actors. These cross-border transactions and the provision of extensive international advice have led to a transfer of new ideas to financial market actors and the creation of new intellectual maps as well as leading to changes in incentives, constraints and available information among domestic market players. With regard to regulators, this has induced a change in the regulatory regime and an internationalisation of regulatory bodies. Both regime organisation and orientation have been impacted by internationalisation, as evidenced in the altered scope, options and mode of regulation, and an increasing alignment of Chinese regulations with international standards and practices. Among domestic financial firms, internationalisation has initiated and fostered a differentiation along the lines of business strategies. Opposition of other vested interests notwithstanding, new kinds of stronger domestic financial firms with new sets of preferences and new objectives, operating more and more under profit considerations, have emerged. Overall, domestic commercial actors, some of them involved in international cooperation or in JVs, have come out increasingly in opposition to administrative controls as they pursue their (commercial) interests more aggressively.

Internationally oriented regulators and the emerging new regulatory regime

With regard to the regulatory regime, the analysis has shown that both regime organisation and orientation have developed in the direction of internationally accepted structures, procedures and standards. The established channels of communication and international exchange have fostered change in the regulatory regime, as have the changes in hiring practices and staff structures of regulatory bodies. Chinese regulators have increasingly internationalised themselves and have become members of a transnational regulatory community, a process that has fostered the emergence of a new (internationally inspired) regulatory culture in China. In total, this has provided the framework for the increasing alignment of formal rules in China's financial markets with international practices and standards, such as the Basel Accord and the IOSCO Objectives of Securities Regulation. Regulators have responded successfully to the challenges posed by internationalisation and this process has rendered them strong and internationally connected organisations in the context of post-Leninist government agencies in China.

The changed actor constellation, modes of interaction and bargaining powers, the more pronounced process of lobbying of different commercial actors and the increasingly international context of regulatory policy-making have considerably altered the framework and process of regulatory policy-making in China. However, with regard to the content of the regulation, indications of a more interventionist approach can be identified alongside more market-oriented regulatory policies. With regard to the nature of the emerging regulatory regime in China's financial markets, the continuing detailed and partly restrictive regulation of foreign firms' market participation, for example, indicates that the Chinese regulatory bodies have not adhered entirely to a market-driven approach to regulation and rather seem to have followed a strategy of coordinated competition and guided market development. Although market players have become more important in the process, financial market regulation does not indicate that regulation in China has moved towards a minimalist market-enhancing regulatory state, but that it has followed a more active interventionist approach.

State-owned domestic financial firms seeking independence from political interference

With regard to domestic financial firms, internationalisation has changed the market environment considerably and has led to differing strategies by firms and thus a differentiation among domestic commercial actors in the market. Most remarkably, as a consequence of the changed environment, some domestic firms have chosen to actively internationalise themselves organisationally as well as with regard to their business strategy, and have started to emerge as internationally oriented financial firms. This process has had a significant impact on their organisational and financial strength and has been accompanied by the emergence of a new (internationally oriented) professional elite in the financial industry. In addition, internationalisation has fostered the provision of more and better financial market information, and has thus reshaped the informational basis of the financial markets. Despite developing in the overall direction of the international system, however, in each segment persistent institutional and organisational particularities of the Chinese system can also be identified; these have had a limiting effect on the impact of internationalisation. On the whole, it has been found that the influence of commercial actors in the process of market development has increased and that they are increasingly playing a larger role in initiating and directing market development.

Promoting institutional change in China's financial markets

On the level of actors, internationalisation has thus fostered three important processes in China's domestic financial markets; firstly, the emergence of regulatory bodies that use new ideas and concepts in regulation and that have increasingly brought China's institutional framework in line with international standards. Secondly, the emergence of new-type domestic financial firms as actors that are increasingly market-oriented and connected to international players. Thirdly, the emergence of new elites on a regulatory and professional level that have links to international financial markets. All three groups of actors were identified as *change agents* with regard to the institutional foundation of China's financial markets, as they favour, foster, promote and demand a more market-oriented and rules-based system. The main conclusion of this analysis has thus been that internationalisation has had a significant impact on domestic actors, including their configuration, internal structure, strategies and interaction, and that this has enabled them to become agents acting towards institutional change.

Interestingly, this change originated from within the set of state and state-owned organisations, rather than from privately owned financial firms; it highlights the relevance of state and state-close actors in the transition to a market economy in China. In this process, particularly with regard to changing the informal institutions in China's financial markets, change in the personnel strategies and the structures of professional staff in both regulatory bodies and domestic financial firms is crucial, as illustrated by the emergence of transnational regulatory communities and new professional elites. In strengthening domestic financial firms and initiating differentiation among them, internationalisation also led market development to move from a leadership-driven to a more market-driven process and from the previous top-down direction of development to one where change originates from below. It can be argued, however, that these developments, as well as the changes in the normal mode of the regulatory regime, will become more clearly observable only after the current reform peak in the banking sector and the related concentrated leadership action is concluded. At the same time, the changing regulatory regime, although more attuned internationally, has not necessarily moved in a less administrative and interventionist direction. In the analysis conducted here, conflicting evidence was presented in this regard; certain policies (in particular during the macroeconomic recontrol campaign) were dominated by administrative force and informal channels of regulation, while on the other hand CBRC rules and plans for the reform of the four SOCBs indicated a credible commitment to a more market-oriented system. This was particularly so in the case of the international listing of the four large SOCBs; that diminished the ability of government bodies and regulators to interfere with their business. Regulatory change and the new market actor constellation have to reinforce each other on the basis of increased transparency; the liberalising and more internationally oriented framework provided by the regulators is not sufficient in itself to alter the dynamic of the entire financial market, and regulators might stop short of ceding control in crucial issues. But while stronger financial firms press for these developments, they might at the same time not necessarily behave in a market-preserving way. Therefore, where domestic players obstruct, oppose and circumvent competition, regulatory bodies need to intervene in a market-oriented and fostering manner, and firms in turn need to push regulators when these lack the impetus, conviction and strength to do so.

In the context of a slowly liberalising regulatory framework and latently unfavourable market conditions, foreign financial firms have not yet emerged as a powerful group of commercial market actors and, notwithstanding their positive impact on market development, they have so far disappointed the hopes placed on them to become significant independent stakeholders in financial market development. As shown in the analysis, changes in financial market policies, as well as moves towards increased market liberalisation, were *not* driven by the market power or lobbying efforts of foreign financial firms, but instead can best be explained by overall changes in the domestically determined priorities of the regulators. It was argued that the trend towards more liberalisation developed in the context of changes in the overall strategy of Chinese regulators to modernise, reform and internationalise the domestic financial market and to make the largest possible use of foreign financial firms in the process. Therefore, while the actor constellation was altered, financial market development and liberalisation in China remained dominated by regulatory actors and thus was domestically determined. The future development of foreign firms' business will therefore most likely be driven by the market-development strategy of the Chinese regulators. Their business presence is likely to expand rapidly only in some business areas and only for some firms. The increasing international orientation of the domestic financial market development strategy offers new business opportunities for foreign firms where their interests and regulatory priorities converge. The domination of financial market development by regulation means that foreign financial firms will grow when and where it suits the development of the Chinese financial market in the eyes of Chinese regulators. Tentatively assessing what drives regulators in formulating domestic financial market development strategies, the analysis conducted emphasised that the allegedly most pressing problem of the Chinese financial market, the reform of the SOBs, was only one part of the story. In a broader perspective, and highlighted by the analysis of the securities industry, the complex nature of problems related to capital account liberalisation and RMB convertibility were also important.

The new actor constellation: remaining challenges

Both external market actors and domestic actors in an internationalised market environment contributed to the creation of more developed, more market-based and more internationally oriented and aligned financial markets in China. In the altered actor constellation, a creative tension between market-oriented regulators and more independent industry players started to emerge. In order to develop this tension and further promote market development, however, one more important factor has to come into full swing. This is the provision of timely, complete and accurate market information that leads to a sufficiently high degree of transparency and thus ensures the accountability of regulators and financial firms alike. A more detailed analysis of the evolving informational foundations of China's financial markets needs to be conducted in order to assess this point fully, but the principal, state-controlled provision of information and media in China, as well as the anecdotal evidence of financial market scandals based on opaqueness of information and the resulting absence of accountability, indicate that the new actor constellation remains to be complemented by new informational institutions that match higher standards of transparency. For market development to proceed in a sustainable fashion and for the creative tension between strong regulators and strong commercial actors to contribute to this in a productive way, openly available information as well as a culture of disclosure and transparency need to grow in China.

Economic impact and political implications of financial market internationalisation

There are at least two noteworthy implications of financial market internationalisation for the structure of the Chinese economy and the allocation of resources in it; firstly, internationalisation has not yet significantly altered the structure of the Chinese financial markets in the sense that, while contributing to the development of China's capital markets, internationalisation has not fostered them over-proportionally to the banking system. As shown, foreign financial firms have, in general, followed the overall reform priorities as set out by the Chinese government and have largely depended on policy changes to extend their business in China. In their regional and sectoral concentration, they have thus enhanced and reinforced the regional and sectoral centres of gravity of economic development that have also been treated favourably by Chinese developmental policies. Foreign financial firms' market participation has followed business interests, but the concentration of foreign firms in the most developed coastal areas and on wealthy customers has been reinforced through regulatory policy decisions. In a way, therefore, while adding to the new foundations of the Chinese market economy, internationalisation has also contributed to widening the already existing and growing gaps of economic development in China because it is regionally focused on the coast and, with regard to customers, focused on foreign-invested or large state-owned enterprises. New strategies to foster the participation of foreign financial firms in the opening of the Western Provinces emerged only in late 2004 and had only a limited effect up to the end of 2006.

Secondly, regarding the efficiency of resource allocation in China's economy, the impact of internationalisation has remained limited so far;

on a macroeconomic level, the implications for resource allocation and economic efficiency based on the limited relative significance of foreign firms' participation in financial transactions was small. In principle, the internationalisation of financial markets achieved what it was intended to achieve from a policy perspective; it channelled additional foreign funds into the Chinese economy and fostered and encouraged foreign and domestic businesses to engage in international trade and FDI. Promoting other large-scale effects on domestic resource allocation was not an identifiable political and regulatory priority. On a microeconomic level, the transfer of management skills and corporate governance standards contributed to improved credit decisions but this was also done only on a limited scale. The positive results that occurred seem, at least so far, to have taken place indirectly and seem to have been related more to the Damocles' sword of the expected WTO-based increase in competition after 2006. In order to significantly change the structures and institutional problems in the Chinese financial markets, though, more and deeper cooperation is still necessary. In sum, therefore, the impact of financial market internationalisation on the allocation of resources in the economy remained limited until the end of 2006.

With regard to one of the most pressing questions in the economic reform process in China, that of currency revaluation, liberalising the exchange rate system and achieving full convertibility of the RMB, financial market internationalisation increased and continues to increase incentives for a more flexible system that would also foster deeper integration with international markets. Yet, although this aspect has not been analysed in depth in this book, it can be said that restrictions on the capital account limited the process of financial market internationalisation where there were limited cross-border transactions.

On the political side, two implications stand out as important consequences of financial market internationalisation in China; firstly, internationalisation altered the process of regulatory policy-making considerably and thus had a significant impact on rule-setting and enforcement in a key sector of the Chinese economy. Secondly, internationalisation contributed to the reduction in the scope for political control over resource allocation through CCP mechanisms in what can be called the 'normal mode' of operations. With regard to the regulatory process, this book has shown that changes in the regulatory regime and the internationalisation of regulators had important implications for the process and content of rule-setting and regulatory politics in the Chinese financial markets. The increasingly international regulators and their framework of regulation led to a realignment of alternatives and choices towards international norms and standards, as well as new perceptions of both problems and possible solutions. On the operational level, regulators and commercial actors started to interact on new terms, a process that was reinforced by the changing constellation and orientation of commercial actors. As more foreign firms enter the market and financially and organisationally stronger domestic firms emerge, the bargaining position of commercial actors *vis-à-vis* regulators is being strengthened.

There are two systemically important consequences of this process with regard to the institutionalisation of the market economy in China; firstly, there is a stronger differentiation among regulators and firms and thus a stronger impetus for the development of independent commercial actors. Secondly, there is an increasingly rules-based mode of interaction between regulators and commercial actors. This implies that regulation is less discretionary and, it can be argued, that it is a process more likely to be accountable to legitimate business interests in the future. Both aspects are important preconditions for the creation of vibrant markets and the regulatory structures to support them over time.

With regard to political control over resource allocation, the willingness of domestic commercial players to cooperate on the old terms of political control and instrumentalisation decreased in the setting described above, and was seen to be likely to do so even more when domestic firms had to compete on a level playing field with transnational actors after 2006. As internationalisation – last but not least fostered by regulators – makes domestic firms more market-oriented, political interference in their business becomes less agreeable for them as it not only reduces profits but becomes a competitive disadvantage *vis-à-vis* (foreign) competitors. As a consequence, interests differentiate and diverge, and conflicts and frictions between political actors and domestic firms increase. After all, the larger organisational strength and market orientation of domestic firms enables them to oppose interference where it hurts their interests, although it might not stop them from seeking political protection where they can profit from it.

While mechanisms of party control over domestic firms, based on the nomenclature system within the CCP and organisational party structures, remain operational, they increasingly exist in parallel to new personnel structures and principles of resource allocation in day-to-day business. In addition, as discussed in this book, mechanisms of party control have become themselves increasingly weakened due to the ongoing financial market reforms; an example is the diminished role of party committees in state-owned banks. The modes of CCP control over domestic firms has thus become seriously challenged; party control needs to adapt to the new structures and needs to become more market compatible when party secretaries sit next to foreign members on the boards of Chinese banks. In addition, internationally listed financial firms face new challenges of information disclosure and transparency; this will create a setting in which party control within banks faces the day-to-day scrutiny of international investors.

In this setting, therefore, on a day-to-day level (in the 'normal mode' of Chinese politics), the ability to use financial firms for political purposes and the political control over resources decreased. Yet, in the course of this book, no indications were found that party structures in the case of crises or in exceptional moments when the stability of the system was endangered lost their effectiveness. The decreasing control was a consequence not only of financial market internationalisation but also of overall commercialisation. In total, it highlighted the relevance of financial market reforms for party control over domestic financial firms. Bearing in mind that this has been an important pillar of political power in China, it reflects the fundamental trade-off Chinese decision-makers faced in the economic reform process and the key contradiction in the current institutional order; on the one side, financial market internationalisation fosters reforms of the financial markets, and thus ensures economic stability and ultimately the ability of political leaders to act, but on the other hand, the reforms limit their ability to use markets and firms for political purposes, increase inherent contradictions and diminish the scope of action of political decision-makers. In a struggle to reform China's banks, the CCP is depriving itself of power, a process that on a larger scale has no historical precedent and that other transition countries have only accomplished after or through political transition. Internationalisation thus highlights the fundamental contradictions in China's financial markets due to the political control over them. It emphasises both the challenges financial market internationalisation poses for CCP rule and the limits posed for further market development if these challenges are not adequately met. In so far as the CCP is or is not able to solve the fundamental conflicts over the principles of resource allocation, further liberalisation, internationalisation and market development is dependent upon political reforms.

Explaining financial market development

Financial market internationalisation in China in this book has been approached as a case study for financial market development in a transition country. From it, some conclusions can be drawn about theories of financial market development and the transition to a market economy. With regard to transition theory, the findings of this book have stressed the need for independent financial firms in the process of financial market development as well as the problems that emerged in China due to the lack of these firms. The book has shown that regulators set incentives in the process of market development, but that financial firms and intermediaries also responded in their own ways to the incentives and constraints created and structured by market opportunities and operational problems. In order for vibrant and stable financial markets to emerge, therefore, regulators and commercial actors have to interact in a creative tension, to the development of which internationalisation contributes.

Comparing these findings with the broader recent literature on regulation in international financial markets, two aspects stand out; firstly, the approach of other studies that have mainly focused on comparing regulation of developed markets, such as Czada and Lütz (2000) and Lütz (2003), is based on a broad definition of regulation highlighting the all-encompassing nature of regulation for market development. While this approach allows a demonstration of the contributions and roles of different actors in the process of rule-setting for markets, this case study has shown that in the transition context a *differentiation* between the process of rule-setting and spontaneous and uncontrolled market development based on commercially determined decisions of industry players is a helpful analytical tool. It allows one to highlight that, particularly in economic transition, regulation is not sufficient for vibrant markets to emerge. Secondly, related to this point, this book has shown that the *interaction* between regulatory and market actors in this regard is an important component. The emergence of independent commercial market actors is a key element of economic transition and the development of financial markets. Commercial actors therefore have to be separated analytically from regulatory actors, notwithstanding the fact that they will not only engage in market behaviour but also try to influence the rules of the market through lobbying. This is not to recommend a shift of the focus away from processes of rule-setting in market development but instead to call for a complementary analysis of industry players' role in the process, both in developed and emerging market economies and with regard to both their lobbying and market conduct.

With regard to theories of financial market development, this book has shown that informal institutions, as the ultimate basis of financial markets, are an important part of market development that can not easily be altered by regulatory decrees. It takes time to foster informal institutional change and there is no way of implanting or importing new informal institutions. Nor can they be built in a top-down manner. From a policy perspective, this has important implications, and some of the mistakes in past financial market reforms could have been avoided if informal institutions had been taken into account, especially in some premature financial liberalisation policies in other transition countries. Well-considered policies on internationalisation, however, as this book has emphasised, can have a fostering effect on informal institutional change through increased interaction and international exchange both on the side of regulators and of commercial actors. Yet, keeping in mind the time needed for institutional change, policy-makers are right to let internationalisation progress slowly.

On the whole, the theoretical approach of this book has thus allowed a highlight on the deep structure of institutional change, the redefinition of state and economic actors in the process of economic transition to a market economy, and the limits to creating markets through regulation during transition. Unlike the conventional wisdom of neo-institutional theory, it has shown that state-owned actors can be key in fostering institutional change. With regard to further research, this book calls for more investigation of the best ways to guide the presence of foreign financial firms in EMEs, in order to avoid detrimental effects and best foster their positive structural contributions. More in-depth comparative studies in transition countries and other large EMEs would be helpful in developing the findings further. With regard to the analysis of institutional change in China's transition to a market economy, this book has highlighted the interrelation of political and economic change. It has shown that financial markets are a major pillar of the Chinese political system and that their reform and development thus have strong political implications. It has pointed out that the political system increasingly needs to respond to economic processes, and has questioned the compatibility of post-Leninist political structures with an open market economy. In order to understand the relation and interaction between changing party power and regulatory as well as state-owned commercial actors more deeply, further research is needed.

This book has also contributed to the analysis of the role international forces and transnational actors have played in the Chinese reform process and has shown that domestic and international processes have to be analysed together because they are interrelated and complementary. Further research is needed on the question of whether an authoritarian state can open its economy to international actors without undergoing fundamental political change. Further research is also needed on the emergence of the regulatory regime in China's financial markets, in itself and also in comparison to the regulation of other economic sectors, in order to understand better the emerging market order *and* its likely impact on the political system.

In contrast to other studies, this book has also shown that a more differentiated approach towards state-owned firms as commercial actors in the transition process is needed; commercial actors are powerful in shaping the structures and rules of markets in China. They have a considerable role in and impact on the political system. Lobbying is an important driving force shaping markets in China. It is likely to gain even more importance as decreasing control over resource allocation will allow all actors to redefine their interests.

Future perspectives of financial market internationalisation in China

Major challenges still lie ahead in financial market reform in China. Political leaders face tough choices. Many experts argue that new non-performing loans will emerge in the future, as a result of the breakneck speed of credit growth during past years of reforms. Financial market reform will also very likely have to take place in a more complex overall economic framework that increasingly needs to respond to social and environment concerns. What are the perspectives for further financial market internationalisation in China in this situation? Three scenarios seem possible.

Scenario 1: Restricted internationalisation

In this scenario, internationalisation would continue on a safe but restricted level. Regulators would choose to balance further market opening closely with the evolving success of ongoing reforms in the domestic financial markets. Internationalisation thus would remain subordinated to domestic political priorities. Foreign firms' market access would be further opened as predetermined by WTO commitments, but possibly slowed down by informal non-tariff barriers. Processes of financial market internationalisation outside the WTO entry commitments, such as investments of Qualified Foreign Institutional Investors in the domestic securities markets or foreign strategic investments in domestic financial firms, would be slowed down. Foreign financial firms would continue to play a positive but limited role. Assuming other factors remain stable, in this 'no-change' scenario China could enjoy continued albeit slowed growth even with limited further reforms in the financial markets. However, structural problems and inefficiencies would aggravate mid- to long-term dangers in the financial markets, depending on the success of domestic financial market reform. Good management of the process could postpone severe implications for another five to ten years.

Scenario 2: Destabilising internationalisation

In this scenario, financial market internationalisation would be speeded up considerably, allowing wide access to foreign financial firms and possibly also capital account liberalisation. Rapid international participation in the Chinese securities markets would lead to destabilising effects in parallel to increased domestic hiccups and distortions, as would the forceful restructuring of some large domestic financial firms in which the largest foreign players would possibly buy (majority) shares. Rapid parallel reform of the SOE sector would create less favourable economic conditions, leading to rising unemployment, unrest and dissatisfaction. The resulting instability would likely deter some foreign financial firms from market participation. Problems of single large foreign financial firms in the Chinese market could lead to a media-intensive market exit of a leading financial firm. Alternatively, domestic banks might not be able to cope with the competitive pressure and could only be saved by large-scale state intervention. In this worst-case scenario, reforms go wrong, remain ineffective or prove to be too slow. The Chinese government could lose control over the process and its capability to act, before new mechanisms of control and governance are fully established and operational. This would have severe detrimental implications for both the Chinese and the world economy.

Scenario 3: Internationalisation and genuine financial market reform

In this best-case scenario, reforms would proceed slowly but successfully in a comprehensive manner. Essential problems such as the corporate governance of domestic financial firms would be successfully tackled, and political consensus would lead to the end of close state-enterprise-bank relations, using the international market participants who offer their help and effectively contribute to genuine financial market reform. Chinese banks would adapt to their challenges and foreign financial firms would enter the market in a fostering way, increasing their market share while cooperating closely with Chinese partners. There would be a gradual but decisive process of transferring control over economic resources away from the CCP, and domestic banks would operate increasingly on a commercial basis. Reforms of the social security system would allow for genuine restructuring of the SOE sector. In this scenario, resources would be increasingly allocated by market mechanisms, while redistribution would be executed mainly through transfer payments financed by an appropriate tax system. The Chinese economy overall could benefit from more efficient resource allocation, leading to high and sustainable growth rates that would compensate for the pains of adaptation. China's growth could contribute to a new boom in the world economy.

Arguably, the future process of financial market internationalisation will be positioned somewhere between scenarios one and three. There are no indications so far of a destabilising internationalisation. Most importantly, the scenarios show that, external factors remaining stable, the process of further internationalisation of China's financial markets will primarily be defined by political and regulatory choices that are also an important factor in determining whether more active internationalisation in the future will occur (Scenario 3) or whether it will stagnate and further accumulate risks in the domestic financial markets (Scenario 1). After all, this has been a main finding throughout the analysis of this book – financial market internationalisation in China is primarily driven by regulatory decisions.

Additionally, the role that international players are likely to have in the process will be determined by the outcome of financial market reform after 2004. So far, the reforms up to 2006 and onwards grew increasingly comprehensive and deep. So far, they have been the most comprehensive and deepest reform efforts in the Chinese financial markets and, as shown in this book, they actively utilise foreign market players' support. Regulators are capable and determined, and there are good overall (macro-) economic conditions for both successful reform and progressive internationalisation. The potential mutual benefit will create incentives both for international firms and for regulators. While the risks of conflicts and loss of control thus remain considerable, economically the reforms are bound to succeed. However, it has also been shown in this book that the principles of resource allocation lie at the heart of the political system in China and that further market-oriented reforms depend on changes in the way in which and the extent to which the CCP exerts control over allocation. This book suggests that, based on the incentive structures already altered by marketisation and internationalisation, there is a fair chance of a gradual and comparatively smooth transformation in this regard, if internal conflicts within the CCP can be minimised and if current favourable external conditions continue.

Interviews

Interview Number	Type of organisation or project the interviewee worked for	Date	Location
1	Domestic securities firm	October 2003	Shanghai
2	Insurance JV	October 2003	Shanghai
3	Academic institution	October 2003	Shanghai
4	Foreign bank	October 2003	Shanghai
5	Foreign bank	October 2003	Shanghai
6	Chamber of Commerce	October 2003	Shanghai
7	Foreign bank	October 2003	Shanghai
8	Domestic securities firm	October 2003	Shanghai
9	Fund management JV	October 2003	Shanghai
10	Academic institution	October 2003	Shanghai
11	Academic institution	October 2003	Shanghai
12	Chamber of Commerce	October 2003	Shanghai
13	Foreign securities firm	October 2003	Shanghai
14	Foreign bank	October 2003	Shanghai
15	Securities JV	October 2003	Shanghai
16	Fund management JV	October 2003	Shanghai
17	Domestic securities firm	October 2003	Shanghai
18	Foreign bank	October 2003	Shanghai
19	Foreign insurance company	October 2003	Shanghai
20	Chamber of Commerce	October 2003	Shanghai
21	Foreign bank	October 2003	Shanghai
22	Domestic securities firm	November 2003	Shanghai
23	Embassy	November 2003	Shanghai
24	Domestic bank	November 2003	Shanghai
25	Fund management JV	November 2003	Shanghai
26	Insurance JV	November 2003	Shanghai
27	Development cooperation	November 2003	Beijing
28	Development cooperation	November 2003	Beijing
29	Embassy	November 2003	Beijing
30	Development cooperation	November 2003	Beijing
31	Foreign bank	November 2003	Beijing
32	Academic institution	November 2003	Beijing
33	Foreign bank	November 2003	Beijing
34	Development cooperation	November 2003	Beijing
35	Development cooperation	November 2003	Beijing
36	Foreign bank	November 2003	Shanghai
37	Foreign insurance company	November 2003	Shanghai

(Continued)

Interview Number	Type of organisation or project the interviewee worked for	Date	Location
38	Domestic bank	November 2003	Shanghai
39	Foreign bank	November 2003	Shanghai
40	VC fund management company	November 2003	Shanghai
41	Stock exchange	November 2003	Shanghai
42	VC fund management company	November 2003	Shanghai
43	Foreign bank	November 2003	Shanghai
44	VC fund management company	November 2003	Shanghai
45	Fund management JV	November 2003	Shanghai
46	VC fund management company	November 2003	Shanghai
47	Domestic securities company	November 2003	Shanghai
48	Securities JV	November 2003	Shanghai
49	Consultancy	November 2003	Shanghai
50	Regulatory institution	June 2004	Beijing
51	Regulatory institution	June 2004	Beijing
52	Regulatory institution	June 2004	Beijing
53	Regulatory institution	June 2004	Beijing
54	Foreign insurance company	June 2004	Beijing
55	Domestic security company	June 2004	Beijing
56	Asset management company	June 2004	Beijing
57	Regulatory institution	June 2004	Beijing
58	Regulatory institution	June 2004	Beijing
59	Media	June 2004	Beijing
60	Media	June 2004	Beijing
61	Domestic fund management company	July 2004	Shanghai
62	Regulatory institution	July 2004	Shanghai
63	Academic institution	July 2004	Shanghai
64	Domestic securities firm	July 2004	Shanghai
65	Academic institution	July 2004	Shanghai
66	Foreign bank	July 2004	Beijing
67	Securities JV	July 2004	Beijing
68	Regulatory institution	July 2004	Beijing
69	Foreign bank	August 2004	via Telephone
70	Academic institution	August 2004	via Telephone
71	Foreign insurance company	August 2004	via Telephone
72	Investment bank	September 2004	London
73	Foreign bank	September 2004	London
74	Research institution	September 2004	London

In addition, 40 interviews were conducted during a long-term research fellowship from April 2005 to June 2006 at the Institute of World Economics and Politics (IWEP), Beijing.

Chinese Laws and Regulations

Beijing Municipal Government/*Beijing Shicheng Zhengfu*

8 December 2000 *Regulations on Zhongguancun Science and Technology Zone*
2 February 2001 *Regulatory Measures on the Registration of Enterprises in Zhongguancun Science and Technology Zone*
21 February 2001 *Regulatory Measures on Limited Partnerships*

China Banking Regulatory Commission/China Securities Regulatory Commission/*Zhongguo Yinhangye Jiandu Guanli Weiyuanhui he Zhongguo Zhengquan Jiandu Guanli Weiyuanhui*

31 December 2003 *Administrative Measures on Overseas Financial Firms Investment in Financial Firms with Chinese Capital*
16 August 2004 *Provisional Measures on Money Market Fund Management*

China Banking Regulatory Commission/*Zhongguo Yinhangye Jiandu Guanli Weiyuanhui* (www.cbrc.gov.cn)

1998 *Administrative Rules for Automotive Consumer Loans*
3 October 2003 *Qiche jinrong gongsi guanli banfa (Administration Rules for Automobile Financing Companies)* Yinjianling 2003, No 4
31 July 2003 *Implementing Rule for the Administrative Measures on Foreign Invested Insurance Companies*
2004 *Administrative Rules for Automotive Loans*
1 March 2004 *Regulation Governing Capital Adequacy of Commercial Banks*
25 July 2004 *Guidelines on Commercial Banks Due Diligence in Credit Business*
26 July 2004 *Zhonghua renmin gongheguo waizijinrongjigou guanli tiaoli shishi xize (Detailed Rules on the Administration of Foreign Invested Financial Institutions)*
2005 *Guidelines on Market Risk Management of Commercial Banks*
February 2005 *Administrative Rules for Pilot Incorporation of Fund Management Companies by Commercial Banks,* The People's Bank of China, China Banking Regulatory Commission and China Securities Regulatory Commission Announcement No. 4

China Securities Regulation Commission/People's Bank of China/*Zhongguo Zhengquan Jiandu Guanli Weiyuanhui he Zhongguo renmin yinhang* (www.csrc.gov.cn)

1 July 2002 *Rules for the Establishment of Foreign-shared Securities Companies*

1 July 2002 *Rules on the Establishment of Foreign-shared Fund Management Companies*

1 March 2002 *Zhengquan gongsi guanli banfa* (*Administration Method for Securities Firms*). Decree No. 5

5 November 2002 *Provisional Measures on Domestic Securities Investments of Qualified Foreign Institutional Investors*

15 December 2003 *Guanyu jiaqiang zhengquan gongsi neibu kongzhi ruogan cuoshi de yijian* (*Notice on Strenghtening Mechanisms for Internal Control of Securities Firms*)

15 December 2003 *Zhengquan gongsi neibu kongzhi zhiyin* (*Guidance on the Internal Risk Control of Securities Firms*). CSRC No. 260

29 December 2003 *Zhenggquan gongsi zhili zhunze* (*Corporate Governance Code for Securities Firms*)

6 January 2004 *Securities Investment Fund Law*

1 March 2004 *Interim Rules on Derivatives Business of Financial Firms*

8 June 2004 *Information Disclosure Rules on Securities Investment Funds*

16 September 2004 *Measures for the Administration of Securities Investment Fund Management Companies*

23 September 2004 *Zhengquan gongsi gaoji guanlirenyuan renzhi zige guanli shenhe chengxu* (*Supervision Measures for Qualified High-Ranking Staff of Securities Firms*)

26 October 2004 *Zhengquan gongsi gaoji guanlirenyuan guanli fangfa* (*Administrative Method on High-Ranking Personnel of Securities Firms*)

Ministry of Finance/*Caizhengbu*

1985 *Accounting System for Sino-Foreign Joint Ventures*

1992 *Basic Accounting Standard*

1993 *Certified Public Accountants Law*

1995 *Generally Accepted Accounting Standards*

1996 *Notice on the Permission for International Accounting Firms Developing Several Member Firms in China*

1996 *Tentative Regulation of the Administration of Sino-foreign Co-operative Accounting Firms*

MOFTEC, MOST, SAIC, SAT and SAFE

30 January 2003 *Rules on the Administration of Foreign Invested Venture Capital Investment Enterprises*

National People's Congress/*Daibiaohui*

29 December 1993 *Company Law of the People's Republic of China. Adopted at the Fifth session of the Standing Committee of the Eighth National People's Congress on December 29, 1993*

29 December 1993 *Accounting Law of the People's Republic of China Originally Adopted at the Ninth Meeting of the Standing Committee of the Sixth National People's Congress on January 21, 1985, Amended at the Fifth Session of the Standing Committee of the Eighth National People's Congress on December 29, 1993*

29 December 1998 *Securities Law of the People's Republic of China, Order of the President of the People's Republic of China No 12, adopted at the 6th Meeting of the Standing Committee of the Ninth National People's Congress of the People's Republic of China on December 29, 1998*

27 December 2003 *Zhonghua renmin gongheguo shangye yinhang fa* (*Law of the People's Republic of China on Commercial Banks*)

27 December 2003 *Zhonghua renmin gongheguo zhongguo renmin yinhang fa* (*Law of the People's Republic of China on the People's Bank of China*)

1 February 2004 *Zhonghua renmin gongheguo yinhangye jiandu guanli fa* (*Law of the People's Republic of China on Banking Regulation and Supervision*)

People's Bank of China/ChinaBanking Regulatory Commission/*Zhongguo Renmin Yinhang he Zhongguo Yinhangye Jiandu Guanli Weiyuanhui*

17 May 2004 *Jingnei waizi yinhang waizai guanli banfa* (*Rule on the Foreign Debt of Foreign Banks in China*) Decree No. 9

People's Bank of China/*Zhongguo Renmin Yinhang* (www.pbc.com)

17 June 1987 *Guanyu jingji tequ waizi yinhang, zhongwai hezi yinhang yewu guanlide ruogan zanxing* (*Guiding Interim Rules on Foreign Banks and Sino-Foreign Cooperation Banks in Special Economic Zones*)

30 April 1996 *Zhonghua renmin gongheguo waizijinrongjigou guanli tiaoli shishi xize* (*Detailed Rules on the Administration of Foreign Invested Financial Institutions*)

2 December 1996 *Shanghai Pudong waizi jinrong jigou jiying renminbi yewu shidian zhixing guanlibanfa (Experimental Rules on the RMB Business of Foreign Financial Institutions in Pudong)*

28 April 1998 *General Office of the People's Bank of China's Approval of Certain Foreign Banks to Participate in National Inter-bank Borrowing*

9 November 2000 *Shangye yinhang biaowa yewu fengxian guanli zhiyin (Guidance on the Risk Management of Commercial Banks' Off-Balance-Sheet Services)*

20 August 2001 *Guidance on the Supervision of Overseas Firms of Commercial Banks*

29 January 2002 *Zhonghua renmin gongheguo waizi jinrong jigou guanli tiaoli shishi xize (Detailed Rules on the Administration of Foreign Invested Financial Institutions)*

27 June 2002 *Waizi jinrongjigou zhu hua daibiao jigou guanli banfa (Rules on the Establishment of Representative Offices of Foreign Financial Institutions)*

18 September 2002 *Shangye yinhang neibu kongzhi zhiyin (Guidance for Internal Control of Commercial Banks)*

26 November 2002 *Draft Interim Measures on the Administration of RMB Interbank Loans*

State Administration of Foreign Exchange (SAFE)/*Guojia waihui guanlibu*

21 June 2004 *Guojia waihui guanlibu guanyu jingneiwaizi yinhang waizhai guanli banfa' youguan wenti de tongzhi (Notice of the State Administration of Foreign Exchange on the Foreign Debt of Foreign Banks in China)*

Shanghai Municipal Government/*Shanghai Shicheng Zhengfu*

5 May 2001 *Several Provisions for Promoting the Development of Zhangjiang High-Tech Park*

Shenzhen Municipal Government/*Shenzhen Shicheng Zhengfu*

Tentative Provisions on Venture Capital Invested in High- and New-technology Enterprises

Standing Committee of the National People's Congress/*Daibiaohui*

26 April 2003 *Quanguo renmin daibiaohui changwu weiyuanhui guanyu zhongguo yinhangye jiandu guanli weiyuanhui lüxing yuanyou zhongguo renmin yinhang lüxing de jiandu guanli zhize de jueding (Decision of the Standing Committee of the National People's Congress on Exerting Supervisory Responsibilities by the China Banking Regulatory Commission, which Formerly Were Exerted by the People's Bank of China)*

1995 *Zhonghua renmin gongheguo shangye yinhangfa* (*Commercial Banking Law of the People's Republic of China*)

State Council/*Guowuyuan*

2 April 1985 *Zhonghua renmin gong heguo jingji tequ waiziyinhang zhongwai hezi guanli tiaoli* (*Regulations of the People's Republic of China on Foreign Banks and Chinese-foreign Cooperation Banks in Special Economic Zones*)

30 September 1998 *Zhongguo zhengquan jiandu guanli weiyuanhui zhineng peizhi, neishe jigou he renyuan bianzhi jueding* (*Decisions on Functions, Inner Structure and Manning Level of the China Securities Regulatory Commission*)

14 November 1998 *Guowuyuan guanyu chengli zhongguo baoxian jiandu guanli weiyuanhui de tongzhi* (*Circular of the State Council about the Establishment of the China Insurance Regulatory Commission*)

20 December 2001 *Zhonghua renmin gonghequo waizi jinrongjigou guanli tiaoli* (*Regulations on the Administration of Foreign Financial Firms*) Decree of the State Council No. 340

Zhuhai Regional Government/*Zhuhai Shicheng Zhengfu*

7 June 2001 *Provisions on Technology Venture Capital Investment*

References

ACFB (1990) *Zhongguo jinrong nianjian (Almanac of China's Finance and Banking)* (Beijing: Zhongguo jinrong chubanshe).

ACFB (2003) *Zhongguo jinrong nianjian (Almanac of China's Finance and Banking)* (Beijing: Zhongguo jinrong chubanshe).

Achhorner, Thomas et al. (2006) *Banking on China* (Boston: Boston Consulting Group).

AmCham (n.d.) American Chamber of Commerce in China at: www.amcham-china.org.cn

AmCham (2003a) *WTO Implementation Report* (Beijing: American Chamber of Commerce in China).

AmCham (2003b) *White Paper: Insurance* (Beijing: American Chamber of Commerce in China).

AmCham (2003c) *White Paper: Banking* (Beijing: American Chamber of Commerce in China)

AmCham (2004a) *AmCham White Paper* (Beijing: American Chamber of Commerce in China).

AmCham (2004b) *AmCham-China Hosts Luncheon Featuring the Chairman of CBRC*, American Chamber of Commerce in China at: www. amcham-china. org.cn/amcham/show/news.php?Id=48&menuid=04&submid=01, accessed 28 March 2008.

AmCham (2004c) *White Paper: Securities* (Beijing: American Chamber of Commerce in China).

AmCham (2007) *White Paper: American Business in China* (Beijing: American Chamber of Commerce in China).

Bank of East Asia (2004) *Banking Reform in the Mainland* (Hong Kong: Bank of East Asia Economic Research Department).

Basel Committee on Banking Supervision (1996) *Amendment to the Basel Capital Accord to Incorporate Market Risk* (Basel: Bank for International Settlements, at: www.bis.org/publ/bcbs24.htm, accessed 28 March 2008).

Basel Committee on Banking Supervision (1997) *Core Principles for Effective Banking Supervision* (Basel: Bank for International Settlements, at: www.bis.org/publ/bcbs30a.pdf, accessed 28 March 2008).

Basel Committee on Banking Supervision (1999) *Enhancing Corporate Governance for Banking Organisations* (Basel: Bank for International Settlements, at: www.bis.org/publ/bcbs56.htm, accessed 28 March 2008).

Basel Committee on Banking Supervision (2000) *Electronic Banking Group Initiatives and White Papers* (Basel: Bank for International Settlements, at: www.bis.org/publ/bcbs76.htm, accessed 28 March 2008).

Basel Committee on Banking Supervision (2003) *Risk Management Principles for Electronic Banking* (Basel: Bank for International Settlements, at: www.bis.org/publ/bcbs98.htm, accessed 28 March 2008).

Basel Committee on Banking Supervision, IOSCO and IAIS (1999) *Supervision of Financial Conglomerates* (Basel: Bank for International Settlements, at: www.bis.org/publ/bcbs47.pdf, accessed 28 March 2008).

Basel Committee on Banking Supervision and IOSCO TC (1998) *Supervisory Information Framework for Derivatives and Trading Activities. Joint Report by the Basel Committee on Banking Supervision and the Technical Committee of the IOSCO* (Basel: Bank for International Settlements, at: www.bis.org/publ/bcbs39.htm, accessed 28 March 2008).

Behrends, Susanne (2001) *Neue Politische Ökonomie* (Munich: Verlag Franz Vahlen).

Bei, Hu (2003) 'Five Banks Win Status as QFII Custodians', *South China Morning Post*, Hong Kong, 1 March.

Bei, Hu (2004a) 'BOC Takes Hammer to Rice Bowl: A Drastic Overhaul Will See 222,000 Staff Re-apply For Their Positions as Civil Service Structure Vanishes', *South China Morning Post*, Hong Kong, 1 October.

Bei, Hu (2004b) 'Party's Influence Waning at Banks', *South China Morning Post*, Hong Kong, 2 December.

Beijing Review (2003) 'Who Is More Competent?' *Beijing Review*, 26 June, pp. 44–6.

Beim, David O. and Charles W. Calomiris (2001) *Emerging Financial Markets* (New York: McGraw-Hill/Irwin).

BIS (1999) *Strengthening the Banking System in China: Issues and Experiences* (Basel: Bank for International Settlements, Monetary and Economic Department).

Bolland, Connie (2004) *Sino-foreign Joint Ventures in Fund Management: It Takes Two to Tango* (Economist Corporate Network, *The Economist*, Hong Kong).

Bonin, John P. and Yiping Huang (2002) 'Foreign Entry into Chinese Banking: Does WTO Membership Threaten Domestic Banks?' *The World Economy*, 25, pp. 1077–93.

Bonin, John P., K. Mizsei, I. P. Szekely and P. Wachtel (1998) *Banking in Transition Economies: Developing Market Oriented Banking Sectors in Eastern Europe* (Cheltenham: Edward Elgar).

Bowles, Paul and Gordon White (1992) 'The Dilemmas of Market Socialism: Capital Market Reform in China – Part 1: Bonds.' *The Journal of Development Studies*, 28: 3, pp. 363–85.

Bowles, Paul and Gordon White (1993) *The Political Economy of China's Financial Reforms: Finance in Late Development* (Boulder, Oxford: Westview Press).

Brehm, Stefan and Christian Macht (2004) 'Implementing Global Standards in the People's Republic of China: The Case of Banking Supervision.' Conference paper presented at Graduate Seminar on China, CUHK, Hong Kong.

Brødsgaard, Kjeld Erik and Yongnian Zheng (eds) (2004) *Bringing the Party Back In: How China is Governed* (Singapore: Eastern University Press).

Burns, John P. (1994) 'Strengthening Central CCP Control of Leadership Selection: The 1990 Nomenklatura.' *China Quarterly*, 138, pp. 458–91.

Byrd, William (1983) *China's Financial System: The Changing Role of Banks* (Boulder: Westview Press).

Caijing (2002) 'Haier Enters the Financial Services Sector.' *Caijing*, 5 February, at: www.chinaonline.com/caijing, accessed 13 March 2003.

Caprio, G., Jonathan Fiechter, Robert E. Litan and Michael Pomerleano (2004) 'The Future of State-Owned Financial Institutions.' Paper presented at The Future of State-Owned Financial Institutions conference, Washington DC, at: www.brookings.edu/comm/conferencereport/cr18.htm, accessed 12 March 2005.

Carmichael, Jeffrey (1999) 'The Framework for Financial Supervision: Macro and Micro Issues', in: BIS (ed.) *Strengthening the Banking System in China: Issues and Experiences* (Basel: Bank for International Settlements, Monetary and Economic Department).

Carmichael, Jeffrey and Michael Pomerleano (2002) *The Development and Regulation of Non-Bank Financial Institutions* (Washington: World Bank).

Carrasco, Bruno (2003) *Challenges in Monetary Policy*, China Special (Frankfurt am Main: Deutsche Bank Research).

CBRC (2003a) 'Answers of a CBRC Official to Questions Raised by the Press Concerning the Promulgation of the Administrative Rules Governing Auto Financing Company', China Banking Regulatory Commission, 4 October, at: www.cbrc.gov.cn/english/module/viewinfo.jsp?infoID=476, accessed 15 March 2004.

CBRC (2003b) 'Council of International Advisers To Be Set Up in the China Banking Regulatory Commission', China Banking Regulatory Commission, 23 May, at: www.cbrc.gov.cn/english/module/viewinfo.jsp?infoID=464, accessed 17 November 2004.

CBRC (2003c) 'The Responses to the Press by the Senior Official of the China Banking Regulatory Commission on Issues Relating to the New Capital Accord', China Banking Regulatory Commission, 14 August, at: www.cbrc.gov.cn/english/module/viewinfo.jsp?infoID=468, accessed 13 May 2004.

CBRC (2004a) 'Chairman Liu Mingkang Answers the Questions Raised by the Press with Respect to Credit Growth', China Banking Regulatory Commission, 23 June, at: www.cbrc.gov.cn/english/module/viewinfo.jsp?infoID=720

CBRC (2004b) 'China's Banking Sector Marches a New Step. Material for the Press Conference of the State Council Information Office', China Banking Regulatory Commission, 1 December, at: www.cbrc.gov.cn/english/module/viewinfo.jsp?infoID=1022, accessed 12 January 2005.

CBRC (2004c) 'Guidelines on Corporate Governance Reforms and Supervision of Bank of China and Construction Bank of China', China Banking Regulatory Commission, 3 November, at: www.cbrc.gov.cn/english/module/viewinfo.jsp?infoID=560, accessed 15 April 2005.

CBRC (2004d) 'Senior Official of the China Banking Regulatory Commission (CBRC) Speaking to the Press on the Newly Issued Regulation Governing Capital Adequacy of Commercial Banks', China Banking Regulatory Commission, 27 February, at: www.cbrc.gov.cn/english/module/viewinfo.jsp?infoID=506, accessed 14 May 2005.

CBRC (2004e) 'The CBRC Promulgated Guidelines on Commercial Banks' Due Diligence in Credit Business', China Banking Regulatory Commission, 25 July, at: www.cbrc.gov.cn/english/module/viewinfo.jsp?infoID=792, accessed 15 February 2005).

CBRC (2004f) 'The CBRC Spokesperson Dismissed the Rumors of Ordering a Stop to Loan Extension', China Banking Regulatory Commission, 29 April, at: www.cbrc.gov.cn/english/module/viewinfo.jsp?infoID=568, accessed 15 May 2004.

CBRC (2005a) 'The CBRC promulgated the Guidelines for Development of Banking Associations', China Banking Regulatory Commission, 2 February, at: www.cbrc.gov.cn/english/module/viewinfo.jsp?infoID=1206, accessed 5 February 2005.

CBRC (2005b) 'The CBRC Senior Official Spoke to the Press on the Newly Issued Guidelines on Market Risk Management of Commercial Banks', China Banking Regulatory Commission, 7 January, at: www. cbrc.gov.cn/english/module/viewinfo.jsp?infoID=1128, accessed 15 February 2005.

CBRC (2006) *Quarterly Statistical Bulletin* (Beijing: China Banking Regulatory Commission).

CBRC (2007) *Report on the Opening of the Chinese Banking Sector* (Beijing: China Banking Regulatory Commission).

Chan-Lee, James, Li-Gang Liu and Masaru Yoshitomi (2002) *Policy Proposals for Sequencing the PRC's Domestic and External Financial Liberalization*, Asian Policy Forum/Asian Development Bank Institute (APF Secretariat), at www.adbi.org/apf_main.html, accessed 28 May 2008.

Chen, Ji and Steve Thomas (2001) 'The Role of Foreign Insurance Companies in China's Emerging Insurance Industry: An FDI Case Study', paper presented at the Financial Sector Reform in China Conference, Harvard University.

Chen, Yao (2004) 'Int'l Banks Share RMB Profits', *China Business Weekly*, 27 July, p. 3, at: www2.chinadaily.com.cn/english/doc/2004-07/27/content_352589. htm, accessed 28 May 2008.

Chen, Zhenzhen (2004) 'China's Watchdog Agencies Need Watchdogs', *Asia Times Online*, 13 August, at: www.atimes.com/atimes/China/FH13Ad02.html, accessed 28 May 2008.

Cheong, Simon (2003) *Acquiring Strategic Stakes in Chinese Banks* (Beijing: Freshfields Bruckhaus Deringer, at: www.freshfields.com/practice/corporate/publications/pdfs/6219.pdf, accessed 13 January 2004).

China Business Weekly (2004) 'QDII Programme To Be Tested.' *China Business Weekly*, 20 June, at: www.chinadaily.com.cn/english/doc/2004-06/20/content_340910.htm, accessed 28 March 2008.

China Daily (2003) 'Draft Law Addresses Bank Supervision, Management', 23 August, at: www.china.org.cn/english/BAT/73069.htm, accessed 28 March 2008.

China Daily (2004a) 'Foreign Early Birds Move into Securities', 5 April, at: http://english.peopledaily.com.cn/200404/05/print20040405_139477.html, accessed 28 March 2008.

China Daily (2004b) 'Newbridge Wins Control of Shenzhen Bank', *China Daily*, Hong Kong Edition, 1 June, p. 15. www.chinadaily.com.cn/english/doc/2004-06/01/content_335396.htm, accessed 10 April 2008.

China Daily (2004c) 'T-bonds Hot among Foreign Banks', 2 June, at: www.chinadaily.com.cn/english/doc/2004-06/02/content_335810.htm, accessed 10 April 2008.

China Daily (2004d) 'China's Banks Should Learn to Say "No"', *China Business Weekly*, 28 June, at: www.chinadaily.com.cn/english/doc/2004-06/28/content_343524.htm, accessed 28 March 2008.

China Daily (2004e) 'China's Stocks Plunge to Five-year Low', 9 September, at: www.chinadaily.com.cn/english/doc/2004-09/09/content_373208.htm, accessed 28 March 2008.

China Daily (2004f) 'HSBC to Launch More Branches', 27 November, at: www.china.org.cn/english/BAT/113367.htm, accessed 28 March 2008.

China Daily (2004g) 'Barclays Bank Gets US$75m QFII Quota', 27 October, at: www.chinadaily.com.cn/english/doc/2004-10/27/content386175.htm, accessed 10 April 2008

China Economic Net (2004) 'Bank of China to Get Strategic Investors', 24 September, at: http://chinastudygroup.org/index.php?action=news&type=view&id=7163, accessed 2 February 2005.

China Minsheng Bank (2007) website at: www.cmbc.com.cn/index_en.shtml

ChinaOnline (2004) 'Wen on Banking Reform', 15 March, at: www.chinaonline.com:80/printfriendly.asp, accessed 17 March 2004.

Chuan, Yu (2004) 'China's Door Now Wide Open for Foreign Banks', 5 August, at: www.chinadaily.com.cn/english/doc/2004-08/05/content_359298.htm, accessed 28 March 2008.

CIEC (2000) *CIEC Industry Report*, Internet Securities, Inc, at: http://site.securities.com/doc.html?pc=CN&print=1&prev_doc_ids=CN13536417, accessed 17 September 2004.

Claessens, Stijn, Asli Demirgüç-Kunt and Harry Huizinga (2001) 'How Does Foreign Entry Affect Domestic Banking Markets?' *Journal of Banking and Finance*, 25: 5, pp. 891–911.

Claessens, Stijn and Tom Glaessner (1998) *Internationalization of Financial Services in Asia*. (Washington: World Bank, at: http://papers.ssrn.com/sol3/papers.cfm?abstract_id=620515, accessed 28 March 2008.

Coase, Ronald H. (1937) 'The Nature of the Firm', *Economica*, 4, pp. 386–405.

Coleman, William D. (1990) 'The Banking Policy Community and Financial Change', in William D. Coleman and Grace Skogstad (eds) *Policy Communities and Public Policy in Canada* (Toronto: Copp Clark Pitman) pp. 91–117.

Cowles, Maria and Thomas Risse (2001) 'Transforming Europe. Conclusions', in Maria Cowles, James Caporaso and Thomas Risse (eds) *Transforming Europe. Europeanization and Domestic Change* (Ithaca: Cornell University Press), pp. 217–37.

Crystal, Jennifer B., B. Gerard Dages and Linda Goldberg (2001) *Does Foreign Ownership Contribute to Sounder Banks in Emerging Markets? The Latin American Experience*, Staff Reports, No 137 (New York: Federal Reserve Bank of New York, at: www.newyorkfed.org/research/staff_reports/sr137.pdf, accessed 28 March 2008).

CSRC (2001) *An Introduction to Overseas Listings* (Beijing: China Securities Regulatory Commission, at: www.csrc.gov.cn/CSRCSite/eng/eol/eolintr.htm, accessed 13 February 2003).

CSRC (2004a) *China's Securities and Futures Markets* (Beijing: China Securities Regulatory Commission, at: www.csrc.gov.cn/cms/uploadFiles/introduction2004edition.1087888443500.doc, accessed 13 December 2004).

CSRC (2004b) *Job Opportunities at China Securities Regulatory Commission (CSRC)* (Beijing: China Securities Regulatory Commission, at: www.csrc.gov.cn/cn/jsp/detail.jsp?infoid=1091437433100&type=CMS.STD&path=ROOT%3ECN%3E%D0%C2%CE%C5%B5%BC%B6%C1, accessed 10 August 2004).

CSRC and SETC (2001) *Code of Corporate Governance for Listed Companies in China* (Beijing: China Securities Regulatory Commission, at: www.csrc.gov.cn/en/jsp/detail.jsp?infoid=1061968722100&type=CMS.STD, accessed 1 February 2004).

Czada, Roland and Lütz, Susanne (eds) (2000) *Die politische Konstitution von Märkten*. (Wiesbaden: Westdeutscher Verlag, at: www.mpi-fg-koeln.mpg.de/pu/mpifg_book/2000_CZ-SL.pdf, accessed 28 March 2008).

Dages, B. Gerard, Linda Goldberg and Daniel Kinney (2000) 'Foreign and Domestic Bank Participation in Emerging Markets: Lessons from Mexico and Argentina', *Federal Reserve Bank of New York Economic Policy Review*, 2000, September, pp. 17–36.

Dai, Xianglong (1999) 'Opening Address', in: BIS (ed.) *Strengthening the Banking System in China: Issues and Experiences* (Basel: Bank for International Settlements, Monetary and Economic Department), pp. 11–15.

Davies, Howard (1999) 'China and Britain: the Developing Financial Partnership', Forum on China's Securities Market and Overseas Listings, at: www.fsa.gov.uk/Pages/Library/Communication/Speeches/1999/sp21.shtml, accessed 28 March 2008.

Davies, Howard (2004) 'Financial Reform in China: The Next Agenda', speech at Fudan University, 19 October 2004, Shanghai.

Dickson, Bruce (2000) 'Cooptation and Corporatism in China: The Logic of Party Adaptation', *Political Science Quarterly*, 115: 4 (2000/01) pp. 517–40.

Dickson, Bruce (2003) *Red Capitalists in China. The Party, Private Entrepreneurs, and Prospects for Political Change* (Cambridge, New York: Cambridge University Press).

Dipchand, Cecil, Yichun Zhang and Mingjia Ma (1994) *The Chinese Financial System* (Westport, London: Greenwood Press).

Dolven, Ben, Howard Winn and David Murphy (2004) 'HSBC Bets Big On China', *Far Eastern Economic Review*, 19 August, at: www.feer.com/articles/2004/0408_19/p042money.html, accessed 28 March 2008.

Duckett, Jane (1996) *Market Reform and the Emergence of the Entrepreneurial State in China: the Case of State Commercial and Real Estate Department in Tianjin* (London: University of London).

Economist, The (2003a) 'Strings Attached: Foreign Financial Firms Would Love to Get into China – without Chinese Partners', 6 March, at: www.economist.com/finance/displayStory.cfm?story_id=1622471, accessed 28 March 2008

Economist, The (2003b) 'On Their Way Back: The Overseas Chinese are Returning to Become Entrepreneurs in the Motherland', 8 November, pp. 59–60, at: www.economist.com/displayStory.cfm?story_id=2193704, accessed 28 March 2008.

Economist, The (2004) 'Newbridge to the Mainland: The First Foreign Takeover of a Chinese Bank Will Be Hard to Copy', 3 June, at: www.economist.com/printedition/PrinterFriendly.cfm?Story_ID=2737033, accessed 28 March 2008.

EIU (2003) *Country Finance China 2003* (London: Economist Intelligence Unit).

Ernst & Young (2004) *Ernst & Young Global IPO Survey 2004* (Ernst & Young, Emerging and Growth Markets).

EU-China Financial Services Cooperation Project (2003) *The EU-China Financial Services Co-operation Project: A Project Introduction* (Beijing).

EUCCC (2003) *EUCCC Position Paper Banking Working Group 2003* (Beijing, Shanghai: European Chamber of Commerce in China).

EUCCC (2004a) *EUCCC Position Paper* (Beijing, Shanghai: European Chamber of Commerce in China).

EUCCC (2004b) *Good Effort, But Could Do Better. Interview with Marc Poirier* (Beijing, Shanghai European Chamber of Commerce in China). www.europeanchamber.com.cn/show/details.php?id=87, accessed 12 March 2005.

Euromoney (2004) *The China Conference: Capital Markets and Corporate Governance*, at: www.euromoneyconferences.com/events/past_event.asp?EventID=59, accessed 28 March 2008.

Evans, P. B., D. Ruschemeyer and T. Skocpol (eds) (1985) *Bringing the State Back In* (Cambridge: Cambridge University Press).

Fan, Fengzhi (2004) 'Shanghai jianshi quoji yinhang yewu zhongxin de lujing he dongli (Shanghai as an international banking center: development and driving forces)', *Jinrong cankao*, 2004-7, pp. 22–6.

Findlay, Christopher, Andrew Watson and Enjiang Cheng (eds) (2003) *Rural Financial Markets in China* (Canberra: Asia Pacific Press).

FIRST (2004a) *China: Strengthening Regulation and Supervision of Securities Firms*, at: www.firstinitiative.org/Projects/projectdisplay.cfm?iProjectID=250, accessed 28 March 2008.

FIRST (2004b) *People's Republic of China: Regulation of the Distribution of Securities Investment Funds*, at: www.firstinitiative.org/Projects/projectdisplay.cfm?iProjectID=297, accessed 28 March 2008.

FSF (2004) *12 Key Standards for Sound Financial Systems*, Financial Stability Forum, at: www.fsforum.org/compendium/key_standards_for_sound_financial_system.html, accessed 12 March 2005.

Gao, Chaosheng (2002) 'The Securities Market in China', *Caijing*, 20 June, at: www.chinaonline.com/caijing, accessed 12 January 2003.

Glionna, John M. (2004) 'Some "Sea Turtles" Find Foreign Degrees Don't Float in China – Graduates Return to Find Intense Competition, Low Wages and a Distaste for Their Western Attitude', *Los Angeles Times*, 8 August, Section I A, p. 5.

Göhler, Gerhard (1997) 'Wie verändern sich Institutionen? Revolutionärer und schleichender Institutionenwandel', in Gerhard Göhler (ed.) *Institutionenwandel* (Opladen: Westdeutscher Verlag), pp. 21–56.

Gourevitch, Peter (1978) 'The Second Image Reversed: the International Sources of Domestic Politics', *International Organization*, 32: 4, pp. 881–911.

Green, Stephen (2003a) '"Two-thirds Privatisation": How China's Listed Companies are – Finally – Privatising', Chatham House Briefing Note (London: Royal Institute of International Affairs).

Green, Stephen (2003b) 'China's Stock Market: Eight Myths and Some Reasons To Be Optimistic', Asia Programme Working Paper (London: Royal Institute of International Affairs).

Green, Stephen (2003c) *China's Stockmarket. A Guide to its Progress, Players and Prospects* (London: Profile Books).

Green, Stephen (2003d) *Drafting the Securities Law: The Role of the National People's Congress in Creating China's Market Economy*, Report from the China Project (London: Royal Institute of International Affairs).

Green, Stephen (2003e) 'Two-thirds Privatisation: Is It Working?', Chatham House Briefing Note (London: Royal Institute of International Affairs).

Green, Stephen (2004a) *Enterprise Reform and Stock Market Development in Mainland China*, China Special (Frankfurt am Main: Deutsche Bank Research: www.dbresearch.com).

Green, Stephen (2004b) *The Development of China's Stock Market, 1984–2002: Equity Politics and Market Institutions* (London: RoutledgeCurzon).

Green, Stephen and Alissa Black (2003) *A Market in Control: Non-tradable Shares Deals in Companies Listed at the Shenzhen Stock Exchange*, Asia Programme Working Paper, No. 11 (London: Royal Institute of International Affairs).

Green, Stephen and Ming He (2004) *China's Stock Market: Out of the Valley in 2004?* Asia Programme Briefing Paper, No. 1 (London: Royal Institute of International Affairs).

Guan, Guofen (2003) 'Corporate Governance and Ownership Reform in China's Banking Industry', Research Papers in Corporate Social Responsibility, No. 4 (London: London Metropolitan University, at: www.socialresponsibility.biz/wp4.pdf, accessed 28 March 2008).

Haas, Peter M. (1992) 'Introduction: Epistemic Communities and International Policy Coordination', *International Organization*, 46: 1 (Winter 1992), pp. 1–35.

Haggard, Stephan and Sylvia Maxfield (1996) 'The Political Economy of Financial Internationalization in the Developing World', *International Organization*, 50: 1, pp. 35–68.

Hall, P. A. and R. C. R. Taylor (1996) 'Political Science and the Three Institutionalisms',Discussion Paper 96/6 (Köln: Max Planck Institut für Gesellschaftsforschung).

Halpern, Nina (1985) *Economic Specialists and the Making of Chinese Economic Policy, 1955–1983* (Ann Arbor, Michigan: University Microfilms International).

Harner, Stephen (2001) *Business Opportunities for Foreign Financial Companies in China's Changing Marketplace: Facts and Figures for Potential Investors* (Munich: Roland Berger, at: www.rolandberger.com/documents/2270659/RB_Business_Opportunities_for_Foreign_Financial_Compa_2001.pdf, accessed 12 March 2005.

Harner, Stephen (2004) 'Bank Reform: Earthquake!', *China Economic Quarterly*, Q3, pp. 42–8.

He, Jianming and Yongzheng Yang (1999) 'The Political Economy of Trade Liberalisation in China', Asia Pacific School of Economics and Management Working Papers, No. 99-1 (Canberra: Asia Pacific Press).

He, Liping (2004) 'Foreign Banks in China: What Impact Would They Bring About?' *China & World Economy*, 12: 1, pp. 50–61.

He, Liping and Xiaohang Fan (2004) 'Foreign Banks in Post-WTO China: An Intermediate Assessment', *China & World Economy*, 12: 5, pp. 3–16.

Heberer, Thomas (2001) *Unternehmer als strategische Gruppen: Zur sozialen und politischen Funktion von Unternehmern in China und Vietnam*, Mitteilungen des Instituts für Asienkunde Hamburg 331 (Hamburg: Institut für Asienkunde).

Heilmann, Sebastian (2001) *Der Aktienmarkt der VR China (I): Staatliche Regulierung und Institutioneller Wandel*, China Analysis, No. 3 (Trier University, Germany: Center for East Asian and Pacific Studies, www.chinapolitik.de).

Heilmann, Sebastian (2002) *Das politische System der Volksrepublik China* (Wiesbaden: Westdeutscher Verlag).

Heilmann, Sebastian (2004) *Regulatory Innovation by Leninist Means: Communist Party Supervision in China's Financial Industry*, China Analysis, No. 38 (Trier: University of Trier, www.chinapolitik.de).

Heilmann, Sebastian and Gottwald, Jörn-Carsten (eds) (2002) *Der Chinesische Aktienmarkt* (Hamburg: Institut für Asienkunde).

Heilmann, Sebastian and Kirchberger, Sarah (2000) *The Chinese Nomenklatura in Transition: A Study Based on Internal Cadre Statistics of the Central Organization Department of the Chinese Communist Party*, China Analysis No. 1 (University of Trier: Center for East Asian and Pacific Studies. www.chinapolitik.de).

Hellman, Joel S., Geraint Jones and Daniel Kaufmann (2002a) '*"Seize the State, Seize the Day": State Capture, Corruption, and Influence in Transition*', Policy Research Working Paper, No. 2444 (Washington: World Bank).

Hellman, Joel S., Geraint Jones and Daniel Kaufmann (2002b) 'Are Foreign Investors and Multinationals Engaging in Corrupt Practices in Transition Economies?' (Washington: World Bank, at: www.worldbank.org/wbi/governance/pdf/fdi_trans_0800.pdf, accessed 28 March 2008).

Hellman, Joel S., Geraint Jones and Daniel Kaufmann (2002c) 'Far From Home: Do Foreign Investors Import Higher Standards of Governance in Transition Economies?', Draft Discussion Paper (Washington: World Bank, at: http://econwpa.wustl.edu:80/eps/dev/papers/0308/0308006.pdf, accessed 28 March 2008).

Herring, R. J. and A. M. Santomero (1999) 'What is Optimal Financial Regulation?', Conference paper presented at the Conference on International Competitiveness of the Swedish Financial Industry, at: http://fic.wharton.upenn.edu/fic/papers/00/0034.pdf, accessed 28 March 2008.

Hertz, Ellen (1998) *The Trading Crowd: an Ethnography of the Shanghai Stock Market* (Cambridge: Cambridge University Press).

HKEx (ed.) (2004) *Institutional Investors in Mainland China, Research & Planning Conference 15 January 2004* (Hong Kong: Hong Kong Stock Exchange, at: www.hkex.com.hk/research/rpapers/IIMC.pdf, accessed 28 March 2008).

Holz, Carsten (1992) *The Role of Central Banking in China's Economic Reforms* (Ithaca: Cornell University Press).

Hope, Nicholas and Fred Hu (2006) 'Reforming China's Banking System: How Much Can Foreign Entry Help?', Working Paper 276 (Stanford: Stanford Center for International Development).

HSBC (2007) Factsheet, at: www.hsbc.com.cn/1/PA_1_2_S5/content/china/about/docs/factsheet_en-Dec07.pdf

Hu, Angang and Li Zhou (2001) 'Market Openness and Good Governance: The Changing Regional Disparity of Financial Development in China (1978–1999)', paper presented at Financial Sector Reform in China conference, Harvard University, 2001, at: www.ksg.harvard.edu/cbg/Conferences/financial_sector/MarketOpennessandGoodGovernance.pdf, accessed 12 December 2003.

Hu, Naiwu and Haifeng Zhang (2004) 'Waizi qiye kehu liushi fenxi ji zhongguo yinhang de yingdui celüe (The vanishing of foreign invested corporate customers and counterstrategies of Chinese banks)', *Jinrong Yanjiu (Journal of Financial Research)*, 286: 4, pp, 88–94.

Hu, Shuli (2002) 'Hu Shuli on the Securites Industry', *Caijing*, 20 June, at: www.chinaonline.com, accessed 12 December 2004.

Hu, Shuli (2004a) 'No Fake Banking Reform', *Caijing*, 20 April, at: www. caijing.com.cn/english/2004/040320/040320editorial.htm, accessed 28 March 2008.

Hu, Shuli (2004b) 'Interest Rates Aren't Useless in Macroeconomic Management', *Caijing*, 20 July, at: www.caijing.com.cn/english/2004/040720/040720editorial. htm, accessed 12 December 2004.

Hu, Shuli (2004c) 'In Bearish Market, a Golden Opportunity for Reform', *Caijing*, 20 September, at: www.caijing.com.cn/english/2004/040920/040920editorial. htm, accessed 21 October 2004.

Hu, Shuli, Shufeng Li and Ning Yu (2002) 'Interview with Wang Jun, CITIC's Chairman of the Board', *Caijing*, 20 August, at: www.chinaonline.com, accessed 12 December 2004.

Hu, Shuli, Fuhua Wei and Wenxin Niu (2002) 'An Interview with Laura Cha, CSRC Vice Chair.' *Caijing*, 23 January, at: www.chinaonline.com, accessed 12 December 2004.

Hu, Tongjie (2003) 'Waizi yinhang zai Zhongguo: yewu jinzheng zhuangkuang yu fazhan qushi (Foreign banks in China: service competition and development trends)', *Zhongguo jinrong banyuekan*, 2003–8, pp. 22–6.

Huang, Daiwei (2002) *Der chinesische Bankensektor im Zeichen des WTO-Beitritt: Reformrückstände und Herausforderungen*, Berichte des Arbeitsbereichs Chinaforschung, No. 17 (Bremen: Universität und Hochschule Bremen, at: www. iwim.uni-bremen.de/publikationen/pdf/c017.pdf, accessed 28 March 2008).

Huang, Jinlao (2003) 'Dangqian zai hua waizi yinhang de zhanlüe fenxi (Analysis of the strategies of foreign banks)', in Feile Wang (ed.) *Guoji jinrong fazhan baogao 2003–2004*, pp. 236–45.

Huang, Yasheng (1996) *Inflation and Investment Controls in China: The Political Economy of Central-Local Relations During the Reform Era* (Cambridge: Cambridge University Press).

Huang, Yasheng (2002) *Selling China: Foreign Direct Investment During the Reform Era* (New York: Cambridge University Press).

Huntington, Samuel P. (1952) 'The Marasmus of the ICC: The Commission, the Railroads, and the Public Interest', *The Yale Law Journal*, 61: 4, pp. 467–509.

Imam, Michael (2004) 'The Chinese Interbank Markets: Cornerstone of Financial Liberalization', *China & World Economy*, 12: 5, pp. 17–33.

Immergut, Ellen M. (1998) 'The Theoretical Core of the New Institutionalism', *Politics & Society*, 26: 1, pp. 5–34.

International Monetary Fund (2003) *Global Stability Report: A Report by the International Capital Markets Department on Market Developments and Issues* (Washington: IMF).

IOSCO (2003) *Objectives and Principles of Securities Regulation* (Madrid: International Organisation on Securities Commissions, at: www.iosco.org/library/ pubdocs/pdf/IOSCOPD154.pdf, accessed 28 March 2008).

Iredale, Robyn and Guo Fei (2001) 'The Transforming Role of Skilled and Business Returnees: Taiwan, China and Bangladesh', paper presented at the 24th IUSSP General Conference, at: www.iussp.org/Brazil2001/s30/S39_04_Iredale.pdf, accessed 28 March 2008.

Iyengar, Jayanthi (2004) 'Goldman Sachs Blazes Trail in China', *Asia Times*, 18 August, at: www.atimes.com/atimes/China/FH19Ad03.html, accessed 28 March 2008.

Jacobson, Harold K. and Michel Oksenberg (1990) *China's Participation in the IMF, the World Bank, and GATT: Toward a Global Economic Order* (Ann Arbor: University of Michigan Press).

Jensen, Michael C. and William H. Meckling (1976) 'Theory of the Firm: Managerial Behaviour, Agency Costs and Ownership Structure', *Journal of Financial Economics*, 3: 4, pp. 305–60.

Ji, Zhaojin (2003) *A History of Modern Shanghai Banking: The Rise and Decline of China's Finance Capitalism* (Armonk, London: M.E. Sharpe).

Kalathil, Shanthi (2003) 'China's New Media Sector: Keeping the State In', *The Pacific Review*, 16: 4, pp. 489–501.

Karmel, Solomon M. (1994) 'Emerging Securities Markets in China: Capitalism with Chinese Characteristics', *The China Quarterly*, 140, pp. 1105–20.

Katz, Christian A. (1997) *Foreign Banks in China* (Singapore: Financial Times Asia Pacific).

Keng, Shu (2004) 'Playing the Devil's Advocate: Finding the Shortcomings in Internationalizing China', *Issues and Studies*, 40: 1, pp. 242–6.

Kennedy, Scott (2004) 'Business Lobbying in China: Aid and Obstacle to Effective Industry Regulation', paper presented at Transforming Institutions in Global China: Past Lessons, Future Challenges, International Symposium, University of Maryland.

Kennedy, Scott (2005) *The Business of Lobbying in China* (Cambridge MA: Harvard University Press).

Keohane, Robert O. and Helen V. Milner (eds) (1996) *Internationalization and Domestic Politics* (Cambridge: Cambridge University Press).

Kim, Yongbeom, Irene S. M. Ho and Mark St Giles (2003) 'Developing Institutional Investors in the People's Republic of China', World Bank Country Study Paper (Washington: World Bank).

Koeble, T. A. (1995) 'The New Institutionalism in Political Science and Sociology', *Comparative Politics*, 27, pp. 221–44.

KPMG (2005) *China's City Commercial Banks: Opportunity Knocks?* (Hong Kong: KMPG Financial Services, at: www.kpmg.com.hk).

Krasner, Stephen (1995) 'Power Politics, Institutions and Transnational Relations', in Thomas Risse-Kappen (ed.) *Bringing Transnational Relations Back In* (Cambridge: Cambridge University Press), pp. 257–79.

Kroszner, Randall S. (1998) 'On the Political Economy of Banking and Financial Regulatory Reform in Emerging Markets', paper presented at Annual Meeting of the Board of Governors of the World Bank Group and the International Monetary Fund, at: http://gsbwww.uchicago.edu/fac/randall.kroszner/more/hk.pdf, accessed 28 March 2008.

Kumar, Anjali (1997) *China's Emerging Capital Market* (Hong Kong: FT Financial Publishing Asia Pacific).

Laffont, Jean-Jacques and Jean Tirole (1991) 'The Politics of Government Decision-Making: A Theory of Regulatory Capture', *Quarterly Journal of Economics*, 106 (1991): 4, pp. 1089–27.

Lange, Thomas (2004) 'Banking in China: Markteintrittsstrategien global tätiger Finanzinstitute', *Die Bank*, 01/2004, pp. 558–65.

Laprès, Daniel Arthur (2000) *The EU-China WTO Deal Compared*, July–August, at: www.chinabusinessreview.com/public/0007/lapres.html, accessed 28 March 2008.

Lardy, Nicholas R. (1998) *China's Unfinished Economic Revolution* (Washington: Brookings Institution).

Lardy, Nicholas R. (1999) 'China in the International Financial System', in Elisabeth Economy and Michel Oksenberg (eds) *China Joins the World: Progress and Prospects* (New York: Council on Foreign Relations).

Lardy, Nicholas R. (2001) 'Foreign Financial Firms in Asia', paper presented at Open Doors: Foreign Participation in Financial Systems in Developing Countries, Brookings/World Bank/International Monetary Fund Conference, April, at: www.brookings.org/dybdocroot/views/papers/lardy/20010720.htm, accessed 20 May 2003.

Lau, Lawrence J. (1999) 'The Macroeconomy and the Reform of the Banking Sector in China', in BIS (ed.) *Strengthening the Banking System in China: Issues and Experiences* (Basel: Bank for International Settlements, Monetary and Economic Department), pp. 59–89.

Lau, Lawrence J. (1998) 'Gain without Pain: Why Economic Reform in China Worked', in Gungwu Wang and John Wong (eds) *China's Political Economy* (Singapore: Singapore University Press and World Scientific), pp. 43–70.

Leckie, Stuart (2003) 'Pension Reform in China', *ChinaOnline*, 25 June, at: www.chinaonline.com/commentary_analysis/C03062536.asp, accessed 4 April 2002.

Lees, Francis and Thomas Liaw (1996) *Foreign Participation in China's Banking and Securities Markets* (Westport, London: Quorum Books).

Levine, Ross (1996) 'Foreign Banks, Financial Development and Economic Growth', in Claude E. Barfield (ed.) *International Financial Markets: Harmonization versus Competition* (Washington: AEI Press).

Li, Cheng (2004) 'Bringing China's Best and Brightest Back Home: Regional Disparities and Political Tensions', *China Leadership Monitor*, 11, Summer, at: www.chinaleadershipmonitor.org/20043/lc.pdf, accessed 12 November 2004.

Li, David D. (2001) 'Beating the Trap of Financial Repression in China', *Cato Journal*, 21: 1 (Spring/Summer), pp. 77–90, at: www.cato.org/pubs/journal/cj21n1/cj21n1-6.pdf, accessed 28 March 2008.

Li, Kui-Wai (1994) *Financial Repression and Economic Reform in China* (Westport, London: Praeger).

Li, Shufeng (2002) 'Discussing the New Regulation for Interbank Lending', *Caijing*, 20 August, at www.chinaonline.com/caijing, accessed 23 November 2004.

Li, Shufeng (2003) 'Shei lai faxing huobi shichang jijin (Who will be able to issue money market funds?)', *Caijing*, 96, pp. 94–5.

Li, Shufeng and Weiping Kang (2003) 'The World's Largest IPO in 2003', *Caijing*, 20 December, at: www.caijing.com.cn/english/2003/1220/1220ipo.htm, accessed 1 March 2004.

Li, Yang and Xingyun Peng (2002) 'The Money Market in China: Theory and Practice', *China & World Economy*, 2002: 3, pp. 3–10, at: www.iwep.org.cn/wec/english/articles/2002_03/2002-3-liyang.pdf, accessed 12 February 2003.

Liao, Xinjun (2004) 'Guoji dahang zhongguo jingbian (Chinese presence of international investment banks)', *21 shiji jingji baogao*, 11 July, at: www.fimr.org/index.php?cid=28&action=showArticle&aid=630, accessed 28 March 2008.

Lieberthal, Kenneth and David Lampton (1992) *Bureaucracy, Politics, and Decision-Making in Post-Mao China* (Berkeley, Oxford, Los Angeles: University of California Press).

Lieberthal, Kenneth and Michel Oksenberg (1988) *Policy Making in China: Leaders, Structures, and Processes* (Princeton: Princeton University Press).

Liew, Leong H. (2004) 'Policy Elites in the Political Economy of China's Exchange Rate Policymaking,' *Journal of Contemporary China*, 13: 38, pp. 21–51.

Lin, Z. Jun and Liyan Wang (2001) 'Financial Disclosure and Accounting Harmonization: Cases of Three Listed Companies in China', *Managerial Accounting Journal*, 16: 5, pp. 263–73.

Ling, Huawei (2004a) 'China Construction Bank Ready for Restructuring', *Caijing*, 20 February, at: www.caijing.com.cn/english/2004/040220/040220ccb.htm, accessed 12 March 2004.

Ling, Huawei (2004b) 'Behind Suspension of Bank Loans', *Caijing*, 5 April, at: www.caijing.com.cn/english/2004/040505/040505behind.htm, accessed 12 March 2003.

Linz, Juan (2000) *Totalitäre und autoritäre Regime* (Berlin: Berliner Debatte Wissenschaftsverlag).

Liu, Meiru (2001) *Administrative Reform in China and Its Impact on the Policy-making Process and Economic Development after Mao* (Lewiston, Queenston: Edwin Mellen Press).

Liu, Mingkang (2003) 'The Letter from Liu Ming Kang, the Chairman of CBRC, to Mr Jaime Caruana, Chairman of the Basel Committee on Banking Supervision', 31 July, China Banking Regulatory Commission, at: www.cbrc.gov.cn/english/module/viewinfo.jsp?infoID=466, accessed 14 July 2004.

Liu, Mingkang (2004a) 'Making all Endeavors to Promote the Opening up of China's Banking. Chairman Liu Mingkang's speech at the Summit Forum on the CEPA and the Local Economic Development of Hunan Province', 12 May (Beijing: China Banking Regulatory Commission, at: www.cbrc.gov.cn/english/module/viewinfo.jsp?infoID=1030, accessed 12 December 2004.

Liu, Mingkang (2004b) 'The State-owned Banks in China: Reform, Corporate Governance and Prospect, Chairman Liu Mingkang's Speech at Beijing International Financial Forum', 19 May (Beijing: China Banking Regulatory Commission, at: www.cbrc.gov.cn/english/module/viewinfo.jsp?infoID=608, accessed 15 February 2004.

Lo, Alexandra Dak-Wai (1999) 'The Practical Implications of the PRC Securities Law: Development of Domestic Market', *Law Lectures for Practitioners*, April, pp. 146–63, at: http://sunzi1.lib.hku.hk/hkjo/view/14/1400255.pdf, accessed 28 March 2008.

Lu, Haoting (2004) 'Experts: Economy Set for "Soft Landing"', China Economic Net, 8 July, at: www.ec.cn/pubnews/2004_07_08/200625/1031188.jsp, accessed 1 December 2004.

Lütz, Susanne (2003) *Der Staat und die Globalisierung von Finanzmärkten: Regulative Politik in Deutschland, Grossbritannien und den USA* (Frankfurt a. M.: Campus Verlag).

Ma, Guonan and Ben S. C. Fung (2002) 'China's Asset Management Corporations', BIS Working Paper, No. 115 (Basel: Monetary and Economic Department, Bank for International Settlements, at: www.bis.org/publ/work115.pdf, accessed 28 March 2008).

March, James G. and Johan P. Olsen (1989) *Rediscovering Institutions: The Organisational Basis of Politics* (New York: The Free Press).

Mathieson, D. C. and J. Roldos (2001) 'Foreign Banks in Emerging Markets', in Robert E. Litan, Paul Masson and Michael Pomerleano (eds) *Open Doors: Foreign Participation in Financial Systems in Developing Countries* (Washington: Brookings Institution), pp. 15–58.

Mayntz, Renate and Fritz W. Scharpf (1995) 'Der Ansatz des akteurzentrierten Institutionalismus', in Renate Mayntz and Fritz W. Scharpf (eds) *Gesellschaftliche Selbstregelung und politische Steuerung* (Frankfurt a. M.: Campus Verlag), pp. 39–72.

McGregor, Richard (2004a) 'Massive Shake-up for Bank of China', *Financial Times*, 16 November, at: http://news.ft.com/cms/s/8c53ee0c-3803-11d9-991f-00000e2511c8.html, accessed 28 March 2008.

McGregor, Richard (2004b) 'Competition in China Keeps Foreign Profits Low', *Financial Times*, 5 December, at http://news.ft.com/cms/s/342499fa-4700-11d9-b099-00000e2511c8.html, accessed 28 March 2008.

McKinnon, Ronald (1973) *Money and Capital in Economic Development* (Washington: Brookings Institution).

McKinnon, Ronald (1992) *The Order of Economic Liberalization: Financial Control in the Transition to a Market Economy* (Baltimore: Johns Hopkins University Press).

Meidinger, Errol (1987) 'Regulatory Culture: A Theoretical Outline', *Law & Policy*, 9: 4, pp. 355–86, at: www.law.buffalo.edu/homepage/eemeid/scholarship/rc.pdf, accessed 28 March 2008.

Meyer, David R. (2000) 'Hong Kong and Shanghai as China's Window to Global Capital', at: www.uic.edu/cuppa/cityfutures/papers/webpapers/cityfuturespapers/session6_4/6_4hongkong.pdf, accessed 28 March 2008.

Meyer-Clement, Elena (2004) 'Institutional Change Under the Impact of an Evolving Private Sector in the PRC – The Case of Opening the Party to Private Entrepreneurs', *ASIEN*, 92, July, pp. 64–80.

Mo, Y. K. (1999) 'A Review of Recent Banking Reforms in China', in BIS (ed.) *Strengthening the Banking System in China: Issues and Experiences* (Basel: Bank for International Settlements, Monetary and Economic Department), pp. 90–109.

Mody, Ashoka (2004) *What Is an Emerging Market?*, IMF Working Paper, No. 04/177 (Washington: International Monetary Fund, at: www.imf.org/external/pubs/ft/wp/2004/wp04177.pdf, accessed 28 March 2008).

Montgomery, Heather (2002) *The Role of Foreign Banks in Post-Crisis Asia* (Tokyo: Asian Development Bank Institute).

Moore, Thomas G. (2002) *China in the World Market: Chinese Industry and International Sources of Reform in the Post-Mao Era* (New York: Cambridge University Press).

Mosley, Layna (2003) *Global Capital and National Governments* (Cambridge: Cambridge University Press).

Naughton, Barry (1995) *Growing out of the Plan: Chinese Economic Reform, 1978–1993* (Cambridge: Cambridge University Press).

Naughton, Barry (2002) 'Selling Down the State Share: Contested Policy, New Rules', *China Leadership Monitor*, 3, Winter, Part 2, at: www.hoover.org/publications/clm/issues/2906811.html, accessed 28 March 2008.

Naughton, Barry (2003a) 'Economic Policy after the 16th Party Congress', *China Leadership Monitor*, 5, Winter, pp. 30–42, at: www.hoover.org/publications/clm/issues/2906361.html, accessed 28 March 2008.

Naughton, Barry (2003b) 'The Emergence of Wen Jiabao', *China Leadership Monitor*, 6, Spring, pp. 36–47, at: www.hoover.org/publications/clm/issues/2906246.html, accessed 28 March 2008.

Naughton, Barry (2003c) 'Government Reorganization: Liu Mingkang and Financial Restructuring', *China Leadership Monitor*, 7, Summer, at: www.hoover.org/publications/clm/issues/2906071.html, accessed 28 March 2008.

Naughton, Barry (2004a) 'Changing the Rules of the Game: Macroeconomic Recontrol and the Struggle for Wealth and Power', *China Leadership Monitor*, Fall, p. 12, at: www.hoover.org/publications/clm/issues/2904011.html, accessed 28 March 2008.

Naughton, Barry (2004b) 'Financial Reconstruction: Methodical Policymaking Moves into the Spotlight', *China Leadership Monitor*, 10, Spring, at: www.hoover.org/publications/clm/issues/2904431.html, accessed 28 March 2008.

Naughton, Barry (2004c) 'Hunkering Down: The Wen Jiabao Administration and Macroeconomic Recontrol', *China Leadership Monitor*, 11, Summer, at: www.hoover.org/publications/clm/issues/2904151.html, accessed 28 March 2008.

Naughton, Barry (2006) 'Waves of Criticism: Debates over Bank Sales to Foreigners and Neo-Liberal Economic Policy', *China Leadership Monitor*, 17, Winter, at: www.hoover.org/publications/clm/issues/2898811.html, accessed 28 March 2008.

Neoh, Anthony (2000) 'China's Domestic Capital Markets in the New Millennium', 21 August, *ChinaOnline*, at: www.som.yale.edu/Faculty/zc25/Emerging Markets/ChinaMktByTonyNeoh.DOC.

North, Douglas (1990) *Institutions, Institutional Change and Economic Performance* (Cambridge: Cambridge University Press).

O'Neill, Mark (2004) 'Rich Tip the Balance for Foreign Banks: Wealthy Depositors Are Defecting from Local Lenders in Favour of Superior Service', *South China Morning Post*, 4 November.

Obinger, Herbert, Uwe Wagschal, and Bernhard Kittel (2003) *Politische Ökonomie* (Opladen: Leske + Budrich).

OECD (2002) *China in the World Economy: The Domestic Policy Challenges* (Paris: OECD).

OECD (2004) *Rural Finance and Credit Infrastructure in China* (Paris: OECD).

Ogden, John and Bei Hu (2002) 'CLSA Investment Bank Joint Venture Approved', *South China Morning Post*, Hong Kong, 20 December.

Olson, Mancur (1965) *The Logic of Collective Action. Public Goods and the Theory of Groups* (Cambridge: Harvard University Press).

Olson, Mancur (2000) *Power and Prosperity: Outgrowing Communist and Capitalist Dictatorships* (New York: Basic Books).

Opper, Sonja (2003) 'Enforcement of China's Accounting Standards: Reflections on Systemic Problems', *Business and Politics*, 5: 2 (August), pp. 151–73.

Overholt, William H. (2004) 'The Lessons of the Asian and Latin American Financial Crises for Chinese Bond Markets', Occasional Paper, Center for Asia Pacific Policy, No. 117, (Santa Monica: RAND Corporation, at: www.rand.org/pubs/occasional_papers/2005/RAND_OP117.pdf, accessed 15 December 2004.

Pang, Cuiping (2005) *Securities Firms in China: Geschäftserfolge und Geschäftsprobleme von Investmentbanken mit unterschiedlichen Eigentumsformen.* Doctoral dissertation, University of Trier.

Parker, Elliott and Thomas F. Cargill (2001) 'Financial Liberalisation in China: Limitations and Lessons of the Japanese Regime', *Journal of the Asia Pacific Economy*, 6: 1, pp. 1–21.

Parkhe, Arvind and Stewart Miller (1998) 'Patterns in the Expansion of US Banks' Foreign Operations', *Journal of International Business Studies*, 29: 2, pp. 359–90.

Pearson, Margaret M. (1991) *Joint Ventures in the Peoples's Republic of China* (Princeton: Princeton University Press).

Pearson, Margaret M. (2003) 'Mapping the Rise of China's Regulatory State: Economic Regulation and Network and Insurance Industries', conference paper presented at the Annual Meeting of the Association of Asian Studies 2003, New York.

Pei, Changhong and Weili Qiu (2002) 'Internationalization of Securities Market After China's WTO Accession', *China & World Economy*, 2002: 4, pp. 24–7.

Pei, M. (1998) 'The Political Economy of Banking Reforms in China: 1993–1997', *Journal of Contemporary China*, 7: 18, pp. 321–50.

Peltzman, Sam (1976) 'Toward a More General Theory of Regulation', *Journal of Law and Economics*, 19, pp. 211–48.

People's Bank of China (2001) 'Zhongyang yinhang yu yinhangye jianguan', *Jinrong Yanjiu Baogao (Neibu) (Internal Research Report of the PBC)*, 2001–37: 635, pp. 1–14.

People's Bank of China (2004a) 'Dui yinjianfenshi hou zhongyang zhineng de renzhen', *Jinrong Yanjiu Baogao (Neibu) (Internal Research Report of the PBC)*, 2004-4: 751, pp. 1–17.

People's Bank of China (2004b) 'Jinrong kongzhi zhong yao miqie guanzhi waizi yinhang yewu fazhan (Watching out for the development of foreign banks services in financial control)', *Jinrong Yanjiu Baogao (Neibu) (Internal Research Report of the PBC)*, 2004: 772, p. 25.

People's Bank of China (2004c) *Quarterly Statistical Bulletin.* No. 04/2004 (Beijing: People's Bank of China).

People's Bank of China (2004d) 'Wo guo rongzi zhongxin de huigu (Reviewing financial centers in China)', *Jinrong Yanjiu Baogao (Neibu) (Internal Research Report of the PBC)*, 2004-9: 756, pp. 1–13.

People's Bank of China (2004e) *Zhongguo renmin yinhang fenzhihang 2005 renyuan luyong kaoshi gonggao (Notice on the 2005 Recruitment Procedures of the PBCs branches).* (Beijing: PBC, at: www.pbc.gov.cn, accessed 21 December 2004).

People's Daily (2002) 'China Would Further Open Financial Market', *People's Daily Online*, 23 March, at: http://english.people.com.cn/200203/22/eng20020322_92606.shtml, accessed 28 March 2008.

People's Daily (2003) 'Stock Market Risk Controls under Discussion: China's Securities Regulators Have Invited Overseas Experts to Help Design a New

Risk Management Scheme for Domestic Securities Companies', *People's Daily Online*, 23 September, at: http://english.people.com.cn/200309/23/eng20030923_124728. shtml, accessed 28 March 2008.

People's Daily (2004a) 'Guowuyuan guanyu tuijin ziben shichang gaige fazhan de jiudian yidian (The State Council's Nine Articles on the development and reform of the stock market)', *People's Daily Online*, 31 January, at: www.people.com.cn/GB/jingji/8215/31550, accessed 28 March 2008.

People's Daily (2004b) 'Construction Bank Names IPO Underwriters', *People's Daily Online*, 15 March, at: www.english.people.com.cn/200403/15/eng20040315_137517.shtml, accessed 28 March 2008.

People's Daily (2004c) 'China Welcomes Overseas Investors to Join Banking Reshuffle', *People's Daily Online*, 31 May, at: http://english.peopledaily.com.cn/200405/31/print20040531_144870.html, accessed 28 March 2008.

People's Daily (2004d) 'CBRC: QDII Policies to Bring More Opportunities for Foreign Banks', *People's Daily Online*, 7 June, at: http://english.people.com.cn/200406/07/eng20040607_145525.html, accessed 28 March 2008.

Ping, Luo (2003) 'Challenges for China's Banking Sector and Policy Responses', conference paper presented at IMF Seminar, New Delhi, at: www.imf.org/external/np/apd/seminars/2003/newdelhi/ping.pdf, accessed 28 March 2008.

Pißler, Knut Benjamin (2002) *Corporate Governance in der VR China: Neue Vorschriften für börsenzugelassene Gesellschaften*, China Analysis, No. 17 (Trier: Center for East Asian and Pacific Studies, Trier University, at: www.chinapolitik.de/studien/china_analysis/no_17.pdf, accessed 28 March 2008).

Pomerleano, Michael and George J. Vojta (2001) 'What Do Foreign Banks Do in Emerging Markets? An Institutional Study', paper presented at 3rd Annual Financial Markets and Development Conference, New York.

PriceWaterhouseCoopers (2006) *Entering the Chinese Investment Management Industry* (London, Shanghai: www.pwc.com).

PriceWaterhouseCoopers (2005) *Foreign Banks in China* (London, Shanghai, Hong Kong: www.pwc.com).

Qing, Wu (2001) 'The Challenges Facing China's Financial Services Industry', in Peter Nolan (ed.) *China and the Global Business Revolution* (Basingstoke: Palgrave), pp. 813–39.

Qu, Hongbin (2004) *Investment Downturn and its Implications*, China Economic Insight No 16, 23 June (Hong Kong: HSBC, at: www.banking.hsbc.com.cn/cn/common/download/aboutus/200406.pdf).

Rajan, Raghuram G. and Luigi Zingales (2003a) 'The Great Reversals: The Politics of Financial Development in the 20th Century', *Journal of Financial Economics*, 69: 1: pp. 5–50.

Rajan, Raghuram G. and Luigi Zingales (2003b) *Saving Capitalism from the Capitalists: Unleashing the Power of Financial Markets to Create Wealth and Spread Opportunity* (New York: Crown Business).

Rawski, Thomas (1999) 'Reforming China's Economy: What Have We Learnt?, *The China Journal*, 41, pp. 139–56.

Reszat, Beate (2002) 'Developing Financial Markets in East Asia – Opportunities and Challenges in the 21st Century', paper presented at Asset

Securitisation Conference, at: www.hwwa.de/Projects/IaD_Programmes/ IDSPs/Asia_Gateway/Developing%20Financial%20Markets%20in%20East%20 Asia.pdf, accessed 2 March 2005.

Richter, Rudolf and Eirik Furubotn (1996) *Neue Institutionenökonomik: Eine Einführung und kritische Würdigung* (Tübingen: Mohr).

Risse-Kappen, Thomas (ed.) (1995) *Bringing Transnational Relations Back in: Non-state Actors, Domestic Structures and International Institutions* (Cambridge: Cambridge University Press).

Rogowski, R. (1989) *Commerce and Coalitions: How Trade Affects Domestic Political Alignments* (Princeton: Princeton University Press).

Rosen, Daniel H. (1999) *Behind the Open Door: Foreign Enterprises in the Chinese Marketplace* (Washington: Institute for International Economics).

Sabatier, Paul (1975) 'Social Movements and Regulatory Agencies: Toward a More Adequate – and Less Pessimistic – Theory of "Clientele Capture"', *Policy Science*, 6, pp. 301–42.

Saez, Lawrence (2004) *Banking Reform in India and China* (New York: Palgrave Macmillan).

Saich, Tony (2001) *Governance and Politics of China* (Houndmills: Palgrave).

Sandschneider, Eberhard (1995) *Stabilität und Transformation politischer Systeme. Politikwissenschaftliche Aspekte einer Theorie der Systemtransformation* (Opladen: Leske + Budrich).

Scharpf, Fritz W. (1997) *Games Real Actors Play: Actor-centered Institutionalism in Policy Research* (London: Westview Press).

Schlichting, Svenja (2004) *Chinas Märkte für Staatsanleihen, 'Financial Bonds' und Unternehmensanleihen*, China Analysis, No. 36 (University of Trier: Center for East Asian and Pacific Studies, www.chinapolitik.de).

Schüller, Margot (1992) 'Der Wertpapiermarkt in China: Entwicklung, Probleme und Perspektiven', *CHINA Aktuell*, March, pp. 163–72.

Schüller, Margot (2002) 'Finanzintermediation und Wirtschaftsentwicklung in der VR China', conference paper presented at Institutionen und wirtschaftliche Entwicklung, Jahrestagung des Ausschusses für Wirtschaftssysteme und Institutionenökonomik des Vereins für Socialpolitik, Kühtai.

SCMP (2004) 'Investment Banks on Mainland Offensive: China IPOs are Expected to More than Triple this Year, and Foreign Arrangers Hope to Grab a Share of the Business', *South China Morning Post*, Hong Kong, 22 April, at: http://biz.scmp.com/bizanalysis/ZZZS4LREXRD.html, accessed 27 November 2004.

Seto, David (2002) *China's Capital Markets Handbook* (Hong Kong: HSBC).

Shanghai Daily (2003) 'Foreign Banks Allowed to Sell RMB Bonds', 5 December, at:www.china.org.cn/english/2003/Dec/81623.htm, accessed 28 March 2008.

Shanghai Jingji Daxue Jinrong Xueyuan (2003) *2003 zhongguo jinrong fazhan baogao (2003 report on China's financial development)* (Shanghai: Shanghai Jinrong Daxue Chubanshe).

Shanhai Pudong Fazhan Yinhang (2002) 'Waizi shangye yinhang jigou fazhan jiaojiu baogao (Report on the development of foreign commercial banks)', *Shanghai Jinrong Nianjian*, 2002, pp. 513–21.

Shaw, Edward (1973) *Financial Deepening in Economic Development* (New York, London: Oxford University Press).

Sheng, Jeffrey L. J., Baochun Li and Jiawen Miao (2003) *Investment in China: Opportunities in Private Equity and Venture Capital* (Beijing: Tsinghua University Press).

Shih, Victor (2001) 'Dishonest Technocrats: The Height of Central Power and the Pathologies of the 1998 Banking Reform', paper presented at the Post-Communist Politics and Economics Workshop, at: www.fas.harvard.edu/~postcomm/papers/2001-02/victor.pdf, accessed 12 December 2003.

Shih, Victor (2004a) 'Factions Matter: Personal Networks and the Distribution of Bank Loans in China', *Journal of Contemporary China*, 13: 38, pp. 3–19.

Shih, Victor (2004b) *Not Quite a Miracle: Factional Conflict, Inflationary Cycles and Non-Performing Loans in China*, Book Manuscript Submission to Cornell University Press.

Shih, Victor, Qi Zhang and Mingxing Liu (2004) *Comparing Chinese Banks: A Principal Component Approach*, at http://pubweb.northwestern.edu/~vsh853/ccb.pdf, accessed 1 December 2004.

Shirai, Sayuri (2004) 'Testing the Three Roles of Equity Markets in Developing Countries: The Case of China', *World Development*, 32: 9, pp. 1467–86.

Shirai, Sayuri and Prithipal Rajasekaran (2001) 'Assessment of China's Financial Reforms', paper presented at ESCAP-ADB Joint Workshop on Mobilizing Domestic Finance for Development: Reassessment of Bank Finance and Debt Markets in Asia and the Pacific, Bangkok.

Shirk, Susan L. (1993) *The Political Logic of Economic Reform in China* (Berkeley: University of California Press).

Shirk, Susan L. (1994) *How China Opened Its Door: The Political Success of the PRC's Foreign Trade and Investment Reforms* (Washington: Brookings Institution).

Slater, Dan (2002a) 'Let the Battle Begin', *FinanceAsia*, pp. 19–21.

Slater, Dan (2002b) 'China's Corporate Bond Market Poised to Book, Says China Expert'. *FinanceAsia.com*, 20 August.

Slater, Dan (2003a) 'Hong Kong Banks' CEP Advantage', *FinanceAsia*, August.

Slater, Dan (2003b) 'Chinese Convertible Bonds: Treat with Care', *FinanceAsia.com*, 5 June.

Slater, Dan (2004) 'China's Big Investor: The IFC is a Surprisingly Big Investor in China, and Is Getting Bigger. But what Is Its Strategy?', *FinanceAsia*, May.

Solvet, Eric (2002) *Banking in China. Sins and Virtues: Appraising the Foundations* (Hong Kong: CLSA Emerging Markets).

Stigler, George J. (1971) 'The Theory of Economic Regulation', *The Bell Journal of Economics and Management Science*, 2, pp. 3–21.

Su, Dongwei (2003) *Chinese Stock Markets: A Research Handbook* (Singapore: World Scientific Publishing).

Sun, Laixiang and Damian Tobin (2003) 'Corporate Governance Reform and International Listing: Case of the Bank of China (Hong Kong)', CeFiMS Discussion Paper, No. 37 (London: Centre for Financial and Management Studies, SOAS, University of London).

Sun, Min (2004) 'Segregation of 3 Financial Branches Should Remain', *China Daily*, 9 August, at: www.chinadaily.com.cn/english/doc/2004-08/09/content_363496.htm, accessed 28 March 2008.

Tam, On Kit (1991) 'Capital Market Development in China', *World Development*, 19: 5, pp. 511–32.

Tang, Shuangning (2001) *Zaihua waizi yinhang gaikuang (Foreign banks in China)* (Beijing: Zhongguo jinrong chubanshe).

Tang, Shuangning (2004) 'Reform of State-owned Commercial Banks In China', China Banking Regulatory Commission, 26 April, at: www.cbrc.gov.cn/english/ module/viewinfo.ijsp?infoID=562, accessed 1 March 2005.

Tenev, Stojan and Chunlin Zhang (2002) *Corporate Governance and Enterprise Reform in China: Building the Institutions of Modern Markets* (Washington: IFC, World Bank).

Tong, Donald D. (2002) *The Heart of Economic Reform: China's Banking Reform and State Enterprise Restructuring* (Burlington: Ashgate).

Tsai, Kellee S. (2002) *Back-Alley Banking: Private Entrepreneurs in China* (Ithaca and London: Cornell University Press).

Underhill, Geoffrey R. D. (1997) 'Private Markets and Public Responsibility in a Global System: Conflict and Co-operation in Transnational Banking and Securities Regulation', in Geoffrey R. D. Underhill (ed.) *The New World Order in International Finance* (Basingstoke: Macmillan), pp. 17–49.

Vogel, Steven K. (1998) *Freer Markets, More Rules: Regulatory Reform in Advanced Industrial Countries* (Ithaca and London: Cornell University Press).

von Beyme, Klaus (1987) 'Institutionentheorie in der neueren Politikwissenschaft', in Gerhard Göhler (ed.) *Grundfragen der Theorie politischer Institutionen: Forschungsstand, Probleme, Perspektiven* (Opladen: Westdeutscher Verlag).

Walter, Carl E. and Fraser J. T. Howie (2003) *Privatizing China: The Stock Markets and Their Role in Corporate China* (Singapore: John Wiley & Sons (Asia)).

Wang, Fanghong (2002a) 'Guonei yinhang lingshou chanpin fenxi yu jiakuai zhong guo (Foreign banks' retail products and its implications for China)', *Guoji jinrong yanjiu*, 2002: 4, pp. 48–52.

Wang, Zhile (2002b) *2002/2003 kuaguo gongsi zai zhongguo touzi baogao (2002/2003 Report on transnational corporations' investment in China)* (Beijing: Waijing maobu guoji jingji yanjiuyuan, kuaguo gongsi yanjiu zhongxin, Zhongguo Jingji Chubanshe).

Weingast, Barry R. (1993) 'Constitutions as Governance Structures: The Political Foundations of Secure Markets', *Journal of Institutional and Theoretical Economics*, 149: 1, pp. 286–311.

Weller, Christian E. (2004) 'Multinational Banks In Developing and Transition Economies', Technical Paper, No. 241, Economic Policy Institute, www.epi.org.

Williamson, O. (1985) *The Economic Institutions of Capitalism* (New York: Free Press).

Wilson, Dominic and Roopa Purushothaman (2003) 'Dreaming with BRICs: The Path to 2050', Global Economics Paper, No. 99 (New York: Goldman Sachs).

Wipper, Svenja (2001) *Möglichkeiten, Grenzen und Erfolgsdeterminanten volkswirtsch aftlicher Regierungsberatung im Reformprozeß der VR China*. Diskussionspapiere/ Freie Universität Berlin, Fachbereich Wirtschaftswissenschaft, Fachgebiet Volkswirtschaft des Vorderen Orients; 85 ed. (Berlin: Schwarz Verlag).

Wong, Jimmie K. S. (2004) 'A Brief Analysis of Mainland and Hong Kong Closer Economic Partnership Arrangement (CEPA)', *China Law*, April, pp. 97–101.

Wong, Y. C. Richard and M. L. Sonia Wong (2001) 'Competition in China's Domestic Banking Industry', *Cato Journal*, 21: 1, pp. 19–41.

World Bank (1995) *Bureaucrats in Business: The Economics and Politics of Government Ownership* (Oxford: Oxford University Press).

World Bank (2003) 'Seminar on Risk Management of PRC Securities and Investment Firms', at: www.worldbank.org.cn/English/content/740f61337941.shtml, 28 March 2008.

WTO (2001a) *Accession of the People's Republic of China* (Geneva: World Trade Organisation, at: http://docsonline.wto.org/imrd/directdoc.asp?DDFDocuments/t/WT/ACC/CHN49.doc, accessed 28 March 2008.

WTO (2001b) *Report of the Working Party on the Accession of China, Addendum: Schedule CLII – The People's Republic of China, Part II – Schedule of Specific Commitments on Services* (Geneva: World Trade Organisation, at: http://docsonline.wto.org/imrd/directdoc.asp?DDFDocuments/t/WT/ACC/CHN49A2.doc, accessed 15 November 2003.

Wu, Jinglian (2002) 'An Alternate Proposal to Reduce State-owned Shares', *Caijing*, 21 January, at: www.chinaonline.com/caijing, accessed 2 February 2003.

Xia, Bin (2001) 'Is China Ready for Adopting a Universal Banking System?', *China & World Economy*, 9: 2, at: http://old.iwep.org.cn/wec/English/articles/2001_02/xiabin.htm, accessed 28 March 2008.

Xie, Duo (2002) 'Analysis of the Development of China's Money Markets', *China & World Economy*, 10: 1, pp. 29–37, at: http://old.iwep.org.cn/wec/english/articles/2002_01/cwe200201-xieduo.pdf, accessed 28 March 2008.

Xinhua (2004) 'Macro-Control of Economy to Continue', *Xinhua Online*, 5 December, at: www.china.org.cn/english/2004/Dec/114037.htm, accessed 28 March 2008.

Xu, Lijing (2004) 'China Encourages Foreign Strategic Investors to Buy Stakes of State-owned Banks', *China Economic Net*, 10 August, at: www.chinastudygroup.org/index.php?type=news&id=6702, accessed 11 August 2004.

Xu, Xiaoping (1998) *China's Financial System under Transition* (Basingstoke: Macmillan).

Yu, Ning and Weiping Kang (2004) 'Shi Meilun: Jianguan de guanjian shi juexin (Laura Sha: the key person of the CSRC made up her mind)', *Caijing*, 20 September, 116, pp. 61–64.

Zeng, Feng (2004) *Venture Capital Investments in China* (Pardee RAND Graduate School/RAND Corporation, at: www.rand.org/publications/RGSD/RGSD180/RAND_RGSD180.pdf, accessed 28 March 2008).

Zhang, Dingmin (2004) 'Foreign Banks Broaden Scope', *China Daily*, 20 July, at: www.chinadaily.com.cn/english/doc/2004-07/20/content_349904.htm, accessed 28 March 2008.

Zhang, Jiwei and Haili Cao (2004) 'Chongzu Jianton Yinhang (Reorganising Bank of Communications'), *Caijing*, 5 June, 109: pp. 27–34.

Zhang, Yongjin (2003) *China's Emerging Global Businesses: Political Economy and Institutional Investigations* (Basingstoke: Palgrave Macmillan).

Zheng, Yongnian (2004) 'Interest Representation and the Transformation of the Chinese Communist Party', in Yongnian Zheng (ed.) *Bringing the Party Back In: How China is Governed* (Singapore: Eastern Universities Press), pp. 269–301.

Zhou, Xiaochuan (2003) 'Explore Market Position to Promote Corporate Bond Development', paper presented at the International Seminar on Bond Market Development: Opportunities and Challenges, at: www.pbc.gov.cn/english/detail.asp?col=6500&ID=20, accessed 28 March 2008.

Zhu, Sanzhu (2000) *Securities Regulation in China* (London, Ardsley: Simmonds & Hill Publishers, Transnational Publishers).

Zweig, David (2002) *Internationalizing China: Domestic Interests and Global Linkages* (Ithaca and London: Cornell University Press).

Notes

1. This book focuses on *economic* institutions, their political control and the interdependence of political and economic change, utilising the framework of North (1990) and incorporating New Political Economy theories (Olson 2000). It stands in the broader context of institutional theories in political science, as developed by March and Olson (1989), Weingast (1993) Immergut (1998), Hall and Taylor (1996), Koeble (1995), von Beyme (1987) and Göhler (1997). See Behrends (2001) and Obinger, Wagschal and Kittel (2003) for a discussion of different approaches in New Political Economy. On neo-institutional economic theory see Richter and Furubotn (1996), as well as the classic works of Williamson (1985), Coase (1937), and Jensen and Meckling (1976). With regard to transition countries see Sandschneider (1995) and Olson (2000).
2. As shown below, regulation in this book is understood as the setting of formal rules for the market through state actors. It encompasses both case-based regulatory intervention and the mid- to long-term-oriented regulatory policies defined by the aims and principles of the regulatory regime (see below). Regulation is understood as a continuous process.
3. This has been discussed by Gourevitch (1978), Risse-Kappen (1995) and Krasner (1995). Also see Keohane and Milner (1996), Rogowski (1989) and Lütz (2003).
4. Financial services in this book are understood to be savings, investments and related products offered by financial firms. Markets on which these services are traded are financial markets. The specific nature of financial services includes severe information asymmetries and a time lag between contract and fulfilment. Systemic risks in financial markets are grounded on the danger that problems in one financial firm lead to (unrelated) problems of another firm. The strategic role of financial markets is based on the functions they fulfil for the economy (Herring and Santomero, 1999).
5. As pointed out above, regulation is a key component in the development of every market. With regard to financial markets, regulation is understood in this book to encompass the rule-setting, monitoring and enforcement as well as the adaptation of rules in order to govern financial transactions and firms that conduct them.
6. While economic approaches to financial market regulation have stressed the need for government intervention in markets that tend to suffer from externalities and the need for government intervention in the public's best interest, they abstract from the nature of regulatory organisations, as well as the incentives created by regulations, and expect the regulators to act in the interest of the public only.
7. More importantly, policy communities in this field are characterised by a closeness and consensus among their members who are primarily experts, as well as the cross-national character of the communities (Underhill, 1997).
8. Emerging market economies (EMEs) in this book are understood to be newly industrialising countries with high growth expectations as well as immature

markets and institutional problems that are reflected in high risks and volatility (Mody, 2004; International Monetary Fund, 2003; Beim and Calomiris, 2001). China is understood to be an EME with regard to its financial markets, because the Chinese financial markets display a number of structural and operational problems that are typical for EMEs. Looking at China as a transition country with regard to economic structure, another perspective chosen in this book, highlights the socialist institutional legacy and the double transition China is undergoing in transforming itself from an isolated underdeveloped planned economy into an internationally integrated industrialised market economy.

9. The groundbreaking works of McKinnon (1973) and Shaw (1973) provide an analytical framework for understanding the specific problems of EMEs, highlighting the common repression of market forces and the state-based structure of financial intermediation that emerged in the post-Second World War period. Among the characteristics of repressed financial markets, the state ownership of banks and other financial firms, the imposition of interest rate ceilings below market prices, as well as restrictions on market entry and directed credit, are prominent. However, ending financial repression through market reform and deregulation after the 1970s often created new problems, as prudential regulation of markets was not developed simultaneously (McKinnon, 1992).

10. Most of the studies on this topic agree, however, that at the same time, structural consequences of foreign financial firms' market entry, such as the segmentation of the local markets, occur in relation to the competitive advantages and disadvantages of the respective foreign and domestic firms. Yet, few studies point to the potential dangers and detrimental effects of foreign bank entry (for an overview see Bonin et al., 1998, pp. 65ff). An exception is Weller (2004).

11. These factors include its political system and the role of the party in the economy, as well as its size and double transition from an underdeveloped to an industrial country and a planned to a market economy.

12. OECD countries – being all successful market economies – for example, vary considerably in the degree to which their financial markets are open to international participation, as well as in the level of actual market entry of foreign financial firms.

13. It shall be noted as well, though, that the level is not exceptional within the Asian context where financial market internationalisation has been regulated tightly for a long time.

14. It shall be noted, though, that historically well-regulated and competitive financial markets seem to depend on a (reasonably) free press and free access to information, which authoritarian regimes are unlikely to allow. See Linz (2000). An important exception in this regard seems to be Singapore where an authoritarian regime hosts vibrant financial markets. It should be kept in mind, though, that Singapore is primarily an offshore financial centre. Countries with a democratic political system experience considerable problems in the financial markets too, as the recent (2008) problems in the USA have illustrated.

15. On the emerging securities markets see Walter and Howie (2003), Green (2004b), Heilmann and Gottwald (2002), Hertz (1998), Su (2003), Zhu (2000) and Schlichting (2004) with regard to bond markets.

16. See Lardy (1998, p. 220) on the stock-flow problematic of NPLs. Unlike most other transition countries, the majority of non-performing loans in China were not inherited from the pre-reform era (Tong, 2002, p. 174).
17. For example see Shih (2004b) in this regard. Heilmann (2002, pp. 43ff) has identified the important distinction between the 'normal mode' of consensual and decentralised policy-making and a 'crisis mode' that is marked by centralisation, ideologisation and political decisions on the basis of decrees.
18. It has also mastered the move from a revolutionary party to a governing party in that process. On the role of the party see Brødsgaard and Zheng (2004), and on the role and change in the *nomenklatura* system see Burns (1994) and Heilmann and Kirchberger (2000).
19. See also Lieberthal and Oksenberg (1988).
20. The key party organ in this regard has been the Central Finance Working Commission (*Zhongyang jinrong gongzuo weiyuanhui*) established after the Asian financial crisis in 1998. It was the central decision-making body and appointed '*a board of supervisors for each of the 16 state-run financial institutions*' (Naughton, 2003c: 3). However, the commission was dismantled in 2003, with personnel and resources integrated in to the regulatory bodies described below (Heilmann, 2004). Instead a Finance and Economic Leading Group (*caijing lingdao xiaozu*) as well as Central Leading Group for Financial Security (*Zhongyang jinrong anquan lingdao xiaozu*) have been set up. For an insightful study on the role and relevance of single commissions and ministries in policy-making and implementation in the case of exchange rate policies see Liew (2004).
21. On the severe conflicts of interest in regulation see Howie and Walter (2003, p. 50). This includes the interlinked ownership: by 1996, the People's Bank of China was the controlling shareholder in 43 of the total 96 nationwide brokerages it regulated.
22. Regional principals played an important role in the establishment of regional banks, development corporations and investment corporations and therefore in the institutional diversification of the Chinese financial system; see Kumar (1997).
23. This 'centerpiece of the overhaul of the banking system' (Saich, 2001, p. 238) aimed at breaking provincial party chiefs' interference in lending decisions. Shih (2004a) identifies a re-centralisation of control through the new PBC structure in the same line of reasoning and stresses that the position of the central government was considerably strengthened by this move.
24. Bowles and White create both a choice- and a power-theoretic framework, outlining the influential paradigms at the earlier stages of financial market reform (market socialism, finance and development, and the NIC model of late development).
25. See the later works of Huang (1996), Shih (2004b) and Green (2004b).
26. However, on the domestic level, the equilibrium is dynamic both with regard to changing priorities of the central-level government and changing power balances between actors. As far as priorities are concerned, three increasingly important problems challenge the existing balance of interests: firstly, highlighted by the decreasing incremental capital output ratio, the financial markets need to allocate resources more efficiently in order to promote, enhance and sustain (politically crucial) high rates of economic growth. Secondly, highlighted by the Asian financial crisis and the

similarities between the Asian economies and China's financial markets, the current order threatens long-term stability. Thirdly, the reform of social and old-age security increasingly depends on financial markets, and social security reform is an important prerequisite of further SOE reform. These factors are all key in changing the interest constellation on a domestic level and lead to altered strategies, most prominently of the State Council (Green 2003b).

27. As pointed out by He and Yang (1999), though, the actual process of lobbying has essentially remained nontransparent. See also Heilmann (2002, pp. 60–3). Kennedy (2004) pointed out that while there has been a reduction in the lobbying by local governments of the central government, there was an increase in the number and relevance of industry players.

28. This has to be seen in relation to the remaining state control over these enterprises as well as the incomplete enterprise reform. Naughton (1995, p. 276) pointed out the presence of SOE directors in the Central Committee of the CCP.

29. As highlighted by Moore (2002) and Shirk (1994). There are numerous works on either the international side *or* on the national side, but not on the impact of internationalisation on the domestic markets. Exceptions are Moore (2002), Zweig (2002) and Zhang (2003).

30. On the pre-1949 history of foreign financial firms in China, see, for example, Ji (2003).

31. Dipchand, Zhang and Ma (1994, p. 176) make the point that it was only due to large budget deficits that China started to borrow internationally from 1979 onwards.

32. These institutions were HSBC, the Chartered Bank, Bank of East Asia and the Overseas Chinese Banking Corporation.

33. Dipchand, Zhang and Ma (1994, p. 178) state instead that the first bank was the Import and Export Bank of Japan.

34. A new major line of business for the international banks in China was the issuance of guarantees for foreign enterprises that were often a condition for domestic banks lending to JVs.

35. Lardy (1999, p. 213) describes the initial (and short) warm welcome international capital markets gave the Chinese government. Re-emerging International Trade and Investments Companies (ITICs) engaged in collecting and channelling international investors' money, often to provinces, bypassing the national credit plan. The first Chinese bond was issued by CITIC in Tokyo in 1982 (Dipchand, Zhang and Ma, 1994).

36. The seven open coastal cities were Dalian, Tianjin, Qingdao, Nanjing, Ningbo, Fuzhou, Guangzhou. The inland cities included Beijing, Shenyang, Shijiazhuang, Xian, Chengdu, Chongjing, Wuhai, Hefei, Hangzhou, Suzhou and Kunming.

37. By December 2002, 112 companies had listed B-shares and 75 companies had listed shares abroad (Green, 2003c, p. 52). In 2001, it was declared that the market would be closed.

38. Foreign financial firms under these regulations included all banks with foreign capital headquartered in China, branches of foreign banks, equity joint ventures between foreign and Chinese financial firms, finance companies with foreign capital headquartered in China and equity joint venture

finance companies (Law governing foreign investment financial firms, Article 2).

39. GITIC was the first major Chinese financial firm to default on its international debt in 1998. It was closed by the central government in a rush to re-centralise control in the Chinese financial markets and to stop the credit expansion of provincial governments.

40. Foreign banks' outstanding RMB loan balance accounted for 0.07% of all RMB credit outstanding at the end of 1999. However, foreign banks had a bigger share in the much smaller market of foreign currency loans, accounting for over 20% of all loans extended by banks in China in 1999.

41. For a detailed list of WTO commitments, and its role and relevance, see the next chapters.

42. On the position of Chinese policy-makers see Tang (2004).

43. In addition to the banks presented above, there are three Policy Banks (the China Development Bank, the Agricultural Development Bank and the Export-Import-Bank), which are not the focus of this analysis. For an overview see Solvet (2002).

44. Notably, some of the smaller banks have expanded their operations geographically; these include the Shanghai Pudong Development Bank which now has a regional licence.

45. See Tsai (2002) on informal private financial firms. On the closure of small private banks, see Cargill and Parker (2001).

46. Operationally, control is primarily exercised through personnel decisions at the top-management level and the CCP *nomenklatura* system (Burns 1994). Important coordination mechanisms in the implementation of policies are quotas and administrative directives, rather than market-based instruments such as interest rates or reserve rates as highlighted by the macroeconomic control campaign in 2003–4 (Naughton, 2004a).

47. Huang (1996) points out that local governments pressured banks to grant credit to local SOEs. This led to monetary expansion and the creation of NPL on the local level.

48. Saez (2004) discusses the case of India, where private banks played an active role in banking reform.

49. For example, PBC controls the number of branches that can be set up by JSCBs and the rules for account opening by SOEs favour state-owned commercial banks (Wong and Wong, 2001, p. 29).

50. Solvet (2002, p. 91) points out that three of the SOCBc are among the largest 50 financial institutions worldwide with regard to (nominal) assets.

51. The CBRC acknowledges the state's responsibility for the occurring losses. These are not only due to political interference but also to the state guarantees for SOEs (Tang, 2004).

52. See Pei (1998) for an extension of this argument. The institutional weakness results from low asset quality, poor risk management, under-capitalisation, poor incentive structures and corporate governance, limited market experience, and low efficiency (BIS, 1999). Smaller banks, such as the city commercial banks, are less affected by the problem, but are not necessarily stronger banks.

53. The ongoing but still insufficient restructuring of the SOE sector and the subsequently remaining state guarantees are the most important structural

problems underlying the troubles of Chinese banks. The banking sector, however, is not only fragmented in the case of banks but is additionally divided between urban and rural financial markets as well as formal and informal markets. For a detailed introduction to the problems of the rural financial sector see Findlay, Watson and Cheng, 2003; OECD, 2004.

54. On this point see OECD (2002). Specifically on the money markets see Li and Peng (2002), Xie (2002) and Imam (2004).

55. However, bank recapitalisation, while necessary, it is unlikely to solve the underlying problems as only major changes in the incentive structures within the banks themselves will impede the emergence of new NPLs. Wong and Wong (2001, p. 38) argue that operational independence depends on the diversification of ownership structures.

56. Tang (2004) acknowledges that 'mandated loans to support industrial policies, system transition and restructuring of State-owned enterprises' were a major cause of the problem, and that 'the loss of Chinese banks is by nature the cost paid for the transition towards a market-oriented economic system'.

57. The transaction was implemented through the establishment of a special fund that has become a strategic shareholder in the banks, with the expectation that its share will be reduced over time. For a detailed discussion see Naughton (2004b). Hu Shuli (2004a) questions its incentive compatibility.

58. Also, the reform does not include a breakup of the banks into smaller banks, ending the oligopolistic structure of the domestic banking sector. See Guan (2003).

59. At the end of June 2004, the RMB-denominated assets of these foreign banks accounted for 84.4 billion RMB (US$10.2 billion), or 1.4% of total banking assets. Aggregated profits from RMB operations were 267 million RMB (US$32 million) in the first half of 2004. Their share of foreign currency loans was 7.4% in 2002, down from 15% in 2001 and recovering to 13% in 2003. See Wang (2002b), ACFB (2003, pp. 723–6) and Tang (2001) for an overview.

60. This categorisation can also be found in several business reports on foreign banks in China, such as PriceWaterhouseCoopers (2005).

61. The country of origin of a bank is also correlated to its business approach, particularly in the case of Japanese banks, which overwhelmingly have focused on following their clients.

62. Following the definition of Parkhe and Miller (1998) and the discussion in Montgomery (2002), subsidiaries of foreign banks are specified as legal entities that are separate from their parent bank in a stand-alone manner, and are fully locally capitalised. Their lending is based on their own capital and, as Montgomery observes, 'the offices resemble host country banks and typically they adopt a local character with local management to obtain access to the local business market'. On the other hand, branches of foreign banks are closer to the foreign parent institution. Their financial policies are mandated by the parent bank.

63. For a discussion of this point see Montgomery (2002).

64. CitiGroup's Buy-and-Build Strategy is an example for this.

65. Wholesale banking is defined as lending to other financial firms for the purpose of on-lending, instead of lending to end-users. The emergence of this trend in China was due to regulatory restrictions and an opaque enterprise

sector. In this context, JP Morgan Chase, for example, established itself as a 'bank of the banks' (interview).

66. Cash management services and international money transfers are part of the non-lending fee-oriented services.

67. On this point and the likely future development see also Solvet (2002) and Harner (2001).

68. For these foreign exchange loans, customers have to be registered through SAFE.

69. The Commercial Banking law prohibits universal banking (that includes investment in securities) but allows trading as an agent for insurance products.

70. A notable exception from the overall strategic positioning and client targeting of foreign banks is the Thai SME Bank, offering credit on a fully commercial basis to Chinese SMEs and thus entering a market segment that is under-serviced by foreign and Chinese banks alike.

71. For an overview of cooperation agreements see Huang (2003).

72. It is noteworthy that this kind of acquisition has been a prominent way of entering the market in other emerging economies, especially in those that now have a large participation of foreign banks.

73. On the role of the IFC, the largest foreign investor in Chinese banks, see Slater (2004).

74. Regulation did not cut off the business potential (and the ability of foreign banks to operate profitably) completely. As pointed out by Harner (2001, pp. 15ff), in 1999–2000, regulation allowed for the readjustment of (some) foreign banks' business towards a larger role of the RMB business.

75. Foreign banks complement the genuine competitive advantages Chinese banks have in their domestic networks of branches, their comprehensive business scope as well as their intimate market and customer knowledge. As Qing (2001, p. 832) states, however, 'a major problem of indigenous Chinese financial firms is that their competitive edge is strongest in those segments of domestic markets that tend to have lower quality customers, with less opportunity to earn high margins and generate large profits'.

76. Foreign banks expect to be bailed out just like Chinese banks if a SOE creditor encounters trouble (interviews).

77. The single most outstanding aspect of the Chinese financial market, the size of the market for savings deposits and credit, therefore has positive and neg-ative aspects from the perspective of foreign banks: with regard to potential customers and business opportunities size may be an asset, but with regard to the capital requirements in order to establish a country-wide network size it can also be a liability.

78. The high costs of doing business were mentioned as a major problem in almost every interview with foreign banks.

79. The discussion of foreign banks' products reflects the strongest arguments in favour of foreign bank entry as outlined by Levine (1996) and discussed by Dages, Goldberg and Kinney (2000). Levine (1996) points out that foreign banks improve the quality, pricing and availability of products, both directly and indirectly.

80. This point is based on anecdotal evidence collected during the inter-views. Several interviewees remarked on the fact that the customer

reception areas in some Chinese banks have been rebuilt to resemble foreign ones after foreign banks had introduced more welcoming spaces.

81. This is not to say that problems may not occur in individual banks and that all the banks are equally strong. On average, however, this judgment seems justified. It is supported by the broader analyses of Dages, Goldberg and Kinney (2000) and Qing (2001).

82. The following comparison based on CAMEL-analysis, assessing the Capital, Asset quality, Management, Earnings, and Liquidity as standards for comparing banks. For a proper in-depth analysis, the necessary information is missing in the case of the Chinese banks, as it is neither published by the banks nor by the CBRC.

83. This aspect is hard to quantify but it can be argued that it is reflected in operating figures.

84. China Minsheng Bank's high loan growth, for example, reflected unsound lending practices, it was argued.

85. No interviewee wanted to discuss this in detail, but foreign banks in general were said not to make large profits (yet). Especially in the case of the fast-growing ones it was widely expected among the interviewees that they would incur considerable losses due to their high costs and speed of expansion (McGregor, 2004b).

86. This is in line with the findings of Claessens, Demirgüç-Kunt and Huizinga (see Claessens and Glaessner, 1998).

87. The discussion here concentrates on equity and bond markets. For Chinese money markets see Imam (2004), Seto (2002), Carrasco (2003), Li and Peng (2002) and Xie (2002).

88. This number accounts for 0.53% of China's GDP. The figure is regarded to be understating the amount, though, as it is derived from balance sheets filed by securities companies (Kim, Ho, and St Giles 2003: 20).

89. For details see Green (2003c, p. 80). Kim, Ho and St Giles (2003, p. 19) point out that restrictions on market entry, on the other hand, generated monopoly rents in this market, especially during boom phases.

90. On the history, as well as earlier forms of funds and scandals that initiated the reform of the industry after 1997, see Walter and Howie (2003, pp. 164ff).

91. On the development of pension funds from the securities market perspective see Kim, Ho and St Giles (2003, pp. 7–12) and Leckie (2003).

92. On the historical development of the Chinese equity market see Tam (1991), Karmel (1994), Schüller (1992), Bowles and White (1993) and Heilmann and Gottwald (2002).

93. On the overall development see Bowles and White (1992), Slater (2002b), Slater (2003b), Overholt (2004) and Schlichting (2004).

94. On the discussion whether a 'market with Chinese characteristics' can be and should be envisaged see the interview with Laura Cha in Hu, Wei and Niu (2002). Cha argued that there is only one universal principle and international standard for efficient market development and everything else is an excuse to justify bad conduct and fraudulent practices. See Green (2004b) for a discussion and a definition of a securities market with socialist characteristics.

95. After WTO entry, foreign brokerages were also allowed to conduct B-share trading without the intermediation of a local brokerage and their representative offices may also become special members of the Chinese stock exchanges.
96. The BOC Hong Kong also set up a JV that was, however, regarded as a special deal as it was connected to the buying of bad debt (Pang, 2005).
97. It has to be pointed out that insurance companies' JVs are an important segment of foreign firms entering Chinese securities markets, as they can also set up fund-management companies.
98. They have thus developed platforms to offer QFII-related brokerage services; for an example, see the Galaxy Securities or the XiangCai Securities' QFII brochures.
99. It is important for large institutional investors to spread their risks internationally even if they do not have a genuine interest in the Chinese market. China is especially important in this regard, as its stock market price movements are correlated to those of other markets only to a very limited extent.
100. The limitations show that caution prevails on the Chinese regulatory side, especially in limiting the amount of investment. This is expected to be relaxed gradually, however, as from the Chinese perspective, the QFII scheme brings the advantages of capital inflows into a stagnant market, a restoration of confidence, positive signalling, and market liquidity.
101. As shown below, the competitive advantages of the foreign partners (and thus their contribution to the JV) is in the business of *international* IPOs, on which they have largely been concentrating so far.
102. Green (2003c, pp. 105ff) names this as one of the four problems of the fund sector in general. 65% to 70% of an average fund's assets were invested in shares at the end of 2003.
103. In this regard, the promulgation of the *Rule of foreign investments in domestic firms* is an indication.
104. Since they are large, internationally operating and competitive firms, it can reasonably be argued that they have these attributes (Qing, 2001).
105. See Bolland (2004) on the general problems in setting up fund-management JVs.
106. This was the case in two investment-fund JVs that were interviewed. It was specifically argued (by the domestic partner) that the regulations had complicated the deal as they did not give enough freedom to structure the agreement. Giving the control to the foreign partner was seen as an active step in fostering the company's future and allowing for a better transfer of knowledge and management skills in the JV.
107. As reported by the Shanghai Securities News (29 December 2004) 'CESL completed a total of 7 sponsor/lead underwriting deals in its first complete business year since inception, hence winning the top spot in the whole industry in terms of the number of sponsoring clients.' CICC is CESL's main competitor in this regard, highlighting the competition not only with purely domestic firms but also among the Sino-foreign JVs.
108. It is however, questionable if and when foreign-invested financial firms will be allowed to participate in the QDII scheme, although they have started lobbying for it, as pointed out in the interviews. Also see *People's Daily* (2004d).

109. This was pointed out by interviewees.
110. Another fear was that the problems would undermine the capital account restrictions, leading to a de facto capital account liberalisation (Chan-Lee, Liu and Yoshitomi, 2002).
111. Disintermediation leads to the transfer of savings deposits into securities markets. The domestic discussion circled around money-market funds that increase competition for savings deposits (Li, 2003).
112. The way the relation between securities markets and the pension system exists is arguable. The potential of pension funds is highlighted by their importance in OECD countries (Kim, Ho and St Giles, 2003).
113. The domination of regulatory bodies through commercial market players and the resulting regulation in the interest of these market players is called regulatory capture (on regulatory capture also see Laffont and Tirole, 1991; Sabatier, 1975; Huntington, 1952). Current work by Hellman, Jones and Kaufmann (2002b) has shown that strong incentives for 'state or regulatory capture' also exist for foreign firms.
114. However, in their work Hellman, Jones and Kaufmann (2002c) focused on illegal measures such as bribery, buying of parliamentary votes and the like in eastern European and middle Asian countries.
115. As this chapter looks at all foreign financial firms, it includes their lobbying efforts *vis-à-vis* PBC, CBRC, CSRC and CIRC, for which *regulators* is used as a collective term here.
116. The knowledge displayed by interviewees varied on these issues. In general, there was a remarkable lack of understanding of the process, the power relations of different actors and their interaction. Therefore it seems justified to say that they perceived it as a black box.
117. Cf. Zweig (2002) for example, on how localities lobby for their interests and exert pressure on the central government, as well as Shirk (1993). On lobbying in general, see Kennedy (2004) and (2005).
118. See Pearson (1991) on foreign-sector business associations. Business organisations in general have been most deeply analysed with regard to private entrepreneurs; for example, see Dickson (2003).
119. The legal status of these organisations remained subordinated to guidance. In the case of the Securities Association, it is a 'non-profit public organisation with the status of a legal person under the professional guidance, supervision and management of CSRC and the Ministry of Civil Affairs of the PRC' (SAC Brochure, p. 5).
120. On the SBA see its website: www.sbacn.org. In addition, there has been the informal Foreign Bankers Association that is primarily a forum for international bankers.
121. In the perception of the interviewees, the aim of the incorporation of the foreign banks in the organisation was to prevent an independent interest representation. One interviewee stated that before the SBA became so prominent, it was easier to voice one's own concerns whereas in the context of the domestic banks it often seemed inappropriate to pressure for the interests of the foreign banks only.
122. On the SAC see its website: www.s-a-c.org.cn. It has four types of members: securities companies, securities investment fund management companies, securities investment consulting agencies and special members.

123. There are tensions in the division of labour between EUCCC and national Chambers of Commerce. Views on the EUCCC differed strikingly, ranging from 'toothless tiger' to 'very effective mode of coordination' (interviews).
124. The insurance and fund-management working group was established in 2004, merging the insurance and the securities and fund-management working groups.
125. An example of this is the AmCham Luncheon with CBRC Chairman Liu Mingkang in October 2004 (AmCham, 2004b).
126. This particularly includes the Commercial Department of the EU Delegation. Passing the position papers up the administrative ladder inside the EU also constitutes a channel of influence for the working groups. Position papers are one of the sources of information for the EU Commissioner of Trade before going on a visit to China. In a similar way, there are national channels, such as in the German case, the Petita of German Industry (*Petita der Deutschen Wirtschaft*).
127. On this point the views of the interviewees differed and no objective information could be obtained.
128. The high relevance of connections and *guanxi* for Chinese firms and foreign firms alike have often been pointed out as a characteristic of doing business in China.
129. On the notion of not prioritising immediate profits but rather stressing the notion of 'old friends' in FDI investment in general see Pearson (1991, pp. 31ff).
130. There have been some issues over the treatment of Taiwan as a sovereign entity; see Green (2003c, p. 203) on the example of CSFB being punished for their misconduct, followed by a Kotao of the CEO in Beijing.
131. The case is in fact a good example of the rampant speculation that surrounds the merits and benefits of these employees: HSBC has not obtained the underwriting deal and there are no indications that the informal ties have been used at all to influence the procedure.
132. Interviewees agreed that the better-connected firms include AIG and Morgan Stanley. It is therefore not regarded as a coincidence that Morgan Stanley was picked to form the first JV investment bank in China.
133. As pointed out by one interviewee, domestically well-connected financial firms are building bridges for the Chinese side to have access to important lobbying opportunities abroad.
134. An exception may be the case of automobile financing, in which extensive formal and informal lobbying has been able to induce market opening.
135. Such as in the case of a German automobile company lobbying during the WTO negotiations to preserve the protected position of its JV.
136. Li (2002) points out that a preliminary version of the draft had also been circulated by the PBC among banks in Shanghai and Shenzhen. However, this has not been confirmed in the interviews.
137. The draft regulation was enacted in 2002, but remained the focus of lobbying at least until 2004, because it seemed unclear whether or not the phase-in would be implemented and enforced.
138. It has to be pointed out here that this perspective was backed by most interviewees.

139. However, they are 'strictly speaking an application of the principle of national treatment', as pointed out by Marc Poirier, the president of the EUCCC banking working group, in an interview posted on the EUCCC website (EUCCC 2004b).

140. These were supplemented by the 'Tentative Procedures on the Implementing Rules on the Administration of the Pilot Operation of Renminbi Business by Foreign Investment Financial Institutions in the Shanghai Pudong New Zone', promulgated by the PBC on 3 November 1997. The emerging funding problems were addressed by the 'General Office of the People's Bank of China's Approval of Certain Foreign Banks to Participate in National Inter-bank Borrowing', a circular issued on 28 April 1998.

141. On the emergence of Shanghai as an international financial centre see Reszat (2002) and Meyer (2000) as well as People's Bank of China (2004d) and Fang (2004).

142. It is important to note that the regulation, albeit regional in effect, was made on the central level through the PBC.

143. The WTO entry-negotiation process was organised as consecutive bilateral negotiations with every bilateral agreement as the foundation of the next round of negotiations based on the most-favoured-nation principle. In this process, the China-USA agreement came first, followed by the China-EU agreement in mid-2000, which meant that the EU negotiations could use the China-USA agreement as a basis as soon as it was reached.

144. On 31 December 2003, the 'Administrative Measures on Overseas Financial Firms Investment in Financial Firms with Chinese Capital' were promulgated.

145. As argued by Shih (2004b).

146. As pointed out by Zhang (2003).

147. For an overview on the institutional history of Chinese regulatory bodies in China's financial markets see Heilmann (2001), Green (2004b) and Walter and Howie (2003) on the CSRC, as well as Holz (1992) on the PBC.

148. The process was not unique for the PBC in China at that time. Other studies have shown that the transfer of market-economy-oriented theories and skills into Chinese ministries has been an important factor not only in providing the technical framework for the market-oriented reform but also in changing the political balance of power among well-established ministries. For a study of the State Planning Commission see Wipper (2001).

149. See Articles 30 to 36 on financial supervision and control. In the 2003 revision, they were changed in their orientation towards specific acts supervised by the PBC such as deposit reserves, the interbank market and gold market transactions, while other functions have been transferred to the CBRC.

150. It remains arguable, however, that the PBC was endowed with much less autonomy.

151. For an early discussion of this topic see People's Bank of China (2001) and (2004a).

152. As reported by the *China Daily*, Liu Mingkang explicitly used the *Core Principles for Effective Banking Supervision* as a reference system when presenting the draft legislation (*China Daily*, 2003). On the split between the PBC and CBRC see Naughton (2003c). For the *Principles* see Basel Committee on Banking Supervision (1997).

153. This has been recommended, among others, by Sir Howard Davies, a member of the newly established international advisory boards of both CSRC and CBRC (*China Daily*, 2004d). Also see Davies (2004).
154. Walter and Howie (2003, pp. 57–8) call this the 'internationalisation of the stock market experiment'. Early international influences also are manifest in a study group going to Hong Kong in order to investigate the possibilities of Chinese companies listing in Hong Kong as early as 1991.
155. See Green (2003d) on the details of the making of the Securities Law.
156. Green (2004b, p. 195) points out that Zhu Rongji is supposed to have 'a personal preference for the American model and so designed China's framework along the same lines'. Also see Green (2004b, pp. 193–207) for an comparison of the CSRC and the SEC.
157. The five principles set out in section A of the IOSCO *Principles* are 1. clear objectives, 2. operationally independent and accountable, 3. adequate power, resources and capabilities, 4. clear processes of regulation, 5. high professional standards (IOSCO, 2003).
158. Chen Zhenzhen (2004) therefore argues that regulatory bodies are primarily an instrument to 'consolidate and strengthen the power' of high-ranking politicians and to ensure the 'continued dominance of the Communist party'.
159. For a conclusive discussion of the role of development assistance in the process of China's internationalisation, see Zweig (2002, pp. 211–58).
160. The World Bank conducted training in the special techniques of project appraisal and evaluation.
161. Jacobson and Oksenberg (1990, p. 122) pointed out that the concept of a balance of payments was introduced during this training.
162. Examples of this can be found in the policy recommendations of the World Bank reports and IMF annual comments that have often been mirrored in the subsequent Chinese economic policy-making.
163. The EU-China Financial Services Cooperation Project (2003) states: 'The aim of the project Is to help develop China's financial services industry through a combination of policy advice, the implementation of a nation-wide training/examination/professional accreditation system and through the provision of access to western financial markets practice via a series of high-level forums, round-table discussion programmes and overseas training seminars'.
164. Sir Howard Davies stated: 'The Chinese authorities have been making major efforts in recent years to enhance the regulatory régime and we have been watching the progress with great interest. I like to think that we in the UK have been able to play some part in that enhancement process. It is true, of course, that financial regulatory standards of best practice are set internationally, by the Basle Committee or by IOSCO, but the reality is that these standards must be given life nationally, and that bilateral links are a crucial element in that equation' (Davies 1999).
165. The members have been keeping a low profile, but in a lecture at London's LSE Davies said that the Chinese regulators make very effective use of the advisers, through asking very specific, predominantly technical questions.
166. See Mayntz and Scharpf (1995) on the need to analyse the individual level in the context of corporate actors.

167. In fact, a number of interview partners themselves fell into the category of Chinese returnees, who had been trained and worked overseas for a number of years.
168. In the case of one interviewee, the way had included at one time an international financial institution, seconded from a Chinese ministry before moving on to the PBC.
169. The international exposure and orientation of top Chinese regulators like Zhou Xiaochuan, Liu Mingkang, and Shang Fulin have been more widely noted, and they are considered to be internationally oriented in their approaches to regulation (Liu 2001). Li (2004) also points out that Liu Mingkang is in fact an overseas returnee as he received an MBA from London University in 1987.
170. Naughton (2003a, p. 34) remarks on Gao Xiqing, vice president of the CSRC, that he had been key as he 'aggressively sought talent from overseas universities and securities companies'. However, Gao was dismissed after Zhou Xiaochuan was promoted to be head of the PBC in 2003. Naughton interprets this fact as a slowdown in the hiring of internationalised staff, but this was not confirmed by the interviews.
171. The post stated: 'With the integration of global economy and capital markets, in order to promote the reform and opening up of China's capital market and to strengthen its regulatory force, the CSRC is cordially inviting overseas Chinese scholars and professionals to join its team of regulators … In accordance with their academic background, working experience and professional ability, overseas scholars and professionals will be appointed to corresponding professional positions in major CSRC functional departments after one year's probation period.' Application deadline was 16 August 2004.
172. Interviewees pointed out, however, that the connotation here may be that an 'ethnic Chinese background' is required. The notion of a Westerner working in a Chinese government body was clearly rejected for positions other than 'overseas advisers' (interviews).
173. Foreign insurers pointed out that while there had been some opening and change, in general CIRC remained a regulatory body closely aligned to the interests of the domestic Chinese insurance providers rather than actively promoting national treatment or increased market opening.
174. On the broader discussion see *Beijing Review* (2003) as well as *The Economist* (2003b).
175. Bowles and White (1993) point out the importance of international ideas on the Chinese leadership.
176. The boundaries of the community remain blurred and also include former officials who now serve in research institutes, government think tanks or financial firms, including Liu Hongru, Xia Bin and Wang Boming. On the overall importance of a coherent regulatory philosophy see Carmichael (1999).
177. See Halpern (1985) on this issue. Policy communities have existed before, but internationalisation has increased their importance.
178. For a list of international standards see the website of the financial stability forum (FSF 2004).
179. For a discussion of this rule see also Brehm and Macht (2004).

180. The essential aim of the Basel Accord, in its earlier version often abbreviated as Basel I, is to ensure the capital adequacy of internationally operating banks. It became an important cornerstone of the regulation of the international banking system, setting the tone in the domestic regulation of banks in numerous EMEs.
181. They are in line with other rules such as the 'Temporary Measures on Monitoring and Examining Non-performing Assets of the Commercial Banks' and the 'Provisional Risk Rating System for Shareholding Commercial Banks'. These rules together mark the systematic shift in regulation, justifying the identification of new regulatory principles.
182. However, the CBRC at the same time has rejected the Basel II Accord as not applicable to China due to a 'lack of rating penetration and robust internal systems' (Liu, 2003; CBRC, 2003c).
183. The structure of the conference, as well as main aims and the target audience can be referred to on the World Bank's China website (World Bank 2003). It is noteworthy that when reporting on this conference the *People's Daily* (2003) title was: 'China's Securities Regulators Have Invited Overseas Experts to Help Design a New Risk Management Scheme for Domestic Securities Companies.'
184. The Financial Sector Reform and Strengthening Initiative (FIRST) is a joint initiative undertaken by the Department for International Development of the United Kingdom, the International Development Agency of Canada, the State Secretariat for Economic Affairs of Switzerland, the Ministry of Foreign Affairs of the Netherlands, the International Bank for Reconstruction and Development and the International Monetary Fund. For more information and the charter see www.firstinitiative.org; on the specific project see FIRST (2004a).
185. In addition, see the 'Several Issues Concerning the Implementation of the Measures on the Administration of Securities Investment Fund Management Companies', promulgated on 21 September 2004, further specifying the above.
186. On the bond market see Zhou (2003).
187. Financial holdings are holding structures whose subsidiaries are financial service providers in at least two of the financial industries of banking, securities and insurance business.
188. The CITIC Holding, for example, controls the Hong Kong-based CITIC Ka Wah Bank, as well as the Beijing-based CITIC Industrial Bank, CITIC securities, and CITIC Prudential Life Insurance, a JV with UK-based Prudential. Wang Jun, CITIC's chairman of the board, stated in an interview that the financial holding was constructed on the basis of a regulatory exception and was modelled on the European mode of universal provision of financial services (Hu, Li and Yu, 2002).
189. Haier Group has set up a JV with New York Life, as well as the Anshan Trust, and is the number one shareholder in Changjiang Securities, while at the same time owning more than 50% of the shares of Qingdao Commercial Bank (Caijing, 2002).
190. The People's Bank of China, China Banking Regulatory Commission and China Securities Regulatory Commission Announcement No. 4 (2005)

'Administrative Rules for Pilot Incorporation of Fund Management Companies by Commercial Banks', February 2005.

191.   Chinese regulators have also realised that they need to allow domestic firms to internationalise. In this regard, the issuance of the 'Guidance on the Supervision of Overseas Firms of Commercial Banks' on 20 August 2001 has been important.

192.   The investment slowdown started in autumn 2003 (HSBC economic outlook, June 2004).

193.   Such as the real estate, steel, cement and aluminium industries. Wen Jiabao explained that the aims of the strategy were to control monetary growth and loan growth, cleaning up ongoing and new projects, countering illegal practices to use land and ensuring the better use of resources (Xinhua, 2004; Naughton, 2004c).

194.   Naughton (2004a) points out that 'this was not a formal directive, and there has been no published document'.

195.   JSCBs had a loan growth ratio of over 20% whereas SOCBs had one of 5%. The JSCBs thus reacted immediately to the "suggestions" of the CBRC (Ling, 2004b).

196.   See People's Bank of China (2004b).

197.   Historically, BOC has been the 'international arm' of the Chinese banking system.

198.   As Katz (1997, pp. 100ff) notes, experiences with interest rate fluctuations were important in this regard.

199.   An example of the wide range of this cooperation is the agreement of 32 foreign banks with China Construction Bank regarding guarantees of credit worthiness (*xinyongzheng danbao*) (Huang, 2003).

200.   The share of the foreign partner is limited to a maximum of 49%. However, some JV arrangements have given operational control to the foreign partner despite its smaller equity contribution. This has been interpreted as a strong impetus to maximise the international component of the JV, but might also reflect the strength of the foreign partner in the negotiations. International cooperation has also been seen as an option to increase independence from state interference. It was mentioned by a number of interviewees that international partners may decrease the probability of political interference in business.

201.   XiangCai claims to have the highest percentage of employees with international experience among Chinese securities firms. At the time of enquiry, the QFII department was staffed with international and Hong Kong staff. In its external presentation such as in brochures and the company's website, XiangCai has strongly highlighted the fact that its team is international and bilingual.

202.   There has been a wide range of speculation as to why foreign strategic investments have become a regulatory policy for commercial banks, but not for securities companies and fund management companies. For example, see Naughton (2006), who argues that the securities companies have developed strategies to oppose a similar policy.

203.   An example of a reforming cooperative bank with foreign strategic investment is the United Rural Cooperative Bank in Hangzhou, which introduced

the Dutch cooperative bank Rabobank as a foreign strategic investor alongside the IFC in 2006.

204. This aspect has been highlighted primarily by the work of the IFC. IFC investments have in turn fostered broader industry-based investments with similar components (Slater, 2004).

205. This also includes board structure and structure, the role of foreign directors, number of meetings per year, relevance of the meetings as well as the position of the boards in the decision-making structure. So far, foreign control over the board can only be taken in domestic banks with a fragmented structure of ownership, such as in the case of the Shenzhen Development Bank.

206. For the case of non-financial SOEs, Sun and Tobin (2003) point out that placing independent non-executive directors on the board succeeded in standardising the relationship between the State Council and the enterprise and led to a convergence with international practices.

207. However, most interviewees remained sceptical on the question of how much of the total shares would float even if more domestic financial firms were listed internationally.

208. On the general problems of 'bureaucrats in business' see World Bank (1995). On the problems of state-owned financial institutions in general see Caprio et al. (2004).

209. A complex and largely opaque system has been established to measure the performance of the personnel in these posts in which loyalty and success in performance indicators are balanced.

210. This has been important with regard to the political connections between the financial firms and policy goals. But even until now, the control mechanisms of personnel appointment as well as party committees in financial firms have not been abolished.

211. In Shanghai, more than 80% of the returnees surveyed by Iredale and Fei (2001) in a comparison of the transforming role of returnees in China, Taiwan and Bangladesh worked in the service sector, including 'information systems, banking and financial services and other conventional services'. Li (2004) mentions that Shanghai and Beijing together accommodate about 58% of all returnees.

212. As mentioned in an article in *The Economist* (2003b), some multinationals turn down applications from returnees who have been abroad for more than two years because they 'no longer know enough about how China works'. For a discussion of the respective merits of locally trained staff and returnees on a broader level see *Beijing Review* (2003); on the problems of returnees also see Glionna (2004).

213. Numerous interviewees mentioned, though, that the command of Mandarin varies greatly among Hong Kong Chinese.

214. Deutsche Bank and Allianz, for example, sponsor chairs for Banking and Finance as well as Insurance and Risk.

215. The project documents state: 'One of the ultimate aims of the project will be the creation of a national training regime which implements a standardised training programme/curriculum. Candidates sitting the programme will be eligible to take an exam or series of exams which, when passed, will verify that the candidate has attained a pre-determined level of competency in the

chosen financial field. Candidates passing the exam programme will qualify for professional recognition and accreditation by the relevant regulatory authority, and as such be eligible to practice in that particular financial business. It is envisaged that eventually it will be a regulatory pre-requisite for practising in the field of banking, insurance or the securities industry that practitioners will need to have obtained entry-level qualifications, with the scope perhaps to go on to take intermediate and advanced-level exams' (EU-China Financial Services Cooperation Project, 2003).

216. As pointed out by interviewees, they have primarily been highlighting the dangers of reform and opening. However, the process has remained largely opaque due to the opaque domestic lobbying system.

217. Interviewees from domestic financial institutions strongly emphasised the fact that more active strategies were the only viable choice. Still, it seems reasonable to assume that some resistance to change has remained.

218. The most successful example of the combination of a proactive international approach with strong political leverage may be the CICC.

219. It is important to note that the trend of increased strength and market orientation and the favouring of a more rules-based system in general will not necessarily hinder the firms from seeking political protection and regulatory exceptions as well. They will not necessarily stop the exploitation of gaps in regulation that they profit from.

220. As pointed out by Pearson (1991, p. 137) on employees in foreign-invested companies: 'They favor not only full marketization and unfettered participation by China in the world economy, but also a greatly reduced role for the state and the party in the economy. They clearly have been influenced by foreign ideologies.'

Index